Bergson, Eliot, and American Literature

Bergson, Eliot,
AND
American Literature

PAUL DOUGLASS

ᏽ THE UNIVERSITY PRESS OF KENTUCKY

Publication of this book has been assisted by a grant from Mercer University.

Editorial and Sales Offices: Lexington, Kentucky 40506-0024

LIBRARY OF CONGRESS CATALOGING-IN-PUBLICATION DATA

Douglass, Paul, 1951–
  Bergson, Eliot, and American literature.

  Bibliography: p.
  Includes index.
  1. American literature—20th century—History and criticism.   2. Bergson, Henri, 1859–1941—Influence.
3. Eliot, T.S. (Thomas Stearns), 1888–1965—Criticism and interpretation.   4. Criticism—United States.
I. Title.
PS228.B47D68   1986   8108.980052   86-9227
ISBN 0-8131-1597-3

To Charlene

CONTENTS

ACKNOWLEDGMENTS

ã   My colleagues and friends Steven Axelrod and Frederick Bur-
wick gave me indispensable support in revising this book. Professor
Richard Lehan has been my mentor, the sort many hope for but few
encounter. In the early stages of my work, the University of California at Los Angeles gave me a travel grant to consult materials in
the Houghton Library of Harvard University, for which I express
my gratitude. I am also grateful to Mercer University for having
provided funds necessary for the completion and typing of this
study.
    I thank Jan Duke and Debbi Legner, who typed and keyed in
the manuscript at different points in its metamorphosis. Professor
Sanford Schwartz generously commented on the manuscript in its
final stages.
    Jeremy and Regan, thank you for being understanding.
    Thought has graciously allowed publication here of material
which had appeared in its pages in slightly different form. I am in
the debt of Mrs. Valerie Eliot and Faber and Faber for permission
to quote from unpublished manuscripts: reprinted by permission of
Valerie Eliot and Faber and Faber Ltd., © copyright Mrs. Valerie
Eliot 1986.

A NOTE ON THE TEXTS

ॐ This study has been informed by reference to the French originals of Bergson's chief works, which are listed in chronological order in the bibliography. The book has been prepared, however, with the nonreader of French in mind, for it focuses on the impact of Bergson on the English-speaking world and especially on American writers—an impact felt mainly through translations. These translations are listed in the bibliography along with the originals. Bergson was fortunate in having some very able translators, and all parenthetical references are to their work. That work was sometimes overseen by the philosopher himself, who made revisions and in some cases added original material for the English versions. In a few cases, especially in the chapters on T.S. Eliot, reference to the original editions has been essential. The reader will find appropriate citations in the notes.

Abbreviations Used

WORKS OF HENRI BERGSON

CE	*Creative Evolution.*
CM	*The Creative Mind.*
IM	*Introduction to Metaphysics.*

L   *Laughter: An Essay on the Meaning of the Comic.*

ME   *Mind-Energy: Lectures and Essays.*

MM   *Matter and Memory.*

TFW   *Time and Free Will: An Essay on the Immediate Data of Consciousness.*

TS   *The Two Sources of Morality and Religion.*

WORKS OF T.S. ELIOT

ASG   *After Strange Gods: A Primer of Modern Heresy.*

CPP   *The Complete Poems and Plays: 1909-1950.*

KE   *Knowledge and Experience in the Philosophy of F. H. Bradley.*

OPP   *On Poetry and Poets.*

SE   *Selected Essays.*

TCC   *To Criticize the Critic and Other Writings.*

UPUC   *The Use of Poetry and the Use of Criticism: Studies in the Relation of Criticism to Poetry in England.*

WORKS OF WILLIAM FAULKNER

AA   *Absalom, Absalom!*

ALD   *As I Lay Dying.*

FIU   *Faulkner in the University.*

LA   *Light in August.*

LIG   *Lion in the Garden: Interviews with William Faulkner, 1926-1962.*

S   *Sanctuary.*

SF   *The Sound and the Fury.*

INTRODUCTION

 है। The aim of this book is to revaluate Bergson's philosophy in relation to American literature. The study does not attempt a comprehensive survey of Bergsonian influences on American writers, a catalogue of which would be voluminous. Rather, it seeks to reintroduce a Bergsonian vocabulary in discussion of American literary Modernism by showing how Bergson's ideas of openness, containment, and tension illuminate the theory and practice of several major American writers. Some of that Bergsonian vocabulary will be recognizable. But if I have done my job well, the reader will find a somewhat unfamiliar Bergson in these pages.

Bergson played an important, perhaps decisive role in the development of an expressly "modern" philosophy and literature. And yet he appears only at the margins of late-twentieth-century philosophy. As Leszek Kolakowski observes, no one seems to follow in Bergson's footsteps, despite the fact that he was "not just a famous thinker and writer; in the eyes of Europe's educated public he was clearly *the* philosopher, the intellectual spokesman *par excellence*." Both Bergson's tremendous impact and his disappearance from the scene are highly significant for understanding twentieth century culture.[1]

His disappearance, however, has troubled attempts to understand his impact, as both Daniel Herman and P.A.Y. Gunter have noted in recent discussions of Bergson's philosophy. That Bergson had a special importance for American writers like Fitzgerald, Eliot, Frost, Cather, Stein, Henry Miller, and Faulkner has long been recognized, and recent books by Piers Gray, John Conder, and Sanford Schwartz discuss Bergson in relation to Eliot, Pound, Faulkner, and other American writers. Articles on Bergson and Anglo-American literature have continued to appear.[2] If I have a quarrel with this fine work, it is that it tends uncritically to accept a common view of Bergson as simply the "time-philosopher," and so it fails to penetrate to the potent and troublesome dualism of Bergsonian thought. Because Bergson has not been "fashionable," for example, no full-length study has systematically explored Bergson's significance for American writers between the wars. And that is, as Kolakowski says, significant in itself.

Fashion is fickle. The buzzwords in 1910 were not "deconstruction" and "intertextuality," but "creativity" and "intuition." *Creative Evolution* (1907; trans. 1911) became one of the most widely discussed books in Europe and America during the prewar years. Following the war, many criticized sharply Bergsonism's apparent irrationalism and faith in "progress"; few wished to be Bergson's "followers." Pilkington's *Bergson and His Influence* (1976) has shown a breadth in Bergson's legacy in French phenomenology and existentialism that many would prefer to ignore, since they still contend that Bergsonian philosophy is guilty of accepting what Jonathan Culler calls the "myth of the innocence of becoming."[3] As I shall show, a false issue is raised when deconstructionism rejects Bergson on the grounds that he ignores the problems of *différence* and *aporia*. The immediate need this study hopes to fill, however, is the lack of a context for certain judgments about American literature.

A recent volume by John Conder provides a good example of what I mean. Professor Conder argues, in *Naturalism in American Fiction*, that Faulkner brings to its final point a tradition of American Naturalism that relies upon an important split in the self (*dédoublement*) described by Bergson: "Hence, by way of Bergson, Faulkner comes into possession of all the component elements of a naturalistic vision that logically allies him to [other American] naturalists."[4] Conder shows (and he has followed many other critics whom I will discuss in chapter six) that it helps to think of Faulkner's characters and themes—of divided selves, of determinism and freedom—in Bergsonian terms. This is fundamentally true, and Faulkner's sympathies with Bergson have proved broader and more helpful than those with American philosophers like Whitehead or James.

But a question presents itself: Can Faulkner be shown to have read Bergson deeply? The answer is, apparently not. So further questions must be asked: Who was Bergson to American writers? What works of his were widely read, and what did his readers make of them? Did Bergsonian ideas somehow become dispersed among American writers in the teens, twenties, and thirties, so that Faulkner's "Bergsonism" is not unique? My study, which began as an attempt to explain this troubling relationship between Bergson and Faulkner, thus expanded its task, and I undertook to follow the history of Bergsonism's dissemination among English-speaking—particularly American—writers, and to set before the reader a fair (if necessarily brief) account of Bergson's place in intellectual history, the difference between "Bergsonism" and Bergsonian philosophy itself, and the influence of Bergsonian ideas upon American writers—especially through the agency of T.S. Eliot and the Southern New Critics. That tells only a part of the story of Bergson in America, but it is the foundation for understanding Bergson's significance for Faulkner, Frost, Henry Miller, and many others.

If anyone consciously set out to transmit Bergsonian thought to the English-speaking world, it was T.E. Hulme, who wrote, in *Speculations*, that Bergson had invented "a much better vocabulary" for talking about artistic creation, one that would justify art as the equal of science in difficulty and importance.[5] As Frank Kermode has said, Bergson was "the almost *inevitable* result of the nineteenth century effort to find room for art amid the encroachments of science."[6] Hulme had seen this and preached Bergson to Pound and Eliot. He had also translated some of Bergson's work into English. John Middleton Murry, too, established *Rhythm* magazine in 1911 with an eye to promulgating a new sort of poetry based on the implications of Bergsonism. But neither Murry nor Hulme was the most important figure in transmitting Bergson across the Atlantic. It was T.S. Eliot, the erstwhile archenemy of evolutionism. He had been in Paris in 1910 and heard Bergson lecture. He had soon begun to draft a paper on Bergson.

Reading this paper suggested an approach to Eliot different from that offered through F.H. Bradley, Babbitt, Nietzsche, or Royce. As I reconsidered Eliot's work, concentrating on his reviews, essays, and philosophical notebooks, I came to see how he had, as he said, been revolutionized by, reacted against, and then come to terms with Bergson's most significant ideas. In spite of himself, Eliot had been profoundly affected by Bergson, and though he is not the only source for Bergson's presence in the work of other American writers—Henry Miller and Robert Frost read *Creative Evolution* themselves—he is still the most important single factor in understanding how Faulkner, for one, came to adopt a Bergsonian vocabulary. Thus the organization of this study evolved: a review of Bergson's career, philosophy, and aesthetics in brief; an exploration of Eliot's career in relation to his reading of Bergson; a tracing of the dispersion of Bergsonian vocabulary and themes among the Southern New Critics, especially Allen Tate, John Crowe Ransom, and Robert Penn Warren; a careful consideration of William Faulkner's style and some of his major works in relation to Bergson; and a brief concluding chapter considering Bergson's meaning for other American writers, like Henry Miller, William Carlos Williams, Robert Frost, and Gertrude Stein.

Bergson spoke to the issue of the twentieth century, that man cannot afford a narrow-minded science: "The workman's tool is the continuation of his arm, the tool-equipment of humanity is therefore a continuation of its body. . . . the body, now larger, calls for a bigger soul" (*TS*, 298-99). Many in England and America in the first decades of this century not only applauded, but were profoundly moved by Bergson's valiant attempt to mediate between hostile camps in philosophy, physics, and aesthetics. It is time we paused to reflect upon the fate of this philosophy that moved so many and ultimately pleased so few. Certainly Bergson remains, as Lewis

Mumford has said, "as essential for the 'biological revolution' as . . . Copernicus, Galileo, and Newton were for the mechanical revolution."[7] Or, one might add, as Saussure for the semiotic revolution.

We have, that is, a well-developed post-Saussurean criticism of modern literature. But there are post-*Darwinian* readings enabled only by a retracing of Bergson's entry into the vocabulary of American writers and critics. Bergson's entanglement in the fabric of American literature between the wars thus goes underappreciated. His aesthetic of "tension," taken in the broad context of his philosophy, is essential to understanding what many American writers were consciously or unconsciously about. His vocabulary unlocks modernist literature, even when it is applied in very different contexts. That is perhaps because the "modern" story, as recorded by American writers, was so much the story of human beings trying to cope with moral issues by material means. This shared vision produced an art like Eliot's and Faulkner's that is ethical in theme, nonspeculative in orientation; it challenges moral assumptions, proposes alternate modes of "knowing," and eventually turns more and more openly to direct treatment of that spiritual life after which it hungers. It doubles back on itself, mastering "dissociation" through mimicry.

In the hermetic writings of Stein, the experimentalism of Williams and of Henry Miller, there lies an implicit faith in the potentiality of language to evoke the paradoxical mystery of memory *knowing itself* in its own containment and openness. The quest to renew language in the play of mind, to create a transcendent poetry that could yet "contain itself," emerges from a Bergsonian heritage, for it was Bergson who had explained how we erroneously extend to memory and time "the obligation of *containing* and *being contained*" which applies exclusively to objects in space (*MM*, 193). The goal of that quest for American writers was a literature of insight, born in "distraction fits," as Eliot put it in *Four Quartets*, when for a moment "in and out of time" consciousness stirs in the unconscious processes of being; and we recognize that time itself is our pseudonym.

ONE

Bergson and Bergsonism

*Open Bergson and new horizons loom on every page; it is
like the breath of the morning and the song of the birds.*
—William James

ᏫᏬ   Born in 1859, the year *Origin of Species* appeared, Bergson
was very much a child of his time. He was first drawn to the sciences, and in 1879 published an article on a problem in geometry
posed by Pascal. But he found mathematics "too absorbing"—that
is, too removed from life—and started reading philosophy. Then,
between 1881 and 1883, something happened to him. In a 1908
letter to William James, Bergson describes his remarkable experience: "I had remained up to that time wholly imbued with mecha-
nistic theories to which I had been led at an early date by the reading of Herbert Spencer, a philosopher to whom I adhered almost
unreservedly. . . . It was the analysis of the notion of time, as it enters into mechanics and physics, which overturned all my ideas. I
saw, to my great astonishment, that scientific time does not *endure*." [1]
Spencer's evolution analyzed change without reference to "change
itself"—the interpenetration of states characteristic of psychic life
(*CM*, 10, 13). Without interpenetration, scientific analysis reflects
no more reality than the frames of a moving picture, and leads inevitably to error. One may think, for example, of the illusion of
backward-spinning wheels created by the strobe effect of the motion

picture camera. Such illusions, like Zeno's Paradox, Bergson labeled "pseudo-problems."

Thus, Bergson began his career in reaction against "scientific
time," and embarked on a path involving, as Anthony Pilkington
has noted, the "phenomenological mode of adhesion to immediate
experience."[2] He prepared the ground for later developments in
French philosophy, from the religious existentialism of Marcel to
the nonreligious existentialism of Sartre and Merleau-Ponty, who
dislike Bergson's old-fashioned values but agree with him in many
ways. They dislike Bergson because he is so rooted in nineteenth
century thought—because his reaction against science is by no
means rejection. But they agree with him, as Merleau-Ponty himself
acknowledges, on his ideas about language and experience.[3] In
1884, shortly after his realization about duration (*durée*), Bergson
published a translation of *De rerum natura* and attached a commentary in which he admired Lucretius's ability to "grasp outright the
two-sided nature of things" and recognize the truth that mankind
seems doomed "to act and not achieve, struggle and not succeed,
and be unwillingly drawn into the vortex of things."[4] The ingenuity
of Bergson's Vitalism, a philosophy of freedom, owes directly to his
profound awareness of the "vortex."

When Bergson returned to Paris in 1888, having taught at Cler-
mont-Ferrand and Angers, he brought with him two doctoral the-
ses: *Quid Aristoteles de loco senserit* and *Essai sur les données immédiates de la conscience*. The first, a study of Aristotle's doctrine
of place, was little noticed.[5] The second, translated in Bergson's
own heyday (1910) as *Time and Free Will*, also attracted little attention, at first. It attacked the "mechanicism" of Spencer, an act
which apparently resulted in subsequent charges of irrationalism
leveled at Bergsonism, charges that have continued to trouble Bergson's reputation as a scientist.

Of course, Bergson was not the only one concerned to attack
confidence in pure rationality. His conviction that reality "transcends intellect" (*CE*, 46) was a common theme among philosophers as various as Meinong, Whitehead, James, Bradley, Russell,
and Peirce, all of whom were engaged in dismantling the nineteenth-century concept of the intellect and showing the falseness of

an unguarded faith in scientific progress.[6] But Bergson was different in that he sought a "new empiricism" based on consciousness; some call it simply psychology, and Bergson simply a "literary philosopher," but it, and he, are more than that. By directing our attention to the immaterial world of the mind, Bergson argued, we can come closer to understanding materiality: biology, evolution, even physics. Bergson proposed a faculty, *intuition philosophique*, to perform the investigative role.

In 1900, after failing twice in attempts to be elected to the Sorbonne, he was given a chair at the College de France. Reaction to his ideas was beginning to be felt. He had already published *Matiére et mémoire* (1896), a sequel to the *Essai sur les données*, and in his first years at the Sorbonne he produced three important books: *Le Rire* (1900) and *Introduction à la metaphysique* (1903), both of which were first serialized, and then *L'Évolution créatrice* (1907), his most famous work. By this time, he had become a celebrity synonymous with *durée*, the rejection of "laboratory time" and the elevation of intuition over intellect. Then, too, he still seemed closely connected with that scientistic evolutionism the foundation of which he had attacked. These contradictory tags have stuck, as a perusal of virtually any general study of modern literature discloses.

Bergson and the Zeitgeist

Bergson is properly a symbol of the late nineteenth-century reaction against what Bertrand Russell called "that scientific optimism which made men believe that the kingdom of heaven was about to break out on earth." [7] Broad studies like Hans Meyerhoff's *Time in Literature* (1955) and Adam Mendilow's *Time and the Novel* (1965) tell this part of the story well—how the "ambitious belief and pious hope" for a "science of history" broke down, and how the schism between intellectual and spiritual life grew.[8] More than ever, rational approaches were needed; more than ever such approaches seemed to render life not worth living, for they remained coldly antithetical to religion, art, culture itself. Bergson's spiritual approach gave hope to many, including the Maritains, who found in it a reason not to keep their suicide pact, and who went on to accomplish a great deal in the same vineyard as Bergson himself. Bergson promised a "new reality," as J. Hillis Miller has noted— one buried right in the old one, waiting to be released through the intuitive responses of trained, sensitive minds.[9] Bergson's time-awareness was a genuinely new one in this sense: that he felt the need to *rescue* time. Those like Hulme, Eliot, the Maritains, Kazantzakis, and Joyce were responding equally to his ideas and to his sense of urgency.

According to Bergson, human time might be reclaimed from the physicists by philosophers and poets convinced that life is growth through metamorphosis rather than "construction," contraries rather than concatenation. Bergson's philosophy, with the work of Freud, Nietzsche, and Einstein, gave a new turn to modern thought, as Mendilow suggests: a turn *inward*.[10] The faculty of intuition became more than a mere debate topic. William James sensed immediate kinship with Bergson. And Jung's psychology owes an important debt to Bergson, one he openly acknowledged in the twenties, but effaced in later editions of his work, apparently because of Bergson's obvious fall from grace.[11] Bergson's philosophy had a widening circle of effects in the work of many writers, including Yeats, Eliot, Woolf, and Joyce, who had become preoccupied with experiences of a quasi-religious nature, and whose art strove toward a liberation from the "nightmare of materialism" and an embrace with "the spiritual life to which art belongs," as Kandinsky wrote in 1912.[12] Like Whitehead and James, Bergson emphasizes that the moment in some sense *creates itself*, and therefore gives augury of something profound and doublesided, something that can know itself as always *more* than itself, a creative act surrounded by forces of repression always deflecting, but never completely stifling that impetus. It is unsurprising, then, that he has been profitably linked with many writers in England and America on this point.[13]

Such connections have helped, but when there are no bones, anyone can carve a goose. Dorothy Richardson sums up Bergson's importance for most criticism of American literature when she says, "No doubt Bergson influenced many minds, if only by putting into words something then dawning on human consciousness: an increased awareness of the inadequacy of the clock-time as time-measurer."[14] That is the view of one who has experienced Bergson-ism, but not Bergson in his profound entanglement with the troublesome issues presented by science and psychology in the years before the war.

By 1907, Bergson's reputation had spread throughout Europe, to England and America. He had already begun a correspondence with William James. That winter, Kazantzakis came to Paris to hear him lecture. Like Hulme, Kazantzakis later translated and wrote about Bergson. Plainly, as Andreas Poulakidas has said, the Greek writer's deep commitment to freedom was shaped by Bergson's "in-spiration."[15] Many besides Hulme and Kazantzakis were listening to Bergson. There were also Piaget and Riechenbach, who share Bergson's epistemology based on biological imperatives.[16] Like Ralph Tyler Flewelling, Maritain began his career with an attack on Bergson's unorthodoxy and irrationalism, but later found himself in substantial agreement with his old master.[17] Bergson lectured in Edinburgh and London on a tour in 1911, when Evelyn Underhill, author of *Mysticism* and later a reviewer for Eliot's *Criterion*, heard him. "I'm still drunk with Bergson," she wrote afterwards, "who sharpened one's mind and swept one off one's feet both at once."[18]

Eliot described the Paris of 1910-11, when he attended Berg-son's lectures: "The predominance of Paris was incontestable . . . Anatole France and Rémy de Gourmont . . . Barrés . . . Péguy. . . . And over all swung the spider-like figure of Bergson."[19] He had gone to Paris, as he told E.J.H. Greene, for no accidental purpose: "Depuis plusieurs années, la France représentait, surtout à mes yeux, la *poésie*."[20] France meant poetry to Eliot, and at that time, Bergson seemed to thread together the diverse and exciting ele-ments that were France. In 1944, Eliot wrote that one simply needed to have been there in the lecture hall to know how fervent was Bergson's following in 1910-11.[21] Bergson's talent for exciting people about ideas had been noticeable from the time he had at-tended the Lycée Condorcet as a youth.[22] And though, as even his critics universally admit, Bergson himself was writing pure philos-ophy, those coming away from his lectures tended to sound a little too drunk on Bergson. Eliot was, as Shiv Kumar has explained, simply one among many who could say "I was certainly very much under Bergson's influence during the year 1910-11 when I attended his lectures and gave close study to the books he had then written."[23]

In this period, Bergson was forced to reserve seats at lectures for his students; journalists, tourists, clergy, foreign students, and even ladies of fashion crowded the hall. Each day the philosopher faced a bewildering logjam of admirers bearing bouquets and gifts, through which he would have to push his way to the podium, on one occasion protesting, "But . . . I am not a dancer!" The news-papers suggested he move his "performances" to the Paris Opera.[24] A copy of one of his books—cover cracked or not—became a not unusual household item. In 1910 the *Essai* of 1889 was translated into English. In 1911, as it was about to go into its tenth French printing, *L'Évolution créatrice* appeared in English, and in this same year *Matière et mémoire* and *Le Rire* were also translated. The following year, 1912, saw two translations of *Introduction à la me-taphysique*: an authorized one by Hulme and an unauthorized by Littman. Bergson devoted considerable time to working with trans-lators. The son of a Polish father and an English mother, he knew English well enough to be greatly frustrated by the difficulties of translating *Creative Evolution*. But this seems to have been his only bad experience. Thankful notes of translators testify to the energy he put into making his work available to English and American readers.

Bergson's frustration over *Creative Evolution* must have stemmed partly from his realization that his major opus would find a troubled reception. On the one hand, there were many "Bergsonists" who had not understood much of Bergson at all. Perhaps Thomas Hanna exaggerates when he says that "if not actually read by every-one, [*Creative Evolution*] was, like the Bible, known by everyone and quoted by all."[25] There can be no doubt, however, that by 1912 Bergson had created a genuine stir in the English-speaking world. Between 1909 and 1911 well over two hundred articles about him appeared in the British press alone. A similar wave of publicity, more of it focused on the man than his philosophy, broke in Amer-ica. As it became harder to find someone who hadn't heard of Bergson, it became harder for Bergson to get the hearing he wanted for his book. He had created what T.S. Eliot later characterized as an "epidemic of Bergsonisms."[26]

The Damnation of Bergson

This notoriety brought out another sort of reader. The Parisian press had already accused Bergson of seeking personal aggrandizement through grandstanding his philosophy (a truly remarkable charge to late-twentieth century ways of thinking!). Across the Channel the view was, in certain quarters, even dimmer. In 1912, Sir Ray Lankester introduced *Modern Science and the Illusions of Prof. Bergson*, by Hugh Elliott, to the British public. In his preface, Lankester decried Bergson's popularity in terms that would be echoed by many others. He called Bergson's books "worthless and unprofitable matter," and characterized their author as a "Confusions-meister ... gifted with an admirable facility of diction [whose] illusions and perversions should be exposed [by] sober science." Bergson's work, Lankester concluded, would remain valuable only for "the student of the aberrations and monstrosities of the mind of man."[27]

There were certainly sympathetic treatments of Bergson published in English, like Wilm's *Henri Bergson: A Study in Radical Evolution* (1914). But a wide stream of virulent anti-Bergsonism had made its appearance, and the rhetoric conditioned much of what was said after World War I. Thomas John Gerrard's *Bergson: An Exposition and Criticism from the Point of View of St. Thomas Aquinas*, for example, concludes with these phrases: "Does M. Bergson tell us that by turning away from intelligence and turning to animal instinct we shall get into touch with life? Pooh! Does he tell us that by retracing the steps which reason has laboriously cut out for us we shall attain to the highest life? Pooh! Pooh!"[28]

George Santayana also used the intemperate rhetoric of anti-Bergsonism in his 1912 study, *Winds of Doctrine*: "I suppose [Bergson] cannot venture to preach the resurrection of the body to this weak-kneed generation; he is too modern and plausible for that. Yet he is too amiable to deny to our dilated nostrils some voluptuous whiffs of immortality. [Bergson's thought is] the work of an astute apologist, a party man, driven to desperate speculation [with] neither good sense, nor rigour, nor candour, nor solidity. It is a brilliant attempt to confuse the lessons of experience."[29] Santayana's charge that Bergson "flatters" us (merely to make us like him?) is the usual one. If not the philosopher himself, then certainly his work, must be condemned because it rejects the operation of "reason." Such, for example, is the rationale employed by Wyndham Lewis in his attacks on Bergson in *Time and Western Man*. Bertrand Russell uses the same knife, and twists it, in an article in *The Monist* of 1912: "There is no room in this philosophy for the moment of contemplative insight when, rising above animal life, we become conscious of the greater ends that redeem man from the life of the brutes."[30]

Nor were the attacks on Bergson solely perpetrated by Anglophiles like Lewis. Julien Benda's career, spanning six decades, was simply one long diatribe against Bergson. An inheritor of the scientistic snobbery of late-nineteenth century positivism, Benda was one of those who, like Santayana and Wyndham Lewis, helped to define the tough thinking of the New Classicism in opposition to that of "soft" humanists like Bergson. Beginning with *Le Bergsonisme* in 1912, Benda wrote against Bergson in virtually all his works. These attacks were personal as well as philosophical. Benda calls Bergson a dandy, a sorcerer, a sophist, a "romantic," and even a descendant of the bloodthirsty and vile Belphegorian sect of the Jews (allusions to Bergson's Jewishness are not infrequent in the attacks of reactionaries like Lankester and Gerrard). Benda went so far as to say that he would joyfully have killed Bergson if in that way his influence could have been stopped.[31]

Benda's and Lewis's position is quintessentially reactionary: They attack Bergson not to propose new concepts of reason and intellect, but to defend old ones against erosion. As most biographers note, this virulent long-term aggression had the inevitable result that Lewis's and Benda's thought was deeply marked by the Bergsonism they attacked. Their philosophical position ends in being what SueEllen Campbell has aptly described as an "equal opposite" of Bergson.[32] Understandably troubled and puzzled by attacks, Bergson maintained silence. In Paris, his colleagues at the Sorbonne rebuked him on the one hand for invoking biology in speculative writing and on the other for importing mysticism into science. In 1914, seeing he could not alter public perception, or speak effectively to the attacks of those like Benda and Hugh El-liott, Bergson resigned his teaching position, hoping the furor would die down.

The war altered everything. As an important public figure, Berg-son found his support wanted for various causes. He did give some patriotic speeches for the French government, which appeared to ally him with the militant nationalists. George Sorel's syndicalists (who were advocating violent revolution at the time) were incensed by this "betrayal."[33] By the end of the war, Bergson was popular with neither faction, nor was he in any better position with his col-leagues at the Sorbonne. The Action Française disliked him as a Jew. The Catholic Church had placed his works on the Index. In 1937, his career over, Bergson wrote to Ralph Tyler Flewelling—a former student who had attacked him, then come to change his mind—"I have serious doubts about the usefulness of controversy in philosophy."[34]

Perhaps P.A.Y. Gunter is right that *any* optimistic or evolutionary philosophy would have been torpedoed by the crisis of the war.[35] But we know that Bergson's "ideology" was denied a fair hearing in many quarters—either through oversimplification of his concepts or through a public revilement not interested in his purely philo-sophical assertions. Bergsonian thought is exploratory, and some of Bergson's key terms, like *élan vital* and *durée réelle*, are not clearly correlated. Yet the charges leveled at him of dilettantism were gen-uinely absurd. Bertrand Russell accused him of creating an imagi-nary picture of the world not capable of proof or disproof—but that is the assessment Russell makes of any philosophy without a posi-tivist bent. Russell also wrote that in the light of Bergsonism, "in-tellect is the misfortune of man, while intuition is seen at its best in ants, bees, and Bergson." And he even charged that Bergson did not understand rudimentary mathematical concepts like "num-ber."[36] To appreciate the insufficiency of this evaluation, one must gain an overview of Bergson's philosophy, particularly its divided commitment to the advance of reason and the preservation of a "ground of being," the *durée réelle*.

Bergson described his philosophy as attempting to bring an empirical approach that would "make philosophy capable of an unlimited progress, like science."[37] This side of Bergson has been ignored. Indeed, few in America know that after the war he undertook a long essay on Einstein's theory of relativity, since that theory appeared to contradict some of *Creative Evolution*'s conclusions. *Durée et simultanéité* (1923) committed two unfortunate errors in transcribing some of Einstein's equations, on which critics gleefully seized. And until recently the book has been considered an inept attempt to deny the new facts of physics. But the facts of physics are not quite what they were in the twenties, and Bergson is now seen as a much more capable scientist and mathematician than he appeared to his (less than dispassionate) reviewers. Certainly, Bergson read in the sciences at a depth and with a regularity that reflected his basic tenet: Philosophy must proceed with a method that grounds it thoroughly in empirical knowledge.

In 1969, *Bergson and the Evolution of Physics* appeared under Gunter's editorship. Gunter shows that Bergson was able to anticipate the consequences of certain revolutions in physics, though few at the time appreciated it: "This is a remarkable achievement, particularly considering Bergson's reputation as an 'antiscientific' or 'literary' intellect; yet, at the present time, Bergson's interpretation of the physical sciences remains one of the least discussed, and least appreciated aspects of his thought." Gunter credits Bergson with "prophetic insights" into particle and astronomical physics, and sees his philosophy as "the affirmation, not the negation of science," suggesting we may yet see Bergson's thought offering further "theoretical advances."[38] Since Gunter's anthology appeared, Bergson's theory that the universe began in a "vital impulse" has indeed found support in research and a wider acceptance among scientists. His insights into particle physics have also been recognized.

According to Milič Čapek's *Bergson and Modern Physics* (1971), Bergson's thought anticipates "the elementary indeterminacy of microphysical processes which limits the applicability of Laplacean determinism to the physical world." Modern physics has, in other words, discovered that Bergson was right that psychological and scientific duration are, in a sense, analogous. And Čapek believes "Bergson's general insights [in his book on relativity] are far more significant than his occasional errors and vacillations, which . . . most frequently resulted from [his] not always fully grasping the implications of his own thought." Čapek recognizes how critics exaggerated Bergson's philosophy of limited free will into one of primitive lawlessness: "Instead of opposing the fictitious indeterminacy of 'free will' to the rigid necessity of the Laplacean type, [Bergson] proposes the theory of different degrees of freedom."[39]

Bergson's philosophy, then, despite what we have been stridently and incessantly told by many over years, is systematic and capable of defense against the charge of "anti-reason." Certainly, there is a legitimate question to be asked: What is the precise character of *durée*, and can it be rescued from an apparent irrationalism? But the charge that he was unsystematic, unscientific, and *irrational* in his approach to philosophy has been answered in the negative by every dispassionate critic.[40] All found a continuity in the philosophical thought. Whether we agree with him or not, Bergson made a system.

Bergson's Philosophy

The vital impulse (*élan vital*) is the cosmic bang with which everything in Bergson begins. Bergson characterizes it as a free, creative *act*. He posits all creation as "merged . . . in growth" (*CE*, 241) The blast of the vital impulse rolls through all things, drawing out of itself always the new. The new always appears, in retrospect, to have been inevitable; it is always actually unpredictable. Like Whitehead, James, and Royce, Bergson cannot make the present fully explicable in terms of the past. The only truth is the whole truth, and this means, for a developing creation, that we are never sure what is Now until we learn what it later becomes. Toward the end of his career, Bergson seems to have acknowledged that his vital impulse must have had a sort of genetically coded end point, conceived by and comprehensible to God alone. In a typically nineteenth-century way, Bergson finds man to be the last word in the evolution of the universe, the end toward which all has pointed. *The Two Sources of Morality and Religion* goes so far as to suggest that the universe is a machine for "the making of gods," and that God undertook Creation in order to "create creators, that He [might] have, besides Himself, beings worthy of His love" (*TS*, 306, 243).

The upward thrust of the vital impulse bifurcates immediately, however; it cannot sweep forward to its target unmitigated in force, for spent energies create a troubling drag of regression. Bergson compares the universe to a giant teakettle spraying steam that condenses into falling drops of water. He draws the further analogy to human consciousness struggling against the slump back to sentience, and divides the animate world into the sentient (plants), instinctive (social insects), and intelligent (vertebrate animals). Though all these forms stem from the mobility of the original *élan vital*, they are only partial expressions of it. And over time, they must fall individually, even if they collectively rise. Thus, the vital impulse we experience is a leap to a fall. Though Bergson asserts that reality is pure mobility, his vision of the universe is fraught with conflict between this mobility and materiality.

Human consciousness, then, is opposed to materiality, for it is "action unceasingly creating and enriching itself, whilst matter is action continually unmaking itself or using itself up" (*CM*, 23). But these opposed processes go on simultaneously. So Bergsonian philosophy is strongly monistic, if one thinks of its source in the *élan vital*. Yet it is also strongly dualistic, when one thinks of this conflict between matter and spirit, a conflict on which Bergson had first focused in his dissertation *Time and Free Will*, which introduced the concept of real duration.

Bergson later reflected that *Time and Free Will* represented the first application of his "method" on the problem of liberty (*CM*, 28). The "method" was philosophical intuition, and it was indeed inseparable from his reaction against the narrow positivistic determinism he attacked in 1889. Intuition reveals how experienced time overrules laboratory time, and shows how the "useful" generally usurps the place of the true in all inquiry, philosophical or scientific. Here

Bergson made an ingenious use of Spencer and Darwin in order to define the functions of intellect and intuition. He also turned the usual argument about memory on its head; that is, we have a great deal more forgetting than remembering to explain.

Real duration Bergson defines as that irreversible succession of heterogeneous states melting into one another and flowing in indivisible process which we experience when we return to our life below, our Being/Becoming. It *is* becoming, as we experience it. To be conscious of real duration, however, is to lose a sense of one's individuality in the world (although Bergson will later say that *durée* is the ultimate source of true individuality). It is to become aware of the continual novelty generated by the vital impulse. Such an overwhelming experience of the heart of life, a revisiting of instinct long buried, contradicts many of our "useful" habits. We discover that our perception of real duration has been buried for a good reason: The intuition of duration is *nonadaptive*. It is a loosening of the mechanisms our organism has evolved in order to survive.

Intellection, an adaptive response to the vertigo of real duration, "rises in revolt" at the "absolute originality and unforeseeability" of the vital impulse (*CE*, 29). Intellect was evolved in order "to limit, with a view to action, the life of the spirit" (*MM*, 233). Its object being survival, not truth, it draws a curtain between us and real duration, taking "cuttings" or snapshots of the flux: "To perceive means to immobilize" if we are speaking of intellectual life (*MM*, 275). Intellect's photographic technique makes it possible for us to hold things still, to plan, learn, to do something with our memories. Unfortunately, a problem arises when we forget that the intellect permits us only a little consciousness of the transfixing light of creation's vital spirit; it offers shadows, not reality. If we forget that intellect places us necessarily in "the discontinuous, in the immobile, in the dead," we lose contact with our fundamental selves (*CE*, 165). The method by which we control and explain our memories can thus end by also controlling our present experience, in which case "automatism will cover over freedom" (*TFW*, 237).

Thus, the *dédoublement* of self arises—the concept that so intrigues Piers Gray in his reading of Eliot and John Conder in his reading of Faulkner as an extension of American Naturalism. According to Bergson, we can *cope* with this doubling or splitting of the self by returning regularly to our primary experience. When we look within, we are reminded that the timeline is merely an exteriorization of a "cutting." It is static, and abolishes freedom, for if we can spread time out in space, all events are co-present. Change by the laboratory model is merely concatenation, and gives rise to determinism. But intuiting life reminds us that there are four dimensions to this reality. Thus, determinism stems from an error of language leading to pseudoquestions about experience. We can analyze things with such tools, but not experiences.

Bergson asserts that "freedom is a fact" (*TFW*, 221). But to know it *as fact* one must admit something like philosophical intuition into the system. Otherwise, how can we avoid the spatializing language of the intellect, which, potent as it is, cannot "think true continuity, real mobility, reciprocal penetration—in a word, that creative evolution which is life" (*CE*, 162)? In proposing philosophical intuition as a "method," Bergson seeks not to answer perennial questions about time, but to show they are mistaken (*TFW*, 74). For this reason, his thought rests on existentialist ground. In Bergson, modes of perception condition our grasp of reality. Mix a little cornstarch with water; the mixture hardens and crumbles when the fingers press it, but flows when let alone. This is the relationship between our mode of perception and the experience we describe. We only grasp an important, verifiable aspect of reality when we let it slip through our fingers. Intuition gives us access to life's flux, so we can grasp its freedom, its novelty. The intellect cannot give this access, since it is interested in sameness, not novelty, in generalities, not experiences. The intellect is interested in *words*, and Bergson protests "against the substitution of concepts for things" (*CM*, 31, 105). On the other hand, he recognizes that the intuitive experience must emerge in the world of words. He carefully defines intuition as "reflection, not feeling," and describes intuition as one of two modes affording two essential "kinds of clarity" in thought (*CM*, 103, 39). Bergson's intuition is thus different from Croce's, in that it is directly connected to apprehension, though it shares with Croce's intuition a cerebral attribute.

In the sense that Bergson's intuition seeks the unique, it is intensely personal. It does not participate in what Bergson saw as the undesirable impersonality of a reductive objectivity. But it is extremely impersonal in the sense that it has no ulterior motives. Intuition is achieved through one's consciously *not* attending (*TFW*, 128). It enters into things and psychological states with detachment, as an "intellectual sympathy" by which one "places oneself within an object [of thought] in order to coincide with what is unique in it and consequently inexpressible. Analysis, on the contrary, . . . reduces the object to elements already known." Thus by a sort of philosophical negative capability, intuition claims to give a clue to freedom, to make possible action that is more closely allied to our "true selves" (*IM*, 7, 74).

We "get back into ourselves," however, by forgetting ourselves. Thus, Bergsonian intuition is the direct forebear of Poulet's intuition, which he describes as a "forgetting myself"—even a kind of "self-alienation," since the intuiter yields up his identity "without . . . reservation, without any desire to preserve [his] independence of judgment. . . . In other words, the kind of comprehension in question here is not a movement from the unknown to the known, from the strange to the familiar, from the outside to the inside. It might rather be called a phenomenon by which mental objects rise up from the depths of consciousness into the light of recognition."[41] Poulet's intuition is, like Bergson's, an act of self-forgetting and self-discovery in one—without contradiction. It restores an alienated inner life. And this is the sort of value Bergson—and Poulet—find in art, particularly the experience of reading. When our inner self has been defended against that social self constantly usurping, we regain some measure of freedom and wholeness: "The deeper psychic states, those which are translated as free acts, express and sum up the whole of our past history" (*TFW*, 185). Precisely through relaxing intentionality do we experience freedom, and for that reason, Bergson says, free acts are exceptional.

Bergsonian intuition is inseparable, then, from Bergson's general view of life as *tension*: The "living and concrete self" is always striving to slough off the "crust" of rationalization it constantly exteriorizes (in the name of survival). The self renews itself by an effluence of primal experience "in which *succeeding each other* means *melt-*

ing into one another and forming an organic whole" (*TFW*, 167, 128). Intuition enables growth, and growth evolution. Intuition cannot do without analysis, nor *vice versa*. Troubled by its own evolutionary heritage, Bergson's intuition still attempts to affirm it, for it represents a sort of Darwinian adaptation to a later stage and higher order of progress than rationalization, which it somehow (paradoxically, critics say) incorporates.

"For a conscious being, to exist is to change, to change is to mature, to mature is to go on creating oneself endlessly. Should the same be said of existence in general?" (*CE*, 7). *Creative Evolution* affirms that it should. Bergson attempts to convince us that freedom is not "spontaneity," but a "synthesis of feelings and ideas, and the evolution which leads to it [is] a *reasonable* evolution" (*MM*, 243; my italics). *Creative Evolution* argues for this "reasonableness" by predicating everything on the dialectically opposed forces, the *tension*, we have just been discussing. Though life is "endlessly continued creation" and "pure mobility," still any "particular manifestations of life accept this mobility reluctantly, and continually lag behind" (*CE*, 178, 128). Indeed, real duration always "gnaws and leaves on them the mark of its tooth" (*CE*, 46). Thus, we are always caught between worlds, one of creation, the other of destruction— at home fully in neither: "The home of matter is space. The home of life is time" (*CE*, 16). But we live in both. The reality Bergson presents us in *Creative Evolution* is thus a coherence in confusion, a disorder in evolution, a reality making itself in a reality *unmaking* itself (*CE*, 251).

The dualism commits Bergson to two views of time, and he formulates evolution as a Charge of the Light Brigade:

All organized beings, from the humblest to the highest, from the first origins of life, to the time in which we are, and in all places as in all times, do but evidence a single impulsion, *the inverse of the movement of matter*, and itself indivisible. All the living hold together, and all yield to the same tremendous push. The animal takes its stand on the plant, man bestrides animality, and the whole of humanity, *in space and time*, is one immense army galloping beside and before and behind each of us in an overwhelming charge able to beat down every resistance and to clear away many obstacles, perhaps even death. [*CE*, 270-71; my italics]

Bergson's vision, contracting evolution into a timeless rush into darkness, is thus divided at the heart, his challenge to death a "perhaps." One thinks of the last lines of Virginia Woolf's *The Waves*: "'And in me too the wave rises. . . . I strike spurs into my horse. Against you I will fling myself, unvanquished and unyielding, O Death!' *The waves broke on the shore*." The cosmic book *may* conclude with a chapter titled "The Triumph of Life," but in the here and now we remain caught, in Eliot's words, "in the form of limitation between unbeing and being" (*CPP*, 122). Bergson's optimism is there, but it has been grossly exaggerated by interpreters—ironically, most often by apologists. According to the reading of Herman and Gallagher, Gunter, Havet, and Scharfstein, Bergson promises only progress through struggle. If we "take things by storm" and "thrust intelligence outside itself by an act of will," we will grow; but only if (*CE*, 193).

Since the "creativity" of evolution lies in a dialectic of competing forces, Bergson is brought to admit both views of time, though he is supposed simply to have disposed of one. "We do not think real duration, but we live it, because life transcends intellect," he writes, and yet, "wherever anything lives, there is open somewhere *a register in which time is being inscribed*" (*CE*, 46, 16; my italics). No attempt to relate Bergson's philosophy and aesthetics to literature can be valid that emphasizes his commitment to the elaboration of the new without recognizing that this novelty exists in a troubled medium *in and out of real duration*. Bergson may be seen in this light to stand not merely on the periphery of Woolf's *The Waves*, but to enter into its very heart. And that is because Bergson's interpretation of experience, like his theory of the self, is double: "Every demand for explanation in regard to the problem of freedom comes back, without our suspecting it, to the following question: 'Can time be adequately represented by space?' To which we answer: Yes, if you are dealing with time flown; No, if you speak of time flowing" (*TFW*, 221). This Yes and this No are the Yin and Yang of Bergson's Creative Evolution—his views of psychic life, culture, literature, philosophy, religion. They do not give simple application. Strangely, they remind one, in their essence, of an aspect of Nietzsche: "We are fundamentally inclined to maintain that the fals-est opinions . . . are the most indispensable to us; that without a recognition of logical fictions, without a comparison of reality with the purely imagined world of the absolute and immutable, without a constant counterfeiting of the world by means of numbers, man could not live—that the renunciation of false opinions would be a renunciation of life, a negation of life" (*Beyond Good and Evil*, I, 4). The conundrum of a *necessary untruth* underlies Bergson's whole philosophy, not merely his intuition of real duration. This fact makes his philosophy richly applicable to a consciously "modern" literature of irony. It is the mind's fictive power, Bergson seems to say, that gathers *temps perdu* and, by thrusting it "compact and un-divided into the present," creates that present.

The Last Years

After his book on Einstein's theory, Bergson published only one full-length study: *The Two Sources of Morality and Religion*. In 1928, when he received the Nobel Prize, rheumatic disease had already begun to limit his physical activity, and by 1935 it had grown so bad that he simply broke off correspondence and left Paris to live in Tours, at St. Cyr-sur-Seine. He was leaning toward the Catholic Church, and *The Two Sources* shows this influence. This latter part of Bergson's career has remained largely in shadow, for it does not accord with the standard view of his philosophy, promoted by Russell and Santayana, among others, a view that fixes Bergson pretty much at the level of his pre-1890 insight, "to perceive means to immobilize." Some, like Jacques Maritain, distinguished finally a "Bergsonism of Intention" from the popularized Bergsonism. Maritain had attacked Bergson's philosophy in *Bergsonian Philoso-phy and Thomism* in 1913, but in later editions had disassociated himself from the climate created by the rhetoric of the New Classi-cists (of which he was, of course, a charter member):

The greater the present vogue for Bergsonism is, the keener will be the reaction—and the more unjust. For no one should forget that at a particularly difficult period Bergson was the only one among the wise ones of this world victoriously to attack agnosticism, Kantianism, and the silly, narrow positivism which reigned unchallenged. In so doing, whatever he may have said of the intellect, he has served intelligence and truth. And many who have come out of the darkness of official atheism owe this to him and to the desire for truth that permeates his teaching.

Maritain recognized finally in Bergson a nineteenth-century mind moving toward faith, and he restricts his criticisms of Bergsonism, in the final analysis, to a quarrel over the place of "intelligence" and the meaning of "intuition"—an area with which, as we shall see, Eliot was also very much concerned.

Maritain believes Bergson's thought, exploratory in principle, moves with increasing clarity toward a humbling of philosophy before the wisdom of the saints and a transcending of his "own system of concepts." Bergson's implicit monism went unrecognized for so long simply because his thought had been "utilized by apologists and theoreticians of dogma," and thus, Maritain says in a note to the last edition of *Bergsonian Philosophy and Thomism*, it is not surprising that Bergson's will (dated Feb. 8, 1937) says, "I would have become a convert [to the Catholic Church], had I not seen in preparation for years the formidable wave of anti-semitism which is to break upon the world. I wanted to remain among those who tomorrow will be persecuted."[42] Bergson died in January 1941 of pneumonia contracted from having stood for hours in line with other Parisian Jews registering with the Nazi government.

Maritain fondly exaggerates Bergson's orthodoxy. What first drew Bergson to Christianity is suggested by a penciled note he made to himself in 1926: "Christianisme = dissatisfaction, *ergo* chambardement, *ergo* action."[43] Still, we have lost some valuable connections between Bergson and the literature of the early twentieth century when we forget that he was not only the "literary" philosopher of *roman fleuve*, but a scientist and ethical thinker whose career took him a long way from its departure point. I.W. Alexander places Bergson in the "time-honored current of non-speculative Christian thinking that runs from St. Augustine to Pascal."[44] James Street Fulton has noted that "Bergson's thinking, despite his criticism of finalism," eventually considers the *élan vital* a manifestation of divine love.[45] And Daniel Herman agrees that the "finality rejected by Bergson is a finality based on utilitarianism. . . . Such a finality is not a true finality . . . since freedom has been eliminated."[46]

Bergson's teleology is more contradictory than Herman is willing to admit. But he performs a valuable service in showing that Bergson's struggle with the irrational is no embrace. Bergson's "free act" entails moral responsibility, and *form* is as important to him as *spirit*. Omission of that fact has allowed many to create an imaginative picture of Bergson, the thinker for whom science is the enemy of art, form the enemy of spirit. In his thought, these dualities exist—and conflict—but finally, they dance as partners, and the music governing them is divine.

TWO

Bergsonian Intuition and Modernist Aesthetics

I believe in the mutability of reality rather than of truth. If we could regulate our faculty of intuition by the mobility of the real, would not this regulating be a stable thing, and would not the truth—which can only be this very regulating—participate in this reality?
—Henri Bergson, letter to William James, 1907

❧   In an essay on the "still movement of poetry," Murray Krieger suggests that Bergson's vitalism offers no key to the "well wrought" aspects of modern art, especially not to poetry's archetypal imagery and symmetrical forms. Though he acknowledges in *The New Apologists for Poetry* the Modernist debt to Bergson for a special concern with freshness and concreteness of language, Krieger nonetheless argues that Bergson cannot earn a *form* beyond fluidity; his philosophy thus gives no satisfactory approach to the Byzantine patterns of much twentieth-century poetry—poetry that seems anxious to become one of the "plastic arts."[1] This view, which makes Bergson the enemy of "form," ignores, as I have already argued, Bergson's dualism. As much as he emphasizes the dynamic and living, Bergson also recognizes the unavoidability, indeed the clear desirability, of formal rigor in literature. Bergson defines "form" differently, however. For him the poem emulates a life-struggle between spirit and flesh, consciousness and sentience. He believes that "the word turns against the idea" (*CE*, 127). But the word remains an enemy only as the common coin of everyday necessity. Words differently employed give better return.

Language wears out over time, losing its value for instruction or insight. The poet wishes to melt down the common coin and forge it new. His object—in Bergson's terms—must be to renew the linguistic system's connectedness to inner life, that self-creating evolution flowing through time. The magic of any linguistic system lies in its ability to evoke this fundamental reality for us, and when the poet succeeds in his endeavor, he may be said to have gotten "hold of the *gold coin,* instead of the silver or copper change for it" (*ME,* 195). In such a moment, language's dry bones live again, for they actually "furnish consciousness with an immaterial body in which to incarnate itself" (*CE,* 265). Language in such a moment is not the enemy, for it has been reinvested with that characteristic impenetrability of the Real. Its mathematics appear mobile, to the consciousness chasing its direction; when consciousness has quickened to its vision, an illusion of *stillness* descends, as when speeding vehicles stand abreast. With its dual emphasis on necessary rigidities of the poet's medium and the pure mobility of experience, Bergson's philosophy and aesthetic theory give important and neglected insight into the practice of many English-speaking writers of this century.

The cause of this neglect is not far to seek: Bergson's hostility to the canon of positivism, on the one hand, and skepticism on the other. As Eliot himself noted as early as 1910, the problem with Bergson is that he always seems bent on occupying a middle ground. Criticism, in contrast, historically goes to extremes. True, confusions about what Bergson really said on aesthetic matters led to the conclusion of Krieger and others; Arthur Szathmary tried in the thirties with a calm and lucid little book on Bergsonian aesthetics to show that Bergson expected art to present "living moments *in precise ordered forms,*" and the artist to express his intuitions in (what else?) "formal structures."[2] The book's failure to be greatly noticed seems unsurprising, in retrospect. It stems from a general opinion that Bergson has a naive view of the potentiality of the linguistic sign. That opinion is in error.

In the *Tractatus Logico-Philosophicus,* Wittgenstein (echoing St. Augustine) sums up the nature of philosophical discussion: "What can be said at all can be said clearly, and what we cannot talk about we must pass over in silence."[3] But, as Augustine asks, are we to say nothing of God, who is "not even to be called 'unspeakable,' because to say even this is to speak of Him"? Augustine notes the "curious contradiction" inherent in such naming, and "yet God, although nothing worthy of His greatness can be said of Him, has condescended to accept the worship of men's mouths, and has de-sired us through the medium of our own words to rejoice in His praise" (*Confessions*, I, 6). In a curious, though I think not finally "contradictory" way, it must be admitted that language suggests something beyond its own "prison house" (to use Nietzsche's phrase). But here we have arrived at the crux of a serious disagree-ment among scholars and critics of literature.

Clearly, no criticism in the skeptical tradition will accept, much less value, an aesthetic theory grounded upon "expression" of any-thing—even skepticism itself. My view stands in direct opposition to that element of deconstructionist criticism which leads to a self-immolating intertextualization of literature. I have in mind such books as Joseph Kronick's recent *American Poetics of History*. "An American poetics of history will . . . be a poetics of reading," the book claims, beginning with Emerson himself, who "finds the world in a book." Typically of such studies, this one reduces its problem, that of "an 'American' identity" to "one of reading, that is, of mapping the exchange of tropes between texts."[4] It would be hard to decide which is the more damaging result, the loss of a human story in the creation of a literary artifact or the extreme dull-ness of a dogmatic approach with essentially one critical technique: "mapping" "interfaces."

On the other hand, I cannot agree with Frank Lentricchia that deconstruction can "tell us how we deceive ourselves, but it has no positive content, no alternative textual work to offer to intellectuals. It has nothing to say."[5] Certainly it does have something very im-portant to say, and that something stems from the same complex and dualistic view of language we see in Bergsonian philosophy. I take it that Bergson would have approved, for example, Paul de Man's judgment that Shelley's readings of literature are great pre-cisely because they defy being "generalized into a system."[6] There is this strong element in deconstructionist writing, skeptical in tone but in content (there is genuinely a content) fundamentally part of the critique of Rationality authored by Russell, James, Bradley, and, of course, Bergson.

There is also a second element in deconstructionism that reflects an unacknowledged heritage of Bergsonism. It is, as W. Wolfgang Holdheim puts it in *The Hermeneutic Mode*, the idea that "getting to know is better than knowing, because the process of learning should never end."[7] This open-endedness is the positive side of a great realization about linguistic systems explored by Saussure. His insight that the linguistic sign unites not things and names, but concepts and sound-images is the point of departure for a criticism based upon the problematics of reading.[8] There is a very big difference, however, between those who interest themselves, with Saussure, in the structure of this mysterious process itself—the self-creating agency of language—and those who interest themselves primarily in the self-consciousness of all linguistic acts, the *dédoublement* as unbridgable chasm.

The difference is summed up beautifully by Hazard Adams in his astonishingly rich, challenging, and humane effort to reconcile the hostile camps, *Philosophy of the Literary Symbolic*. Paul de Man appears to make "communication of a previous truth or reality definitive, then [declare] the impossibility of it," says Adams; he, on the other hand, takes *creation* as definitive. De Man, as Adams sees him, represents "a continuation of that profound disillusionment with language that is one dominant mood of romanticism and perhaps comes to its logical conclusion in Derrida's *reductio ad absurdum*. Derrida seems to play the role with respect to structuralism that Berkeley did in the empiricist movement. There comes a time in each case, however, when someone must kick a stone or recast the terms of argument. Therefore, I look at another romantic mood that continually seeks to formulate the full range of the possibilities of language."[9] Adams has indeed reformulated the terms of the argument, and in a way that sets him partly in the tradition of *Creative Evolution*, since he is determined to see language as Bergson, Whitehead, and James saw it: as the creation of a new definiteness that must constantly be recreated, renewed.

There is a cost to Adams's effort, however. In transferring the issue to an entirely man-made realm, Adams has given up the no-

tion of the Divine Word, capable of bearing an intuition of visionary experience. That is a crucial decision, and one that separates
Adams—and perhaps our age—from the mood in which *The
Waste Land* and *The Sound and the Fury* were written. Having
countered Derrida's conundrum that language is the site of a paradoxical absence, Adams has let go of the idea of a general ground
of Being and of a "transcendental signified." Bruce Kawin's *The
Mind of the Novel* suggests that language's value may yet be linked
to a sense of the "ineffable" experience. His view preserves an Augustinian tradition of wonder and bafflement at language and memory: "Great is this force of memory, O my God; a large and bound-
less chamber! Who ever sounded the bottom thereof? Yet is this a
power of mine, and belongs unto my nature; nor do I myself comprehend all that I am. Therefore is the mind too strait to contain
itself. And where should that be, which it containeth not of itself?
Is it without it, and not within?" (*Confessions*, X, 15). Kawin's is
also the view more in direct descent from the Modernist aesthetic
Bergson bequeathed to Hulme and Eliot.[10]

T.E. Hulme, who observed that art is the "key to Bergson's
thought," made Bergson's thought a key to art, becoming a translator—though not much a popularizer—of Bergson's metaphysics.
Bergson provides, Hulme said in *Speculations*, a way for "theory to
be stated accurately," a way to explain art's importance to culture,
and a "much better vocabulary" for talking about the "indescribable
process of artistic creation."[11] Whether we prefer to view language's
potential in these terms now—and I have suggested that the option
is by no means closed, as some will have it—we must face the fact
that they were the terms of the pre- and post-war period. Certainly
Pound commented sarcastically on Hulme's boring him endlessly
with Bergson. But as Frank Kermode wrote some years ago,
Hulme's ideas were far more influential than popular: "Hulme
hands over to the English tradition a modernized but essentially
traditional, aesthetic of Symbolism . . . the magic Image, or Romantic anti-positivism, and of the excluded artist. We are so accustomed
to regard Hulme as the classicising, anti-Romantic thinker, that we
tend to ignore [this]."[12] In the aesthetic theory of Hulme, clearly
Bergson's "intuition" is the most important term.

In Hulme's intuitive revery, the artist contacts a reality, pure duration, which transcends intellect. He has, then, a sense of being
outside of time—and yet of having entered it profoundly, merging
with a flux in which he sees "the blending of many ideas which,
when once dissociated, seem to exclude one other as logically contradictory" (*TFW*, 136). Moreover, intuition seems to distil "enormous periods of an infinitely diluted existence into a few more dif-
ferentiated moments of intenser life, and in this summing up a very
long history" (*MM*, 275). Intuition then may give almost prophetic
powers (*TFW*, 198). It certainly bestows on the artist of Hulme's
imagining a privileged view, a primary position.

According to Bergson and Hulme the artist begins with the
"humming of life's depths" (*CM*, 176). He combats the visceral
reaction of the mind to flux. But for Bergson—and this is the point
of confusion for the critics of Bergsonian "formlessness"—the
depths that defy analysis are not without logic. Consciousness flows
like a sheet of water in "an unbroken stream of images which pass
from one into another," but this "interpenetration of images does
not come about by chance. It obeys laws . . . which hold the same
relation to imagination that logic does to thought" (*L*, 41-2). With
Kant, Bergson opposes to practical logic the science of the *form of
thinking* ("die Wissenschaft von der blossen Form des Denkens
überhaupt"). Logic as practically used, Kant says, "can be nothing
other than a scholastic technique," which he assigns to pedagogy,
reserving his *applied logic* to psychology. The latter is the science
of the necessary laws or "rigidities" ("notwendigen Gesetzen") of
the understanding and the reason, which have their own formality.[13]
Intuition allows study of this "logic of the imagination that is not
the logic of reason" (*L*, 41).

The artist of Bergson and Hulme is thus a sort of psychic spe-
lunker, advance scout for the new empiricism Bergson hoped to
found on the "immediate data of consciousness." For this reason art
assumes tremendous importance in Bergson's philosophy. One may
see this pattern develop in subsequent French thought, like that of
Sartre, which actually turns to art to find a vocabulary for its insights, since philosophical discussion must pass over them in silence. Philosophy dependent upon elements of art (and artifice) be-

comes tractable as well to the needs of art, as Hulme discovered: "The creative artist, the innovator, leaves the level where things are crystallized out into these definite shapes, and, diving down into the inner flux, comes back with a new shape which he endeavours to fix. He cannot be said to have created it *but to have discovered it,* because when he has definitely expressed it we recognize it as true." [14] The poet-empiricist visits the river *beneath* the static forms reflected from its surface; that river, like Eliot's in "Dry Salvages," is "within us," a "reminder of what men choose to forget." Hulme's consonance with Bergson here is not a contradiction, if we recognize that Bergsonian intuition brings with it a "passionate desire for accuracy," a deep wonder, and hunger to locate the "universal in the particular"—the Reality beneath reality. [15]

In *The Contrived Corridor,* Harvey Gross develops the thesis that Modernist writers are essentially mental explorers searching for a vocabulary adequate to their experience of "radical reality," their knowledge gained through having "lived in history as functioning organs of the world's body." Gross sees Modernism as a literature of the "blood and nerves," derived "more from insight than theory." [16] The encyclopedic detail and psychological intensity of the *Cantos, The Waste Land, Ulysses, The Waves,* and *Absalom, Absalom!* give credence to Gross's view. He sees "victims" of insight who present moments of an intenser life, one that often creates a sense of moral and intellectual crisis, as does *Paterson,* for example. The moments often contract long histories into short spaces, attempting to reveal continuities between widely disparate people and places. More importantly, Modernist literature entertains the hope that through understanding the necessary laws of the myth-making, or poetic consciousness, we may find a means to "make sense" of the chaos of memory and history.

This literature adopts the Bergsonian principle that the past has a real, sensual presence—though it is not visualizable in the scholastic jargon. In order to communicate this intimate sense of history Now, they try to make their poetry reify the smelting, flowing character of the deeper consciousness Hulme discusses. They amalgamate archetypal figures with pungently contemporary characters; they strive to evoke images beneath images, even re-fusing words, as Joyce does in *Finnegans Wake*. Such exploratory literature meets, as Bergson suggests, the challenge of communication with revolu-tionary use of language, and at first "disconcerts, then teaches us to see art differently, and finally precipitates itself as, [in retrospect] work of genius" (*TS*, 66, 33).

Such works, that challenge linguistic structures, that suggest a "self-deconstruction," call attention simply to a paradox and limita-tion characteristic of all linguistic acts. As Kawin argues, it depends upon your interpretation of such gross disturbances as the intrusion of rude, anachronistic voices in the *Cantos*: Does the cacophony suggest an "absence" at the heart of the text—or is the heart "inef-fable"? When Pound says he cannot "make it cohere" (Canto CXVI), does he write the final word on the palimpsest, encourag-ing us to believe that language itself is alienated from "meaning"? Or should we not look at the *Cantos* as an effort—though failed—predicated upon a very different idea of the significance of the lin-guistic act: "I have tried to write Paradise" (fragment of Canto CXX).

Of course, it was against just such ambitiousness for art's respon-sibilities that Eliot reacted in "Experiment in Criticism" (1929). In that essay, Eliot recommended a return to literature intended to give "refined pleasure to persons of sufficient leisure and breeding," rather than one with pretensions to "eliciting truth or acquiring knowledge." Eliot put much of the blame for this dramatic increase in art's responsibilities upon Coleridge, a thinker with whom he also strongly identified.[17] Though Eliot protested the move toward an art with empirical and metaphysical responsibilities, he had to confront its claims. A poem like *Four Quartets* takes those respon-sibilities very seriously, recording one poet's "findings" in a career that asks very much to be read as a search for what Kenneth Burke calls the "title of titles."[18] The poetic voice of *Four Quartets* recurs often to the intractability of language to inner experience. Indeed, this seems characteristic of the Modernist long poem generally: that it images "the radiant gist that / Resists the final crystallization" (*Paterson*, book 3).

"Precisely," critics of Bergson's aesthetic will say. Such an artist can salvage nothing from his intuitive experience. He will stand in speechless awe before the revelation: "Spirit, duration, pure change" (*CM*, 37). How can he, in any case, suggest the nonverbal through the verbal, the dynamic through the static forms of language; how can he communicate the "ineffable"? Must not Bergson oppose words themselves? He does tie language to the same imperatives that condition the intellect. Words "intervene" between us and reality, and "even our own mental states are screened from us" by language (*L*, 153). Words, as pre-cut molds for thought, automatically convert tangible experience into frangible objects (*TFW*, 130). The word, in Bergson's evolutionary theory, is essentially utilitarian, reducing novelty to "commonplace forms," expressing the new only as "rearrangement of the old" (*CM*, 94-96). It would seem that for Bergson the artist's intuition cannot be cast into words at all without its fluidity being arrested and its uniqueness converted to public property. The poet tries in vain "to force the living into this or that one of his molds. All the molds crack. They are too narrow, above all too rigid for what [he tries] to put in them" (*CE*, x).

From this standpoint poetry is a hopeless project; and Bergson recognizes the pose of failure as fitting for the artist. Faulkner claimed the honor of failure; Eliot speaks of the "raid on the inarticulate / With shabby equipment always deteriorating" (*FIU*, 4; *CPP*, 128). But there is another point of view consistent with Bergson from which the project is not hopeless. Intuition gave "birth to poetry . . . and converted into instruments of art words which, at first, were only signals" (*CM*, 94). From this standpoint the artist is sovereign in language's realm, a real Power—in the Coleridgean sense—who poses as god. This artist performs the task of taking the coin of everyday speech handed down by evolution and "making it new." Once he has intuited duration and felt the necessities of action drop away, the artist becomes infused with the desire to create. "Anyone engaged in writing," says Bergson, "has been in a position to feel the difference between an intelligence left to itself and that which burns with the fire of an original and unique emotion, born of the identification of the author with his subject, that is to say, of intuition" (*TS*, 38). The artist finds "he cares no more for praise and feels above glory, because *he* is a creator" (*ME*, 70). In fact, Bergson's aesthetic theory stands in a long tradition of viewing the artist as a secular creator.

Such a theory was traced by Renaissance aestheticians to Aristotle himself—this was their interpretation of the charge Aristotle gave poetry to "imitate only ideal truth." Spingarn notes that Scaliger (1540-1609) was the key figure to make this "adjustment" in Aristotle's view of poetry for the sake of justifying poetry against charges of sacrilege. Puttenham and Sidney clearly drew on Scaliger's defense of Dante, Petrarch, and Boccaccio in their own "defenses" of poetry. Poets, according to Scaliger, viewed theology itself as a form of their art—"the poetry of God." For Boccaccio, Petrarch, Dante, "the poet's function . . . was to hide and obscure the actual truth behind a wall of beautiful fictions." Through obfuscation, the poet created "another nature better than ever nature itself brought forth," thus giving a suggestion of God's own *unimaginable* glory. For Renaissance aestheticians, then, the argument was that poetry's impulse was "at one with God Himself."[19] Bergson has not fundamentally changed the original argument: The poet's power derives from contact with the universe's creative center; the poet's function is to suggest a truth beyond everyday powers of seeing, to utter a word that suggests, but does not usurp or evacuate, the unspeakable center itself. For Bergson, too, the height of God's creation is the creative human being. But for Bergson, the most important illusion an artist can create (and he does understand it can be only illusion) is that we have briefly penetrated the veil.

Not that the veil must be destroyed: "Fortunate are we to have this obstacle, infinitely precious to us is the veil" (*ME*, 70). Without automatic responses, stock ideas, dead language, we would actually stand unable to function in a world requiring action, action, action. But though we should not stare into the sun, we need light. We visit the world art creates to be reminded that the curtains occasionally part, and the artist creating the reminder is the uncommon man, one who has remained close to his origin, like Wordsworth's child, retaining an ability to reconcile "in a harmony sensitive to the heart terms perhaps irreconcilable to the intelligence" (*CM*, 299). For the most part, we live in the "practical" world, and this tends to divide us from ourselves. The artist shaking the veil reasserts the feeling inner part of our nature against the utilitarian outer part. That intuitive facet of our nature is the key to growth. Bergson sees the artist as having "no other object than to brush aside the utilitarian symbols, the conventional and socially accepted generalities, in short, everything that veils reality from us" (*L*, 157). "Reality," for Bergson, is self-discovery and self-creation. And Bergson suggests a technique for brushing aside the veil.

It is indirection. The higher the consciousness of the poet, the greater will be the *tension* between any partial notation of Becoming and the "paradoxical permanence of ceaseless change."[20] Inspired by insight, the poet must "catch up" his readers by employing rigorous techniques of *omission*, making use of the inherent paradox of language itself. His poem must resist us, just as language resists his poetry. This is not merely his curse, the site of a paradoxical absence, but his triumph also, for the incidental forms of the poem can regulate our intuition by the mobility of the real, the stability of truly "ceaseless change." Bergson's artist does not introduce feelings or ideas into us, but "introduces us into them, as passersby are forced into a street dance" (*TS*, 32). Not the bits of dust and paper in the Metro, but the wind that stirs them should attract our attention; yet it is only through the bits and pieces that the wind makes itself known to us. Great literature, according to Bergson, catches us up in its voice, bringing our thoughts into a dance, so that we "fall into step" (*CM*, 102). If the poet distracts us from practical life, the border blurs, and we merge (with him) in intuitive revery, seeing and feeling what he wishes to suggest (*TFW*, 14).

Thus Bergson offers a vocabulary for describing how the well-wrought poem may embrace its medium and yet achieve an epiphany of spirit. The poem's unity of form is achieved by mental—that is, scholastic—effort, but the poet is precisely that person who has kept his "ideas in touch with his feelings and his soul in touch with life" (*L*, 106). Intellectual effort, in the common sense, is comparatively easy "and can be prolonged at will," but the intuition of the artist is "arduous and cannot last" (*CM*, 39). Such effort can achieve however "the unity of a 'directive idea' common to a great number of organized elements," "the very unity of life" (*ME*, 225). In the center of the winds of flux, there is an eye, a still point.

"Above the word and above the sentence there is something much more simple than a sentence or even a word: the meaning, which is less a thing than a movement of thought, less a movement than a direction" (*CM*, 143). Through properly constructed art, we may achieve fleeting contact with something like this directive prin-ciple, according to which, as Wittgenstein says, words mean what they do.

Bergson ascribes to the poem a logic reifying the logic of dreams, of memory itself left to itself. For him, the experience of a poem is virtually indistinguishable from that of memory, and the power of the proper poem can be released only when the reader exercises heightened powers of *memorization* in order to intuit the presence of a directive idea. With practice, says Bergson, we can memorize instantaneously even a complex temporal sequence, grasping the timeless unity of the timebound series. This means "making all the ideas, all the images, all the words converge in one single point. *It is getting hold of the gold coin*, instead of the silver or copper change for it. What is the gold coin? How are so many images held together in one simple idea?" (*ME*, 195). This is the simplicity costing "not less than everything," as Eliot has it. To make all converge on a single point is a physical impossibility for the poet printing letters on a page, but it is a psychological possibility for the poet putting images into our heads. It likely remains only a possibility, but po-etry ought to push us—beyond appearances, back toward some-thing primordial and instinctive. It ought, according to Bergson, to help us locate original novelty, freshness, and vitality.

Such moments of contact with reality's heart were of great im-portance to Modernist writers, like Pound, who called them mo-ments of "magic," in which we break through "from the quotidian into 'divine or permanent world.'"[21] For Joyce, they are moments when an object of thought yields its "soul, its whatness . . . from the vestment of its appearance."[22] Aldous Huxley, whose theory of perception owes a great deal to Bergson, defined them as revelations of "the impossible paradox and supreme truth—that perception is (or at least can be, ought to be) the same as Revelation, that Reality shines out of every appearance, that the One is totally, infinitely present in all particulars."[23] The well-wrought poem must, then, give the feeling that its finite parts make an infinite whole. Its pattern must resist reduction to a roadmap. That is why Joseph Frank's pioneering essay on spatial form in modern literature misleads us when it asserts that Joyce seeks in *Ulysses* "to give the reader a picture of Dublin seen as a whole," and that the book can therefore not really be "read" but only "reread."[24] *Ulysses* is no picture of Dublin. Rather, it is an attempt to reveal the Dublin of Joyce's intuitive experience. The novel invites us to take stock of the interrelationship of its parts, to fabricate alternative maps of parts of the city, but never offers us the resolution of a picture spread out in space. Frank's essay emphasizes one side of reading *Ulysses* at the expense of the other. It would be truer to say that we cannot reread *Ulysses*—only experience it anew. And that is its magic.

To create such magic, Bergson says, the artist must stay perpetually aware of the tension between intuition and the forged implements of language. The artist's work, like any manifestation of life, accepts mobility "reluctantly" (*CE*, 128). The reader's attention must be directed incessantly beyond what is immediately in view, to attend as on a moonless night to what lies just beside the object of apprehension. In *The Spirit of Romance* (1910) Pound distinguished this concern of the artist carefully from that of the scientist—implying thereby that art shares something with science. Art, he wrote, is not unlike a river "perturbed at times by the quality of the riverbed, [but] in a way independent of that bed. . . . Stationary objects are reflected, but the quality of motion is of the river. The scientist is concerned with all these things, the artist with that which flows." Of course, Pound knew that traditional science was not unconcerned with what "flows," and that the artist hoping to evoke the river had better know a great deal about the reflections on the surface. But his artist enters a "divine or permanent world," and his poem must invite vision that penetrates static forms evoked by nouns to the sweeping verbal flux of the river. The arts are always "dynamic," Pound writes, "not passive, nor static, nor in a sense reflective, though reflection may assist at their birth."[25]

The "reflections" here conduct to intuitive knowledge. At this early stage of his career, Pound appears to be repeating the sorts of things Hulme might have been saying about Bergson's aesthetics.

That is the guess of William Harmon, who points out that the central concern of all Pound's early criticism—the criticism that helped
forge Vorticist and Imagist dogma—was "discovering the means for
subverting the temporal sequence of language so that images can
present the essence or effect of sudden illuminations that transcend
space and time."[26] A poem like "In a Station of the Metro" seeks
not to reflect on such illuminations, but to give their effect. Many
other contemporary writers seem to have had the same concern with
moments of illumination. And most found it necessary to take
Pound's subversive approach—Eliot seeks, for example, to dislocate "language into his meaning" (*SE*, 248).

Bergson's *Introduction to Metaphysics* had certainly provided
Hulme with an obvious vocabulary to talk about the necessity for
this incessant exhausting reorientation of vision poetry demands of
its readers. The poet's images "keep us in the concrete. No image
can replace the intuition of duration, but many diverse images, bor-
rowed from very diverse orders of things, may, by the convergence
of their action, direct consciousness to the point where there is a
certain intuition to be seized" (*IM*, 15-16). Here is the Imagist
aesthetic passed on by Hulme, who acted as both translator and
promoter of the book in which it appeared. It helps explain both
Pound's revisions of *The Waste Land*, where he ruthlessly pared
away context and elaboration, and his own strategies of "indirection" in the *Cantos*.

It also helps us understand William Carlos Williams's heterodox
structures in *Paterson* (as it finally *evolved*). There, Williams gives
us the formula "No ideas but in things" (book 1). Yes, "thingness"
is a trap in aesthetic discussion; it is static; it freezes. But *living*
things transcend their formal limitations, leaving us with more than
empty form. By a cunning arrangement of the images of things—
that is, after all, what Williams's dictum boils down to in poetic
practice—the poet may direct the reader's consciousness toward an
experience language cannot directly touch. The arrangement must
be intuitive, following the logic of dreams. It must seem random,
novel, incomplete . . . For it is a developing whole. But it will not
resolve its many tensions. They are the "point." Through that tech-

nique, it may end in evoking for us something—we usually call it emotion, but it is an amalgam of feeling and thought.

Eliot's "objective correlative" is rooted in a Bergsonian aesthetic. It proposes a "chain of events which shall be the formula of that particular emotion" poetry evokes (*SE*, 124). Faulkner, too, spoke of aesthetics as a science, like chemistry, with certain scientific rules which, when properly applied, will produce great art as surely as certain chemical elements combined in the proper proportions will produce certain reactions."[27] Pound also spoke of poetry as a "sort of inspired mathematics, which gives us equations not for abstract figures, triangles, spheres, and the like, but equations of human emotions."[28] This desire to compete with science, to turn the powers of intelligence on unexplored psychic territory, is profoundly Bergsonian, and its strong presence in the work of trendsetters like Pound and Eliot (and later Faulkner) changes our view of the sequence by which certain literary techniques were developed and promulgated among American writers. The ubiquitousness of this pseudoscientific rhetoric has often been noted, but always with the emphasis on either the "mathematics" or the "inspiration." In Bergson the impulses coexist. For him, the artist must use "equations," but they must not be allowed to resolve. Rather, the language must preserve what Ernst Cassirer calls the "magic circle with which consciousness surrounds it."[29] The poet's equations, that is, must maintain a sufficient degree of impenetrability for the intellect if they are to evoke intuition.

The poet does not aim merely to make it hard on readers, but he must insist on a mode of reading. He must, as Eliot put it, create a "living and developing scheme," and even risk going "too far" in the direction of complexity and obscurity to do so.[30] In Bergson's vocabulary, the poet must coin new words, create new ideas, though he will stand accused of "no longer communicating," not even "writing" (*TS*, 242). The reader of such poetry does indeed find it demanding. He too must adopt a new method. Eliot describes it in his introduction to Perse's *Anabasis*. One must allow "the images to fall into . . . memory successively without questioning the *reasonableness* of each at the moment; so that at the end, a total effect is produced. Such a selection of images and ideas has nothing chaotic about it. . . . The reader of a poem should take at least as much trouble as a barrister reading an important decision on a complicated case."[31] The difficulty comes in shifting gears from courtroom logic to intuition. To open memory after Eliot's fashion requires an act of will by which intelligence is "thrust outside itself" and the mind is left in a state of active receptivity.

Thus, Bergsonian aesthetics help us understand why that artifact, the Modernist text, comes to look and feel the way it does. M.L. Rosenthal and Sally Gall have actually claimed that there is a "modern poetic sequence" that is a genre in itself (like the sonnet).[32] Whether we accept this or not, certainly there is a common vocabulary among many Modernist poets that springs from the root we are tracing, and one might as well call it a "sequence" whose goal is to keep alive the intuitive "formulation" of the poet through the conscious creation of tensions: "By choosing images as dissimilar as possible, we shall prevent any one of them from usurping the place of the intuition it is intended to call up, since it would then be driven away at once by its rivals. By providing that . . . they all require from the mind the same kind of attention, and in short the same degree of *tension*, we shall gradually accustom consciousness to a particular and clearly defined disposition—that precisely which it must adopt in order to appear to itself as it really is, without any veil" (*IM*, 16-17; my italics). The poet reveals us to ourselves. To evoke this experience, the poem must consciously not name it. The whole poem is the Name. The method of the poem is universal, and yet it will result in totally different *sequences*, depending upon the intuition to which the poet hopes it leads. And a part of the revelation will always be linguistic; that is, the poet's revelation of inner life will also incorporate the tensions he himself feels between the poem's parts (word, phrase, image, stanza) and its entelechy, between the partial notations and the vector.

Bergson's aesthetic theory, then, is not naive about formal artifice. When the poet directs consciousness to that point at which there is an intuition to be seized, we are filled with admiration. He has torn aside the veil, "the cleverly woven curtain of our conventional ego," showing us our fundamental selves in their "infinite permeation of a thousand different impressions which have already ceased to exist the instant they are named." Naturally, we laud the artist for having known us "better than we knew ourselves. *This is not the case, however*" (*TFW*, 133; my italics). Those who think Bergson's aesthetic theory begins and ends in the pure innocence of Becoming have simply not read far enough. We realize, on reflection, that we have been given another veil, another illusion: "The very fact that [the poet] spreads out our feelings in homogeneous time and expresses its elements by words shows that he in turn is offering us only its shadow" (*ibid.*). Great art overcomes this obstacle through its very provisionality.

It does so by returning to the incessant process of discovery— the disorientation and reorientation of life. Witnesses of the poet's foray, we are brought back into our own presence finally by the *process* of our interaction with the text, which can restore our sense of connectedness to both nature and culture. In this, Bergson anticipates Paul Tillich's assertion that the literary symbol is a "sacrament," one that "opens up levels of reality which are otherwise closed for us [and] also unlocks dimensions and elements of our soul which correspond to the dimensions and elements of reality."[33] Literature can open these depths precisely because it participates in the reality to which it points—the words mean what they *do*. For Bergson, too, art can evoke living selfhood through its very artificiality, for as we peel back layers, seeking meaning, we are perpetually surprised at how meanings are, in Eliot's phrase, "perpetually *eingeschachtelt* into meanings" (*SE*, 195). To become engaged, through literature, in this unending process of discovery is precisely to contact again at its most salient point the nature of our own being.

At this point, the artist steps aside. He merely catalyzes. For Eliot, he is platinum filament, for Bergson a reagent bringing out latent images in film, revealing the canvas's *pentimenti*. The experimental method cannot guarantee success; the equation may not have result. For some readers (Bergson says) the poet's language will seem vague, "and so it is in what it expresses. Others feel it precise, because they experience everything it suggests" (*CM*, 299). Poetry concerns itself mainly with suggestion and impression, not expression, the utilitarian "message." It concerns itself with experiences, not concepts (though perhaps with the experience of a concept). If we cannot have presentation of the original in art, we can still have what Bergson—and after him Hulme, Eliot, Pound and others—called the "emotional equivalent" of it (*TFW*, 15). The reader with such an object in view will perhaps not mind changing his method, being patient, dispensing with some of his old expectations.

He will not mind adjusting other things. His definitions of memory and history, for example. *Ulysses, The Waves, Paterson, The Waste Land, The Cantos,* and *Absalom, Absalom!* collapse space and time, suggesting that past, present, and future are Now, that all personalities are continuous. They point to an underlying reality refracted through moments of intense experience that ask to be accepted as "sacraments" and revelations. They include much that might be considered "trivial," because of the poet's strategy of selection leading to tensions. Thrown into such an encyclopedia of psychic, mythic, historical data, the reader must fall back on instinct, must read intuitively. This literature's zeitgeist, as it turns out, is the very concept of a zeitgeist—or perhaps we should use Pound's term, *paideuma,* which insists upon its flowing and developing character. Such art makes large claims to craftsmanship and vision.

One of the greatest American craftsmen to come in the wake of the Bergsonian tradition is Wallace Stevens. "The poems of Stevens," Frank Doggett comments, "remind us of the intuition of Bergson . . . an intuition that is both gnomic and intelligible," an intuition reflecting "the flux of experience."[34] Stevens's poetry gets at the psychic sensuality of intuition through a rigorous and dispassionate probing that is keenly alive to the sensual world. It lulls and directs with its great care for the place of the syllable, the flow of sound into sound. Yet its voice is intensely cerebral. Gnomic with the mystery of process, Stevens's poetry is finally intelligible only to those who understand something of its heritage, and therefore of its intent. The final image of poem XI of "The Man with the Blue Guitar" refers us to this territory: "Deeper within the belly's dark /

Of time, time grows upon the rock." Here stands the rock of ceaseless change, gnawed by time, the moment's pregnancy.

For Bergsonian aesthetics, the mystery of any poem lies in the
tension between coolheaded laboratory techniques and the noise of
creation, the "humming of life's depths." Breaking down barriers,
rending veils, the poem yet maintains its self-consciousness, its distance. It claims to rediscover a spirit from which it gains authority,
and somehow to overcome the contradiction between that spirit's
dynamism and its own rigid form. Frost wrote that "the greatest of
all attempts is to say one thing in terms of another, is the philosophical attempt to say matter in terms of spirit, or spirit in terms of
matter, to make the final unity.[35] The philosopher tries to say it, the
poet to make it. In order to do this, he claims the ability of seeing
more deeply and clearly how "every moment is a window on all
time," as Wolfe says in *Look Homeward Angel*.[36] Bergson's aesthetic
is consonant with a long tradition behind watchers from privileged
windows.

The window offered by intuition is, ultimately, a revelation of
Self and Nature—it is their confluence. The "other world" of
prophecy subsumes our own. But is it a world of fatality or of self-
creation, as it appears in Modernist writing? Is it, as some would
say, a world hermetically sealed off from meaning, or is it a world
such as the Greek oracles saw, a finished work? For Modernist writers there is perhaps no one good answer to this question. It is important to note, however, that for them it is at least true that there
could not be a fatalism denying growth. Growth might cancel itself
out in the long run; it might take place in a nonsensical relation to
its own medium, but growth was life, or life (and art) were not
worth pursuing. Bergson's own background of study in Spencer
and Lucretius reflects the divided allegiances of Modernist writers
like Faulkner, for whom free will "functions against a Greek background of fate" (*FIU*, 38). Modernist writing involves a pathos
born of this dual awareness of the form and the spirit. Thus the
Modernist lays claim equally to craftsmanship and prophecy; learns
what Scaliger called the "poetry of God," those rhetorical ploys that
create belief, insight, faith. Some, like Thomas Wolfe, bear their

testimony with self-conscious drama. Others, hoping to be more convincing, perhaps, make lesser claims.

When Lily Briscoe sits, mulling over memory and art in the middle of *To the Lighthouse*, she finds herself wondering "what is the meaning of life?" She realizes that no great revelation is likely to arrive, yet believes that "little daily miracles, illuminations, matches struck in the dark," point the way. The mind wishes to compose life, to see it whole, as a logical form with practical relations. But the spirit brooks no permanent "form": "Mrs. Ramsay saying 'Life stand still here'; Mrs. Ramsay making of the moment something permanent (as in another sphere Lily herself tried to make of the moment something permanent)—this was of the nature of a revelation. In the midst of chaos there was shape; this eternal passing and flowing (she looked at the clouds going and the leaves shaking) was struck into stability. Life stand still here, Mrs. Ramsay said."[37] Lily's desire for permanence leads her intuitively toward this shape. She tries to master ineluctable processes, just as Mrs. Ramsay, as wife and mother, seeks mastery of her family's lives. Lily "strikes" on the moment, and the moment is "struck" like a coin into a stable image: her painting. Her "stand still" must remain ambiguous so that it does not deny the dynamism it seizes. Only thus can it strike *us* with "sudden intensity" on the book's final page. Lily has come to finish her painting. She adds a simple line she feels intuitively goes in the center. Her experience of insight is the one toward which the entire book tries to point the reader, but it is an experience that is not and cannot be explained.

Lily's "stand still" sounds like a conscious echo of the phrase that should have damned Goethe's Faust at the end of part two. Faust had agreed that if he ever uttered those words, ever came to a moment so full that he wanted only to prolong it indefinitely, Mephistopheles would have his soul. With his legalistic mind, Mephistopheles hears only the direct reference of the phrase: "Verweile doch, du bist so schön." He thinks Faust wants the scene to remain just as it is. But Faust's attention is on the *way the scene is changing*. He wants it to go on changing still, to remain ever in process. The principle of change is its stability, in his eyes. For Modernist writers, Wallace Stevens's dictum in "Notes Toward a Supreme Fiction" that "it must change" names a fact and a requisite. Poetry must change; it cannot help but change. More than that, it is a distillation of change and time (our pseudonyms).

Bergson, who came out of the self-building philosophies of the nineteenth century, is a key link in the chain of metamorphoses bringing us Modernist poet-prophets, the "victims" of an inspiring voice (*TS*, 243).[38] The craft of their work is born of that tension between creative spirit and partial notations—the "change of Philomel" (voice of poetry) in *The Waste Land*, for example: "Under the firelight, under the brush, her hair / Spread out in fiery points / Glowed into words, then would be savagely still." Poems of an earlier age might be monuments or portraits; those of Modernism are "experiences" of what is "still and still moving" (*CPP*, 119). Such poetry works directly with its awareness that final form owes to a molten core of creation that "glows into words." It seeks to make readers understand something of the process by which fluidity is captured so that it may flow again. Putting the coin of everyday language to the fire, it seeks a renewed medium of exchange, one closer to the heart of the matter, one which will "suffice" (Stevens' term) until it must again be submitted to the flame. The majority of men, Eliot wrote in his early sarcastic piece on philosophies of art, "Eeldrop and Appleplex" (1917), use terms which are merely "good for so much reality; they never see the actual coinage."[39] Modernist literature tries to return us just such "change."

Unwilling to be written off, to ascribe to the imagination powers weaker and less rigorous than those of science, Modernist writers required a vocabulary amalgamated of aesthetics, mathematics, physics—just the sort of vocabulary Bergson offered. If even those whose works were profoundly affected by this change, the climate in which it took place, the reactions against it, and the popularization of certain aspects of Bergson's philosophy—if even these writers sometimes fail to recognize that Bergson's science of philosophy does not predicate itself upon an abandonment to the superstition of the life-force, that is no reason for us to ignore the fact that Bergson signifies. He elaborated aesthetic theories that had once served to defend art against charges of immorality and anti-religiosity, creating a defense for modern art against the charges of a science-obsessed age. To us he bequeathed terminology that explains the Modernist drive toward a new sense of "formality," one that would be regulated by the truth of duration, mediated by language, but *patterned* by intuition.

THREE

Eliot's Unacknowledged Debt

The greatest debts are not always the most evident.
—T. S. Eliot

𝕒 Lyndall Gordon has rightly remarked that in the years 1911-14 Eliot formulated his most characteristic ideas and attitudes.[1] But though Philip Le Brun has convincingly argued that Eliot's "major formulations about poetry" were influenced by Bergson, Bergson's influence on Eliot has generally been seen as limited to the narrowly defined period of 1910-11.[2] In the view of most, Bradleyan philosophy eclipses Bergson in Eliot's thought. Staffan Bergsten, for example, writes in *Time and Eternity* that Eliot's concept of tradition as an "ideal order" in the Bradleyan vein "may be interpreted as a rejection of Bergson's doctrine of time." And yet Bergsten is forced to admit that though "as a critic Eliot thus seems to have rejected Bergson's philosophy . . . as a poet he has no doubt been influenced by him."[3]

Similarly Piers Gray has shown how we may trace a certain "argument" among different philosophical views of the self and experience going on in the 1910-12 writing.[4] Gray finds Eliot's mind essentially skeptical, and says he rapidly moved beyond Bergson's concepts of time and experience. Indeed, Gray believes Eliot first "out-ironies Laforgue," subsequently (in *Prufrock and Other Observations*) expresses his profound experience of reading Bergson (as an overlay, now, to Laforguian irony), and then, in a typical shift, becomes "dissatisfied" with Bergson—so much so that he simply "stopped writing poetry between 1911 and 1913." The Eliot that emerges after this dry spell has, in Gray's view, become thoroughly skeptical about what can be known of the self and memory and what can be said within any linguistic tradition. Thus, Gray places Eliot in a "sceptical relationship" with the tradition of St. Paul, Lancelot Andrewes, Josiah Royce—and of course Bergson. Gray reads *The Waste Land* provocatively, as a poem of ironics, the last of which is that we are left speculating on the unmeaning syllables "Shantih Shantih Shantih," which "feebly translated into our language, promise the unimaginable."[5]

Bradley versus Bergson?

Gray's sensitive and intense readings show the utility of Bergson in explication. His analysis leaves us, however, with an essentially unchanged picture: that Eliot passed through a brief period of enthusiasm for Bergson but rapidly came under the influence of Bradley's skepticism and remained of that camp thereafter. A review of Eliot's poetry and criticism during this period and immediately after shows that there is a problem with the Bradley-Bergson polarity, and that Eliot knew it.

First, there is the important and neglected distinction between Bergson and Bergsonism—Bergson's disciples were not always students of his philosophy. If Eliot passed out of discipleship, that hardly means he no longer found Bergson's works illuminating. Second, it is tempting to draw too harsh a distinction between Bergson and Bradley, who certainly reach profoundly different conclusions, but also share some very important convictions and strategies.

Hugh Kenner was the first to claim that Bradley helped Eliot to achieve "a view of the past, a view of himself and other persons, a view of the nature of what we call statement and communication."[6] Eliot's doctoral dissertation had been dug out of the archives at Harvard in the late fifties and published in 1964, spawning many articles and books about Bradley's influence. Sean Lucy echoed Kenner in asserting that Bradley was the primary source for Eliot's idea of tradition.[7] Eric Thompson's *T.S. Eliot: The Metaphysical Perspective* was the first full-length study devoted to Bradley's influence on Eliot. Written without benefit of the dissertation, it is much less adequate than Lewis Freed's *T.S. Eliot: The Critic as Philosopher*.[8] Russell Kirk summarized a great deal of what is to be found in these studies (including Gray's) when he wrote that Eliot got from Bradley: 1) a concept of the self as an artificial construction and 2) a hunger for the Absolute which deepened the schism in his thought between the world of experience and the world of permanent values. According to Kirk, Eliot also acquired defenses against utilitarianism and dry intellectualism.[9]

Anyone who has tackled Bradley's *Appearance and Reality* or Eliot's dissertation, which spends a good deal of time on the object-theory of Alexius Meinong and is thus somewhat unhappily titled, will agree with Freed that what can be done with Bradley's philosophy in relation to Eliot's criticism is, though occasionally very revealing, still extremely limited.[10] Richard Wollheim has warned that "*Knowledge and Experience* is a painfully obscure work. Criticism which sets out to understand Eliot's work as a poet and critic by reference to it is likely, fairly soon, to admit bewilderment, or else, overtly or covertly, to reverse the enterprise." Wollheim draws tentative conclusions, but offers them as merely general tendencies "in Eliot's writing, particularly his critical writing . . . that also occur in Bradley, so that we can say of them that, even if they were not transmitted from Bradley to Eliot, they would have been reinforced in Eliot by his reading of Bradley." At the same time, Wollheim admits, "to trace the influence of Bradley's philosophy upon Eliot any way beyond such generalities seems to be a most hazardous and uncertain undertaking."[11]

Thompson suggests that "Eliot may have been doing what F.H. Bradley suggests every metaphysician does: finding bad reasons for believing what the poet knows on instinct." And Kirk makes a parallel argument: Bradley "confirmed" for Eliot "that the past is not a thing frozen."[12] Such claims keep to the general level recommended by Wollheim; they do not ask us to believe that Bradley was a source for Eliot's ideas, though some have argued that "Tradition and the Individual Talent" is a Bradleyan piece. Of course, the idea that the "past is not a thing frozen" seems as much a Bergsonian as a Bradleyan notion. Indeed, Bergson and Bradley share a great deal more than is generally recognized by those who have, mostly in vain, sought to make sense of Eliot's poetics in the light of Bradley's Absolute.

Like Bergson, Bradley reacted against materialism, particularly that of John Stuart Mill. Bradley debunked the Greatest Happiness principle by showing how it depended on positing terms which, because they come from the intellect, are inevitably self-contradictory. Wollheim notes in his book on Bradley's philosophy that a "comparison has often been drawn between Bradley and his contemporary Bergson, for Bergson, too, was preoccupied with the inadequacy of Thought to Reality, with the way in which concepts and abstractions of discursive thinking mutilate and do violence to the continuum of experience."[13] Like Bergson, Bradley viewed the concepts of time, space, object, and self as essentially suspect because they were the vision of a cyclopean eye: the intellect. Bertrand Russell drew the parallel: "What Bergson is trying to do is uphold the reality of flux in experience as against the travesty of rigid forms that pertain to reason and its picture of the world. Thus far the problem of Bergson is reminiscent of Bradley. But the solution is here quite different. . . . Bradley may be described as a rationalist and Bergson as an irrationalist."[14] Since Bradley and Bergson contrast profoundly in their solutions to the problem, their fundamental agreement on that problem's character is often forgotten.

William James, who admired Bergson, also saw that Bradley and Bergson shared a view of primary experience. "Bradley's thought and Bergson's run parallel for such a distance, and yet diverge so utterly at last," James wrote in 1910, with this in mind.[15] For both Bradley and Bergson, primary experience is something with which we almost intentionally lose touch, a nonverbal darkness out of which consciousness emerges mysteriously. Eliot refers to it repeatedly in his dissertation: "Immediate experience . . . is a timeless . . . unity. . . . Immediate experience, at either the beginning or end of our journey, is annihilation and utter night" (*KE*, 31). Bradley's immediate experience, then, like Bergson's, is primary, irreducible: "There is no further point of view from which it can be inspected" (*KE*, 22). It is a state in which all distinction between self and other is lost. Bradley defines the finite center somewhat contradictorily, according to Eliot; finally, it is inseparable from immediate experience, *durée*, the eternal present. Thus, expressing some puzzlement, Eliot admits that "the Finite Center, so far as I can pretend to understand it, *is* immediate experience" (*KE*, appendix 2). The finite center—what common sense defines as consciousness or the self—must then be a thing transpiring.

And yet Bradley insists that immediate experience is also an illusion. Unlike Bergson—a thinker admittedly younger and with different orientation—Bradley felt one must adopt a permanently quizzical view of experience. William James found this aspect of Bradley's thought puzzling. For Bradley, somehow "not to enter life is a higher vocation than to enter it," and the knowledge of immediate experience is replaced in Bradley's system by a "trans-conceptual evaporation . . . the absolute."[16] Bradley's extreme skepticism bothered even his disciples, who attempted to make the philosophy more supportive of the religious impulse—at least, Bosanquet tried to adjust Bradley's theories in that direction. In his final metaphysics, Bradley denies that his Absolute is at all related to personal experience, denies freedom and keeps a distance on the idea of immortality for the individual human soul. *Appearance and Reality* defines the Absolute as neither personal nor beautiful nor moral nor "true." It also argues that the aesthetic experience, because it involves pleasure, can never conduct to the Absolute.

These are not small matters for Eliot's own theories of poetry and experience. The trajectory of his career leads Eliot away from Bradley's skepticism and toward faith; but more than that, his critical and philosophical writings show an affinity with Bergson's thought that vindicates Le Brun's view. Eliot's reaction against Bergson is no simple matter of rejection. His insistence on permanence and conscious mind is balanced by belief in the importance of flux and unconscious process.

Reading Eliot Reading Bergson

For the young Eliot, just graduated from Harvard, Bergson seems to have been a path chosen impulsively. During the winter of 1910-11, Eliot had direct contact with Bergson's ideas and style when he went to Paris to hear him lecture at the Sorbonne. He was already identifying Bergson as a mystic, as we shall see. Later, he associated himself publicly with two men on whom Bergson's influence had been profound: T.E. Hulme and Jacques Maritain. And in 1916 Eliot lectured on Bergson through the Oxford University Extension Program, identifying Bergsonian philosophy as essentially mystical and optimistic.[17] In 1948, he admitted that his only "real conversion, by the deliberate influence of any individual, was a temporary conversion to Bergsonism," and in 1952 he wrote of "a longing for the appearance of a philosopher whose writings, lectures and personality will arouse the imagination as Bergson, for instance, aroused it forty years ago."[18] This sense of having been "converted" produced a genuine negative reaction to Bergsonism in the twenties and thirties, when Eliot came to identify it as "heresy."

Bradley, in contrast, was a cerebral choice, though it is hard to believe Eliot took Bradleyan philosophy seriously as a "path." Bradley's philosophy, Eliot would write in 1924, seemed to give him everything he asked, but render it not worth having.[19] "I spent three years, when young, in the study of philosophy," he later wrote. "What remains to me of these studies? The style of three philosophers. Bradley's English, Spinoza's Latin, and Plato's Greek" (*TCC*, 20-21). Bradley, whom Eliot called master of "the finest philosophical style in our language," influenced profoundly Eliot's prose style and his manner of solving problems.[20] From Bradley Eliot acquired a prose and a habit of thought at once hedging and fearless—unafraid to confront uncertainties fully and to leave them, though fully explored, still uncertain. This mark of Bradley on both the criticism and the poetry is deep. It gives Eliot's work an extraordinary quality of courage, since he faces reality's "irreducible contradictions and irreconcilable points of view" with such poise (*KE*, 112). Bradley's is the voice we hear when Eliot discusses impenetrable problems: "The admission of inconsistencies, sometimes ridiculed as indifference to logic and coherence, of which the English mind is often accused, may be largely the admission of inconsistencies inherent in life itself, and the impossibility of overcoming them by the imposition of a uniformity greater than life can bear" (*SE*, 332). Thus, Eliot in Bradleyan tones asserts "it may be the man who affirms the apparently incompatible who is right" (*OPP*, 142). But Eliot does not finally embrace Bradley, though he remains posed as the wide-eyed pessimist. He admires Bradley for having written a philosophy in which "acute intellect and passionate feeling preserve a classic balance."[21] And this rigor clearly changed his own approach as a writer.

But Bergson, whose style Eliot also admired as one of "intense addiction to an intellectual passion," influenced him in a more profound way: It gave him a vivid sense of his own age's optimism. His reaction against that optimism was out of proportion to its presence in Bergson's thought precisely because it touched a nerve in his own struggle to clarify his moral and spiritual values. Thus, Bergson became, for the *Criterion*'s readers—and especially after Eliot had converted to the Anglican Church in 1927—a "heresy." Eliot came to describe Bergson as a sophist who had "invented new sensations from metaphysics." And Bergson's "time-doctrine" he called "wholly destructive," for in it "everything may be admired, because nothing is permanent."[22] Though Eliot never reached the stratosphere of bombast navigated by Lewis, Benda, Lankester, and Santayana, he did use hyperbole when it came to Bergson: "The potent ju-ju of the Life-Force is a gross superstition."[23] When, in the late twenties, a portion of several issues of the monthly *Criterion* was given over to a debate on humanism, Eliot squared off with J. Middleton Murry, Ramon Fernandez, and others. He disliked their vocabulary: "Words like *emergent, organism, biological unit of life,* simply do not arouse the right 'response' in my breast."[24] But he disliked even more the residue of Bergson*ism* he detected in their theories: "It is possible, of course, that evolution will bring the human race to such a point that thinking will no longer be necessary. Thinking is painful and requires toil and is a mark of human incompleteness."[25] Bergson, he implies, has encouraged men to think they are complete in themselves. Given a choice between the "unthinking" intuition of Bergsonists and the unpopular but honest intellectual labor of Bradleyans, Eliot's public position could not be other than it was.

He placed Bergson in the tradition of late-nineteenth-century progressives whose thought had been "harnessed to Spencer and Darwin." In this progressivism he detected the heresy of human-ism: "The hope of immortality is confused (typically of the period) with the hope of the gradual and steady improvement of this world" (*SE*, 293). Bergsonism helped spread this optimism in the twen-tieth century, and Eliot damns it as a form of fatalism: "To assume that everything has changed, is changing, and must change, accord-ing to forces which are not human, and that all a person who cares about the future must or can do is to adapt himself to the change is a fatalism which is unacceptable. It is an exemplification of the modern time-philosophy discussed by Mr. Wyndham Lewis. . . . Man is morally responsible for his present and his immediate fu-ture."[26] Eliot certainly should have been clear, as Le Brun argues, that this attack could be justified against Bergson's disciples, but not the philosopher himself.[27] Still, Bergson had created a sort of "epidemic" of which Eliot himself had, fortunately, been cured.[28] Eliot's essays in the *Criterion* after 1927 recur often to this trouble-some optimism with which Bergsonists seem infected. In Eliot's eyes, they are fools looking for the easy way out, "pious pilgrims" of progress, "cheerfully plodding the road from nowhere to no-where, trolling their hymns, satisfied so long as they may be 'on the march'" (*SE*, 325).

On the face of it, Eliot certainly had a point, for Bergson was optimistic about progress, even in the late stage of his career, when he asserted that "the essential function of the universe is a machine for the making of gods" (*TS*, 306). Such statements gave credence to attacks charging Bergson with encouraging fascism.[29] The charge that Bergson's Vitalism ignores moral responsibility is a se-rious and troubling one. Bergson himself seems to have been con-cerned with working out other problems than his philosophy's moral commitments until the publication of his last major book, *The Two Sources of Morality and Religion*, in 1932, when for most the question had already been settled in the negative. This book considers two principles in moral life: "a system of orders dictated by impersonal social requirements, and a series of appeals made to the conscience of each of us by persons who represent the best there is in humanity" (*TS*, 75). Religion is indispensable to society, according to Bergson, because it educates men to see that "obedience to duty means resistance to self" (*TS*, 12). Religion institutionalizes conscience. The "pressure" it creates is the first force of the book's title.

And the second is the "aspiration" we feel when we contemplate the lives of saints and mystics. This volume shows the profound influence Christian mysticism was having on Bergson: "Christianity is the latest advance in justice," he wrote, for it preaches "that all men are brothers." And Christian mysticism is the only complete mysticism, full of "divine humility" (*TS*, 68, 216-17, 220). Bergson said in 1907 that "to change is to mature" (*CE*, 7), yet came to believe that "men do not sufficiently realize that the future is in their own hands" (*TS*, 200). And, in what seems an uncharacteristically pessimistic tone, he wrote that man is nearly "identical" underneath "with his remotest ancestors" (*TS*, 262). Finally, Bergson is in substantial agreement with Eliot that the artist's standpoint is, though important, "not final. . . . The standpoint of the moralist is higher" (*ME*, 31). And in his final works, Bergson exhibits a strong idealist vein: "The great moral figures that have made their mark on history join hands across the centuries, above our human cities; they unite into a divine city which they bid us enter . . . . from the real society in which we live we betake ourselves in thought to this ideal society" (*TS*, 59).

Very likely, Eliot never came to recognize the Augustinian side of Bergson's thought (few have), although the *Criterion* gave *The Two Sources of Morality and Religion* a positive review. One imagines that Eliot would have been surprised to learn of Bergson's intention to convert to Catholicism.

He would have been surprised because he believed Bergson stood clearly on the opposite side of what Eliot came to think was "the real issue of our time," namely, that between the "secularists—whatever political or moral philosophy they support—and the antisecularists: between those who believe only in values realizable in

time and on earth, and those who believe also in values realized
only out of time."[30] It is important that we note the word "also," for
Eliot has a special sense in which he uses the concept of secularism:
Secularists profess views that are heretical. And a heretic is "a person who seizes upon a truth and pushes it to the point at which it
becomes a falsehood." The secularist has lost the sense of tension
between what is true in time and on earth and that "absolute to
which man can never attain" (*SE*, 436-37). This does not necessarily mean that the "anti-secularist" denies secular wisdom; he simple
inserts it in a broader context that mitigates its truth.[31]

Had Eliot not come to see his early experience with Bergson's
philosophy as a flirtation with heresy, he might have acknowledged
a broad parallel between his and Bergson's careers. Each ends by
humbling philosophy and poetry before the wisdom of the saints.
And if he had seen this broad parallel, Eliot might have been readier
to acknowledge that Bergson offered a way, in 1910, to clarify his
spiritual values and his commitment to the importance of intuitive
insights. Le Brun believes that in Eliot's failure to recognize what
he gained from Bergson there may have been "some process of
repression." It is a matter for wonder that Eliot does not distinguish
more carefully between Bergson and Bergsonists. But the reasons
for this are really more interesting than they are important. Whatever Eliot has said, the evidence shows that Bergson helped him
phrase to himself questions that occupied him through most of his
career as a critic and poet. If he inserted Bergson's insights in a
broader context that supplies the moral stance he desired even in
1910, that does not in the least diminish the validity of those insights, just as Einstein's Theory of Relativity does not cancel the
validity of Newtonian physics for the man who (in Faulkner's
terms) is trying to nail together a chicken house in a windstorm.
Bergson provided Eliot with ground on which to build, and most
importantly, with a mark of the era's confluence of thought, to
which, however he may struggle against it, Eliot also belongs.

Two manuscripts from Eliot's stay in Paris and subsequent work
on Bergson provide us with our own necessary mark to steer by in
evaluating Bergson's significance to Eliot. The first is a booklet of
notes (entirely in French) from Bergson's lectures heard mostly in

January and February of 1911. The notes are neatly copied in complete but grammatically crude sentences—a reconstruction, one
supposes, from fragmentary jottings made during the lecture. We
cannot know, of course, how much Eliot selected and edited. There
are virtually no marks indicating his opinions or impressions, only
an occasional question mark. The notebook records a familiar sort
of introductory course in the philosophy of self and personality.
Bergson discusses Mill, Spencer, Hume, and Kant, spending most
time on the latter, whose thought Eliot notes Bergson apparently
found "extrêmement profonde est tres instructive." Bergson's own
observations reflect directly the thrust of his work: "Le moi est un
unité mais n'est pas l'unité d'un chose mais d'un forme."[32] The notebook suggests a thoroughness in Eliot's study of Bergson that a
second manuscript at Harvard confirms.

Sometime after returning to Harvard, he drafted a paper in English on Bergson's philosophy. We cannot precisely date the essay,
nor is it certain whether he wrote it for purposes of lecture or with
the idea of publication. Lyndall Gordon guesses that it was composed in 1913 or 1914, since it is not in Eliot's 1910-11 handwriting (he changed handwriting styles after leaving Paris). The essay
exposes some of Bergson's apparent contradictions, especially his
use of the spatializing language condemned in *Time and Free Will*,
and suggests that Bergsonian intuition (pure perception) cannot itself escape the dictum of *Matter and Memory*: "percevoir signifie
immobiliser" (to perceive means to immobilize).[33] If we accept this,
Eliot asks, "then how can perception be identical with the object,
which, in itself, is pure motion? Where, again, is the reality,—in
the consciousness, or in that which is perceived? Where is the
one reality to subsume both of these, and can we or can we not
know it?"

Eliot's chief criticism, in this essay, is that Bergson has failed to
make good his "claim to mediate between idealism and realism." In
insisting on this disjunction, Eliot has already achieved the orientation of his later thought. Indeed, the bone he has to pick with
Bergson never changes hereafter: Bergson denies the polarity by
which alone man determines value. (Eliot has not yet called Bergson a "secularist.") Of course, Eliot has already been reading Brad-

ley—at one point, Bradley's name gets written down by mistake, then is corrected to "Bergson." And in the paper's conclusion Brad-ley comes forth as a crucial part of the interpretation Eliot gives to Bergson's philosophy.

Eliot identifies "the last part of M + M [*Matter and Memory*]—cap [*sic*] iv + conclusion" as "a very remarkable and provocative—indeed tantalizing—piece of writing—I find one of the most inter-esting + most important parts of Bergson's work."[34] This, the pen-ultimate section of the book, discusses imagery, perception, and matter. Eliot recapitulates it in some detail, concentrating on driving home two points. First, that Bergson would have movement prior to both matter and consciousness. Second, that Bergson's "pure memory" is the significant mediating factor in his equations for the extended and unextended, quantity and quality. Eliot disposes of the first point by asserting that motion cannot exist "without a con-sciousness to perceive," and that "perception means immobilisa-tion." He thus appears to catch Bergson in the bind of having used "perception" covertly in the very sense he wishes to avoid. Eliot's approach to the second point is more complicated and much more interesting.

The crux of the problem, as Eliot sees it, is that Bergson has tried to establish a middle ground between idealism and realism, and has been led to put consciousness (consciousness's most salient characteristic, for Bergson, is, of course, memory) in two roles: "as half of the dichotomy and also as potentially absolute. . . . Bergson's philosophy must stand as a kind of pluralism and a kind of realism as well. This is the one side of the case, and this is the side I have chiefly emphasized, because it is the side which I am interested to oppose." (The words "in attacking" were crossed out here and re-placed by "to oppose.") Bergson's middle way cannot avoid slipping to one side or the other, according to Eliot. Pure memory cannot, he contends, be held to reach a level at which it is no longer part of a relational chain: perceiver, object, perception. Thus, Bergson's at-tempt to "occupy a middle ground" is inadequate, and the *durée réelle* must be viewed as "simply not final."[35]

"Yet there are," Eliot goes on immediately to say, "as I have inti-mated, suggestions, more than suggestions, of leading toward an absolute; suggestions which have often led Bergson's critics to call him a mystic. With this appellation I am not disposed to quarrel; though, as at present elaborated in Bergson's [sic] it is a rather weakling mysticism." Eliot notes the implicit monism of Bergson's philosophy, which "tends toward an absolute which sees eternity in a single moment." He regards the "evolutionary" doctrines of Bergson's work as having somehow obscured its real tendency, though having certainly contributed "largely to Bergson's popularity." And he ends by asking the reader to "consider Bergson in the light of neo-Platonism," a rather astonishing request. Eliot then claims that Bergson's attempt to institute a philosophy of pure change has only "reinaugurated" the timeless and eternal in a new form. Spatialisation gives one the illusion of timelessness, yes, but let the flux of inner states more and more concentrate as the "tension" of the perceiving mind contracts history into what Bergson called a few moments of more intense life—let those inner states press more and more into each other and they "approximate nearer + nearer to one state," Eliot claims. And thus the "limit will only be a single eternal present. Timelessness of another sort." Eliot echoes his foe of later years, John Middleton Murry, who had published in 1911 a brief essay saying that Bergson was "declaring once more today" the Platonic truth of the "eternality of art."[36]

In his conclusion, Eliot argues (as Maritain also argued) that Bergson does not himself understand clearly toward what his philosophy leads. "If Bergson, then, had begun his philosophy with the duration of pure identity which I have suggested, the descent into the world of plurality + externality would appear not as a quickening, but as an arrest. Reversing the apparent conclusions of his theory, time would be the child of space; the formula being time = eternity/space. And this I call neo-Platonism. . . . In such a system—Bergson Resartus—science in the narrower sense of the word would of course find short shrift." Science is Eliot's real target here. It can never be complete, nor can memory complete through partial notations the infinite. And he accepts the dead end this implies: "Finally, nothing essentially new can ever happen; the absolute, as Bradley says, bears buds + flowers + fruit at once; time gives the *Menue monnaie* ad infinitum."[37]

Now this is indeed, as Eliot admits, "Bergson Resartus," and Bergson would certainly not have agreed to Eliot's conclusions, not even at the end of his career, when his idealism came more to the forefront. At first, one is impressed almost wholly by the consistency of Eliot's view with his later pronouncements on history, the absolute, evolutionism, etc. Here it all is, with remarkable consistency, before he had achieved any recognition as a poet and critic, before his conversion, before "Burnt Norton,"where the Bradleyan Absolute ("buds + flowers + fruit at once") appears in the lotos vision. It is easy to forget the most salient characteristic of Eliot's whole discussion, namely, that he attributes these views to Bergson himself. Eliot's essay is an attempt to get the two philosophical systems to overlap. It is not a straight attack on Bergson, for it does not condemn the philosopher's views, but strives to adjust them.

Above all, Eliot seems to be assessing the significance and power of memory and intuition, two profoundly interrelated concepts in Bergson's philosophy. He wishes to preserve these principles. But he also wishes to assert that from a certain "point of view," memory is "a futile attempt to emulate the completed infinite by a sequential infinite." Though memory is "a tool of tremendous effect in practical life," if one seeks "what Parmenides would call truth, it is no more possible that truth should be gained by these means than that a man should ever catch sight of himself with his eyes closed."[38] And later, in his debate with Middleton Murry, he writes of intuition: "I do not at all wish to expunge the word 'intuition' from the dictionary . . . I mean that intuition must have its place in a world of discourse." The issue here is really a simple one. Eliot does not reject the "native gift of intuition" (*OPP*, 257). But he insists that one should not make it "the key to the universe."[39]

In his notes for Philosophy 24A at Harvard in 1913-14 Eliot says that "the lotos alone is perfect, because it has many flowers and many fruits *at once* . . . mutual relation of final reality and manifestation."[40] This image of what is both in *and* out of time represented itself in Eliot's work on Bergson himself at approximately the same time we have assumed he embraced Bradley. But Eliot was still working seriously on Bergson long after he had been reading Bradley. Eloise Knapp Hay explains the presence of the lotos vision in the Bergson paper at Harvard by saying Eliot wrote the paper after giving the philosophy class and taking Royce's seminar, so that the lotos vision had obviously "stayed on Eliot's mind."[41] But the paper may predate the class notes. And in any case, what are we to do with Eliot's working on his reading of Bergson *three years after having left Paris—and supposedly Bergson—behind?* We have been so convinced that Eliot's mind works by progressive consideration and rejection of ideas that we are almost prepared to ignore the facts. Piers Gray's book is structured entirely on this view of Eliot's intellect: that it grew by digesting and then expelling philosophies and literary devices whole. But it seems to me Eliot grew differently. He selected as well as rejected. He kept what he could not or would not throw away, and in this fashion *evolved* a solution over many years to a central problem already becoming fairly clearly defined in 1910-11: the polarity between "final reality and manifestation" that just had to be accepted somehow.

Eliot's essay gives Bergson's philosophy of change importance where merely "practical" considerations obtain, but denies its having approached "truth." We make a great mistake, I think, if we take Eliot's pronouncements on truth and the Absolute to mean he wholly condemns Bergson's empirical approach. After all, whether we are poets, mechanics, or politicians, our lives consist mainly of "practical considerations." Only the mystic or the saint, as Eliot wrote in *Four Quartets*, takes the Absolute as his vocation. The practical effect Bergson had on Eliot's thinking was, finally, profound. "Change as process," Elizabeth Schneider observes, "may have engaged Eliot at a deeper level even than did its content or result—deeper, that is, than the actual Christian view of life arrived at."[42]

Some of Eliot's most perspicacious critics have long acknowledged the broad parallels between Bergson and the poet/critic.[43] In what follows, I have sought to make that parallel specific, to show how Eliot's vocabulary and operative principles owe a debt to Bergson's thought. It would be well to say, at the outset, that while no single point in what follows will convince overwhelmingly, the weight of the points taken together does convince, even if one allows for the fact that there are no new ideas under the sun, and that

Eliot could conceivably have gotten some of them elsewhere or independently.

Bergsonian Concepts in Eliot's Criticism

For Eliot, as for Bergson, change is the defining characteristic of
life and its most fundamental experience. And while the change
transpiring in nature may appear random, it is not so when it is
manifested in a truly vital life-form. Vital life always changes into
something both new and continuous with the past—life develops
into novelty by a continuous inner-directed growth, passing forward constantly into the unpredictable. Bergson and Eliot agree on
these points concerning the world and experience. And they agree
on two points about the nature of the perceiving mind that con-
fronts experience: that the fundamental tendency of the mind is to
shield us from reality by falsifying it, and that art is one of our most
important weapons in combating this tendency which would eventually rob us of our vitality and our ability to grow. Finally, Bergson
and Eliot share a theory that language has a dual source: It comes
partly from the evolutionary heritage, partly from divinity. In this
theory, language can be rejuvenated only by constant recurrence to
the personal and unique. For this reason, Eliot, like Bergson, puts
the poet in the roles of explorer and prophet, "catalyst" and vehicle.
For Eliot, as for Bergson, language begins and ends not in the utilitarian concept of the "message," but in a dimly known realm of
experience made available to us by intuition.

Bergson identified change with life itself; he even denied that
change needed anything to operate upon. For him, "there are
changes, but there are underneath the changes no things which
change: change has no need of a support . . . movement does not
imply a mobile" (*CM*, 173). This fundamental process in creation
could never be susceptible to reason, and it became in Bergson's
philosophy the single absolute criterion of existence. For Eliot, too,
mobility equals existence, and this is a value prior to any moral or
ethical standards. Immobility for Eliot means death. In "The Pen-

sees of Pascal" (1931) he writes, "So far as we are human, what we do must be either evil or good; so far as we do evil or good, we are human; and it is better, in a paradoxical way, to do evil than to do nothing: at least we exist" (*SE*, 379-80).

This principle, that inactivity is synonymous with inexistence, is at the heart of Eliot's view of society and literature, and he draws a distinct line between those whose work concerns living things— like literature—and those who deal with a conceptualized (spatial-ized and hence immobile) world like that of mathematics or specu-lative philosophy. "On my side of the line," he says, "one is con-cerned with living things which have their own laws of growth, which are not always reasonable, but must just be accepted by the reason: things which cannot be neatly planned and put in order any more than the winds and the rains and the seasons can be disci-plined" (*OPP*, 15). The poet's business is with such mysteries; he himself is part of them. According to Eliot, "the poet makes poetry, the metaphysician makes metaphysics, the bee makes honey, the spider secretes a filament; you can hardly say that any of these agents believes: He merely does" (*SE*, 118). A curious view for one who condemned the "fatalism" of Bergson's creative evolution!

So Eliot may have decried Bergson's emphasis on the "organic" and "emergent," but in his own theories of language and experience he exhibits a strong streak of Vitalism. When we read poetry, he advises, we must try to grasp what it is "aiming to be . . . its *ente-lechy*" (*OPP*, 122). The poem's principle of inner development is its vitality, and "we must be patient to be able" to perceive "vitality in it, to recognize that real vitality is never aimless, yet not to spec-ulate upon the aim itself."[44] We must read, then, for this vitality with our intuition, for the poem itself began with the intuition of vitality, with "nothing so definite as an emotion, in the ordinary sense," but "still more certainly not an idea" (*OPP*, 106). Eliot's paper on Bergson chided the philosopher for having reduced con-sciousness "to a matter of rhythm."[45] But *On Poetry and Poets* ar-gues that rhythm may be the essence of the poetic consciousness: "A poem, or a passage of a poem, may tend to realize itself first as a particular rhythm before it reaches expression in words," and "this rhythm may bring to birth the idea and the image" (*OPP*, 32). This theory appears to make poetry an activity predicated on glimpses into the heart of change.

It is, a closer look at Eliot's language theory reveals, only one of many theories based on the criterion of change; Eliot seems to have had the principle continuously in mind. "It is, of course, a necessary condition for the continuance of a literature that the language should be in constant change. If it is changing, it is alive" (*TCC*, 49). Many words, he notes, "*must* change their meaning, because it is . . . their changes in meaning that keep a language *alive*, or rather, that indicate that a language *is* alive" (*TCC*, 65; Eliot's italics). This principle found a direct application in the *Criterion* itself, when Eliot, as editor, proclaimed that the magazine would aim "to be perpetually in change and development, to alter . . . with the phases of the contemporary world for which and in which it lives."[46]

Both Bergson and Eliot seem to have drawn the logical conclusion from this belief in change as the criterion of life that to pin down things is to render them lifeless. This stricture applies equally against determinist science and literary theory: "Any theory which relates poetry very closely to a religious or social scheme of things aims, probably, to explain poetry by discovering its natural laws; but it is in danger of binding poetry by legislation to be observed—and poetry can recognize no such laws" (*UPUC*, 139). Poetry can recognize no such laws, for to bring into consciousness the unconscious processes of life and art kills them. We become conscious of social traditions *qua* traditions, for example, "only after they have begun to fall into desuetude" (*ASG*, 25, 19). "Experience," wrote Eliot in his dissertation, "both begins and ends in something which is not conscious" (*KE*, 28). To bring living things into consciousness is to tempt fate, and if we wish to preserve the living spirit of our culture and our art, we must "scrupulously guard ourselves against measuring living art and mind by the dead laws of order."[47]

Here Eliot makes the Bergsonian distinction between intellect and the world-in-experience. Unless we recognize that intellect kills things in order to "understand" them, we can do justice neither to culture nor to art, for both involve inherently emotional processes.

So Eliot is led to say that poetry's function is "not intellectual, but emotional," that it cannot therefore "be defined adequately in intellectual terms" (*SE*, 118). But more than that, aesthetics is dangerous business for poets, as "it may make us conscious of what operates better unconsciously."[48] Eliot, like Bergson, touches here the mainstream of the Romantic reaction against rationalism; Goethe's Mephistopheles put it thus glibly:

> Wer will was Lebendiges erkennen und beschreiben
> Sucht erst den Geist herauszutreiben.
> Denn hat er die Teile in seiner Hand . . .
> Fehlt, leider! nur das geistige Band.
>
> [*Faust*, I, 1936-39]

Eliot's commitment to the Romantic view on this question helps explain the preference he announces in his social as well as aesthetic criticism for unconsciousness over consciousness. Thus, despite his contempt for those who make intuition the "key to the universe," Eliot is driven to admit that "meaning is of the intellect, poetry is not."[49] And in this Eliot distinguishes himself markedly from Pound, who responds, "Saxpence reward for any authenticated case of intellect having stopped a chap's writing poesy! You might as well claim that railway tracks stop the engine."[50]

Eliot does believe that intellect raises obstacles to poetry, however. And he believes this because he subscribes to a theory of experience that parallels Bergson's. For Eliot, as for Bergson, life has an inherent direction of growth that is graspable only intuitively. Poetry captures, emulates, or embodies this living process. Eliot says of the mature literature of a nation, for example, that it participates in a process of self-realization not explainable by historians: "A mature literature . . . has a history behind it . . . that is not merely a chronicle, an accumulation of manuscripts and writings of this kind and that, but an *ordered though unconscious progress* of a language to realize its own potentialities within its limitations" (*OPP*, 55; italics mine).[51]

Many have been puzzled by this streak of Romantic organicism in Eliot, who remarks, in *To Criticize the Critic*, that he inclines toward an "organic" view of the conservative tradition, or writes, in

The Use of Poetry and the Use of Criticism, that we should consider the critical tradition not as "a sequence of random conjectures, but as readaptation" (*TCC*, 139-41; *UPUC*, 27). Unable to see the true continuity of Eliot's stance, commentators have often opted for the standard Hazlittian dissection. George Bornstein, for example, tells us candidly that "like his mind, Eliot's poetry divides against itself."[52] Bornstein argues that Eliot covertly wrote poetry in the Romantic tradition while attacking Romanticism in his criticism, and he characterizes *Four Quartets* as "romantic against the grain," by which he seems to mean that *Four Quartets* rehearses a dialectic between Eliot's drive to write a poetry of novelty and his critical orthodoxy. Bornstein explains this apparent contradiction between Eliot's Romantic imagination and his Pauline intellect as a simple case of id versus superego: "Eliot's response to feared forces within himself [was] denial, restraint, projection."[53] To the extent that Romanticism is associated, in his thought, with abandonment to the confusion of primary experience, Eliot felt the dangers Bornstein discusses were very real. And there is, of course, no way to deny a theory of repression, in which latency takes on sinister hues. But Eliot's criticism is simply not "orthodox" in this sense, as Edward Lobb's *T.S. Eliot and the Romantic Critical Tradition* makes clear.[54]

I believe the criticism—I will refrain from addressing the poetry, for the moment—has a public and a private face, and the public face does indeed argue for restraint, self-denial, and orthodoxy; but not necessarily because these repressions were felt as necessary in the poet's life. Eliot seems to have felt that they were essential to the survival of culture. The private face, however, clearly sets itself in the Romantic tradition, and argues vehemently against the abuse of that tradition. We have already partly explored the crux of the matter here: Eliot and Bergson share with the Romantics of the previous century a belief that life is process, and especially a process directed by an inner principle not capable of legislation by the intellect. The artist is thus instinctive—for Bergson "intuitive." Eliot seems to have had no trouble realizing this consciously. When he praised Wyndham Lewis's *Tarr* in 1918, he said the book gives one "direct contact with the senses, perception of the world of immediate experience," and went on to offer a theory of the artist as "more primitive, as well as more civilized, than his contemporaries. . . . Primitive instincts, and the acquired habits of ages are confounded in ordinary men. In the work of Mr. Lewis we recognize the thought of the modern and the energy of the cave-man."[55]

When it comes to the Romantic poets themselves, Eliot identifies most strongly with Coleridge. "The criticism of today," Eliot writes, "may be said to be in direct descent from Coleridge," and he has in mind here especially Coleridge's writings on Shakespeare (*OPP*, 115). Coleridge pushed criticism in the direction of other disciplines, toward the academy, where it has found its home in this century (*OPP*, 127). The artist has been affected too; he must, sometimes against his will, look to politics, economics, religion, and philosophy, in addition to consulting the monuments of his art.[56] But most importantly, Coleridge explained why the artist must never rest, must seek always the flowing of that inner development, a power behind all that evolves, whether in the natural or the psychic world.

This is where Bergson fits in the Romantic tradition. As Michael Roberts noted in his early book on T.E. Hulme, "In substance, both Hulme and Bergson were trying to restore to 'reason' the meaning it had for Coleridge and the Cambridge Platonists." For Hulme and Bergson, Roberts says, the mind is more than a logic machine; "it is a power that controls and coordinates."[57] Bergson adopts the Coleridgean concept of the imagination's power: "True genius does not merely restructure the given, but melts and reshapes things" (*TS*, 38). And Eliot must also incorporate this idea in his theory of poetry.

To evoke the richness of the parallel between Coleridge, Bergson, and Eliot on this point, let me quote a well-known passage from Coleridge's criticism of Shakespeare:

No work of true genius dares want its appropriate form, neither indeed is there any danger of this. As it must not, so genius cannot be lawless; for it is even this that constitutes its genius—the power of acting creatively under laws of its own origination. . . . the mistake lies in confounding mechanical regularity with organic form. The form is mechanic, when on any given material we impress a predetermined form, not necessarily arising out of the properties of the material; as when to a wet mass of clay we give whatever shape we wish it to retain when hardened. The organic form, on the other hand, is innate; it shapes, as it develops, itself from within, and the fulness of its development is one and the same with the perfection of its outward form. Such as the life is, such is the form.[58]

This reflects Eliot's belief that "real vitality is never aimless." It also sheds light on Eliot's own criticism of Shakespeare, which takes as its major principle the fact that Shakespeare's career is one continuously developing whole and makes that a standard by which lesser poets may be judged. Eliot agreed with Coleridge that a poem or play is an indivisible whole. He then extended the theory Coleridge had put forth on individual plays to Shakespeare's whole career.

Shakespeare set a standard for poets, "that of a continuous development from first to last. . . . We must know all of Shakespeare's work to know any of it" (*SE*, 170). Again and again Eliot applies this principle in his criticism: "The test is this: does every part of a man's work help us to understand the rest?" (*OPP*, 249). Every poet must strive to give expression to that continuous development that is the highest criterion of life and art. His work must always have "significant unity," changing, but not merely changing, rather "evolving" through time, so that we may say it is "united by one, consistent, and developing personality," as Shakespeare's was: "The whole of Shakespeare's work is one poem" (*SE*, 179). From very early in his career Eliot applied this standard—to the work of Pound, for example, which he found can only be evaluated if we "acknowledge the whole design."[59] "The music of verse," Eliot argues, "is not a line by line matter, but a question of the whole poem" (*OPP*, 30). What is true of the poem is also true of the poet's career—and finally true of poetry generally. Only the poet conscious of tradition can further the development of his nation's literature, for the "continuity of a literature is essential to its greatness" (*TCC*, 146-47). And yet, as Bergson says, "in all continuity there is confusion" (*ME*, 28). We come to understand true continuity only retrospectively. This is precisely what Eliot meant when he wrote in this dissertation that "the only real truth is the whole truth" (*KE*, 163). To know what something is, we must know what it will become.

And Bergson and Eliot agree we cannot know this in advance. For both, true continuity must be characterized by genuine novelty. How else could Eliot have held the view that "the conscious present is an awareness of the past . . . which the past's awareness of itself cannot show" (*SE*, 17)? Because there is genuine novelty, "the past has to be reinterpreted for each generation" (*TCC*, 119). This rein-terpretation is no mere "review"; it is a rebirth and rediscovery in one. Eliot's view rests on the same foundation as Bergson's argu-ment against determinism: The "possible" is known only retrospec-tively as such (*CM*, 22). "Premonitory" signs appear only after we know the conclusion (*CM*, 24-25). Bergson and Eliot have, in a sense, transferred the Romantic Sublime from a symbolic location out there in the world—in cataracts, ice-floes, and alps—directly to the interior place, the location of immediate experience, the "place of passage" as Bergson calls it in *Matter and Memory* (*MM*, 196-97). And here the same failures of imagination and language that occupied the Romantics occupy Eliot and Bergson. For them, the present is always a heart of darkness; in life, we must always wait to understand. A work of art, for example, becomes only "ret-rospectively a work of genius" (*TS*, 66). We talk of the occurrences of the present, but "practically, we perceive only in the past" (*MM*, 194). In short, novelty eludes us because we always confront it *post facto*. That, of course, is for our own protection, according to Berg-son. We need time, as Eliot says, in order to know what we have experienced (*OPP*, 50).

Bergson would agree completely with Eliot that the forward thrust of life's vitality into the future acts directly on the past. Eliot writes that "a living literature is always in process of change. . . . It is not that we have repudiated the past, as the obstinate enemies— and also the stupidest supporters—of any new movement like to believe; but that we have enlarged our conception of the past; and that in the light of what is new we see the past in a new pattern" (*TCC*, 57). That new pattern usually shows a more heterogeneous character. "A simple state can, in remaining what it is," writes Berg-son, "become a compound state solely because evolution will have created new viewpoints from which to consider it" (*CM*, 27). The appearance of the Romantics, for example, caused the Classicists to appear retrospectively to divide into subgroups, one of which we began to think of as "pre-Romantic" (*CM*, 24-26). And Eliot makes a similar statement about nineteenth-century American writers, who could never have conceived of their "Americanness" as we do, for "it is only in retrospect that their Americanness is fully visible" (*TCC*, 51-52). This newly patterned past is real enough; but it is an illusion to imagine a secret Americanness having been in preparation during the eighteenth century. That is, though American literature has continuity, there are still genuinely new events transpiring in its history, so that, finally, both prediction and explanation must remain problematic.

Yet we still cling to the illusion of "pre-Romanticism." And Eliot would agree with Bergson's explanation for our obstinate faith: Man prefers to conceptualize immediate experience rather than intuit it. He conceives time as a line, searches for and finds patterns in it. But this knowledge "imposes a pattern and falsifies," as "East Coker" warns: "For the pattern is new in every moment / And every moment is a new and shocking / Valuation of all we have been" (*CPP*, 125). That our intellectual constructs of experience are repeatedly and inevitably rendered provisional teaches, admittedly, different but related lessons for Bergson and Eliot. For Bergson, it means we have pursued knowledge by the wrong means. For Eliot, it is proof of our incomplete knowledge of God's ways and works. "The only way in which we can handle reality intellectually," Eliot writes, "is to turn it into objects. . . . At the same time we are forced to admit that the construction is not always successful" (*KE*, 159). But while for the philosopher "intuition attains the absolute" (*IM*, 74), for the later Eliot, intuition is merely better than intellectualization, for there is an absolute "to which man can never attain" (*SE*, 437).

One must remember that Eliot asserts this unattainable absolute in addition to, not instead of, Bergson's *durée*. That Bergson's was not the whole truth did not invalidate his insights. For both Eliot and Bergson the "organ of attention to life," the intellect, is a potential "obstacle to perception" (*ME*, 59; *TS*, 303). One must go by the path of the intuition to overcome the obstacle. And when one does, Eliot and Bergson agree, one sees that object and subject are by no means distinguishable entities. "The self, we find," Eliot writes, "seems to depend on a world which in turn depends on it; and nowhere, I repeat, can we find anything original and ultimate" (*KE*, 146). For everyday purposes, we act as if this were not so: "We perceive an object . . . in a special relation to our body" (*KE*, 155). The body's relationship to an external world is a fabrication that both Eliot and Bergson attack, though both admit that it "protects mankind" (*CPP*, 119). The intellect is of great practical value. But its supposedly "objective" truth is merely a shadow, merely "relative truth; all we care about is how it works" (*KE*, 169). As we shall see, the artist's intuition comes to the aid of both philosopher and poet here, suggesting a way of talking about primary experience that does not succumb to the falsifications of the intellect's concepts.

Eliot's aesthetic, Ronald Schuchard has said, appears to come partly from T.E. Hulme, Bergson's student and translator. I agree with Schuchard that Hulme may be seen to have placed the "keystone for [Eliot's] classicism."[60] Hulme's aesthetic and poetic, as formulated in *Speculations*, fit Eliot's theories. We have already reviewed part of this ground in chapter two, where we observed that Hulme sees the artist as "leaving the level where things are crystallized out into these definite shapes, and, diving down into the inner flux, [coming] back with a new shape." Once the artist has made this new form, anyone can see what he has seen. He is only able to "break the moulds and . . . make new ones" because he has detached himself from the practical, or "objective" view of the intellect. The artist struggles against the "stock types" that undermine his work, the tendency of language to become the "lowest common denominator." The artist seeks, in a "passionate desire for accuracy," to communicate something of the true individuality and novelty of primary experience.[61]

Hulme's aesthetic, in which the artist opens a door from objectivity into the flux of reality, showing us that to which intellect blinds us, is remarkably close to Eliot's.[62] The theory is detectable in a general form in Eliot's dissertation, where primary experience is defined. And later, Eliot states directly that the artist seeks "some new experience, some fresh understanding of the familiar, or the expression of something we have experienced, but have no words for" (*OPP*, 7). For Eliot, the poet must "explore." He must try "to find words for the inarticulate, to capture those feelings which people can hardly feel because they have no words for them" (*TCC*, 134). Poetry, "if it is not to be a lifeless repetition of forms, must be constantly exploring "the frontiers of the spirit."[63] It should, for Eliot, remind us of the "deeper unnamed feelings which form the substratum of our being, to which we rarely penetrate; for our lives are mostly a constant evasion of ourselves, and an evasion of the visible and sensible world" (*UPUC*, 155). Now there really can be no way to this kind of truth save through intuition, through re- nouncing practical ends and allowing the mind to contemplate what Bergson says "it has a material interest in not seeing" (*CM*, 161).

Eliot's poet cannot avoid exploring, digging "below the surface of contact between the self and external objects . . . to the depths of the organized and living intelligence" (*TFW*, 136). It is another country he enters: "Beyond the nameable, classifiable emotions and motives of our conscious life when directed toward action . . . there is a fringe . . . of feeling of which we are only aware in a kind of temporary detachment from action" (*OPP*, 86). Authentic poetry penetrates to such depths through the disinterested state of intui- tion; sailing into the unconscious, it offers our only hope of avoiding a "relapse into unconsciousness."[64] The poet exercises that detach- ment professionally, for the sake of raising to consciousness both individual experience and cultural heritage, things his poem must have in its bones. Indeed, a great poem may carry something in its mere rhythm; a poem in a language unfamiliar to us thus may leap directly into the mind: "In poetry you can, now and then, penetrate into another country, so to speak, before your passport has been issued or your ticket taken" (*OPP*, 14). It can only offer us this if it was born of intuition, of a renouncing of the "processes which we generally employ for practical ends" (*IM*, 67). Sometimes, appar- ently, we can achieve those "moments of inattention and detach- ment" in which we "perceive a pattern behind the pattern" by ser- endipity (*SE*, 232). More often, we must earn them.

In Eliot's life, one such moment, brought about by illness, en- gendered a section of *The Waste Land*. "A piece of writing meditated apparently without progress for months or years," he wrote, "may suddenly take shape and word; and in this state (brought on by illness) long passages may be produced which require little or no retouch. . . . He to whom this happens assuredly has the sensa- tion of being a vehicle rather than a maker" (*SE*, 358). The poet's sensation of being a vehicle rather than a creator follows naturally from Bergson's concept of intuition as a negative function of con- sciousness. Where the stamina to effect this conscious relaxation of the intellect lacks, illness may serve as a helpmeet; this it appears to have done for Eliot in 1920, when he experienced an "efflux of poetry." "To me," he later wrote, "it seems that in these moments, which are characterized by the sudden lifting of the burden of anx- iety and fear which press upon our daily life so steadily that we are unaware of it, what happens is something negative: that is to say, not 'inspiration' as we commonly think of it, but the breaking down of habitual barriers—which tend to reform very quickly" (*UPUC*, 139). These "habitual barriers" that make daily living possible buffer us from the wellspring of poetry, which may visit us if we let it. And Eliot appears to have found that, for him, writing good po- etry was the art of courting this serendipity. He quotes Housman admiringly: "'I have seldom,' he says, 'written poetry unless I was rather out of health.' I believe I understand that sentence. If I do, it is a guarantee . . . of the quality of Mr. Housman's poetry."[65] Thus, paradoxically, genius is a sort of self-effacement which, "driven on . . . by an inner necessity," yields to what "had to express itself" (*ASG*, 25; *TS*, 38).

Bergson's *intuition philosophique* is thus profoundly helpful in understanding Eliot's view of personality and the act of writing. The ground for this view remains, of course, the "primary experi- ence" defined in Eliot's early philosophical writings: "In feeling the subject and object are one," and primary experience cannot there- fore be "mine" for "I am only I in relation to objects." Because this relation disappears in primary experience, so must our commonly held views of the self and the world. In immediate experience, the self merges in a "timeless unity" with the whole world.[66] Thus, the most universal truth is the most intensely personal: "Each [mind or finite center] expanded to completion, to the full latent reality within it, *would be identical with the whole universe"* (*KE*, 202; my italics). For Eliot, this transformation of personality is an "impersonality" more significant than the impersonality of craft with word and form. The poet can always think of his work as like the "turning of a jug or a table leg" (*SE*, 96). It is harder to achieve the rendering of highly personal matter in a way that brings out its universality, reminding us of the unity behind our world of "subject and object." The more profound impersonality "is that of the poet who, out of intense and personal experience, is able to express a general truth; retaining all the particularity of his experience, to make of it a general symbol" (*OPP*, 299). Yeats, Eliot said, had achieved this. By becoming more Irish, Yeats became more universal, and Eliot called the line in which Yeats named his own age in a poem "a triumph" (*OPP*, 300-301).

There is no conflict between the theorist of "impersonality" and the poet who writes about his trips on the London tube in "Burnt Norton." There has only been a misunderstanding about what impersonality meant to Eliot. It is the impersonality of intuition, an "extinction of personality" in the face of and for the sake of revealing an underlying reality. No good poetry, Eliot tells us in his introduction to Valéry's *Le Serpent*, is "divorced from personal experience and passion." "Indeed," he says, "the virtue, the marvel of Lucretius is the passionate act by which he annihilates himself in a system and unites himself with it, giving something greater than himself."[67] The artist struggles not to deny the value of personal experience, not to abandon the world of "appearance," but to "transmute his personal and private agonies into something rich and strange, something universal and impersonal" (*SE*, 117). Universal does not mean "public."

But language is a public medium of "exchange"; it gives the illusion that it is substantial coin. So the first problem the modern poet faces is making a new relationship between primary experience and these outward signs. Like Bergson, Eliot recognizes that words inevitably tend to sink away from that vital beginning and come to substitute for experience rather than evoke it. In his dissertation he had asserted that the symbol is "continuous with that which it symbolizes," and that name and object form a "mystic mar-

riage" (*KE*, 104, 132, 135). But Eliot's criticism is really more con-
cerned with the divorce of these things, with the difficulty of rec-
onciling them. In his essay on Swinburne (1920) he asserts that
"language in a healthy state presents the object, is so close to the
object that the two are identified" (*SE*, 285). So long as language
is in a "healthy state," meaning, which "cannot be merely contemplated, but must be *erlebt*," keeps its immediacy and life (*KE*, 94).
Unfortunately, language must be continually restored to health, for
it becomes with time a "shabby equipment always deteriorating / In
the general mess of imprecision of feeling" (*CPP*, 128).

In a sense, for Eliot the poet must murder to create; he must
smash the precut molds for thought, the language for which experience has ceased to exist. He must shake the arras of this "utilitarian" language as the madman shakes his geranium in "Rhapsody
on a Windy Night." He must fight the tendency of words to convert
the unique (that is, the universal) into public property. That is what
Eliot had in mind when he wrote that "all significant truths are
private truths. As they become public, they cease to become truths;
they become facts, or at best, part of the public character; or at
worst, catchwords" (*KE*, 165). For Eliot, intellectual "objectivity"
can never capture living truth. The poet must thus become subversive, must plot to overcome the natural tendency of language. He
must "become more and more comprehensive, more allusive, more
indirect, in order to force, to dislocate, if necessary, language into
his meaning" (*SE*, 248). This dislocation of language—not meaning—is tantamount to a smashing of molds. A poem thus re-shaped
jerks us out of our depersonalized, stereoptican world into the world
of mutating, interpenetrating forms the artist has exposed by his
impersonal vision. We do not merely contemplate a message presented to us with proper etiquette; we find ourselves "forced into a
street dance" (*TS*, 32).

The poet does not interfere in this *erlebnis*; he designs it and
catalyzes it. He has in mind not so much "communication" as invoking memory. He must use language in new ways if he hopes to
have any effect at all, for otherwise the language will bury again
what he has unearthed. He cannot literally recreate the experience,
and should not pretend to. He can only go so far in "dislocating"

language without losing his reader entirely and careening wildly past the universal into the cryptic. But he is left with one great tool: the image. Here lies the burning fountain of poetry as Philip Wheelwright calls it. We have already discussed the similarities between Eliot's "objective correlative" and Bergson's image theory presented in Hulme's translation of *Introduction à la metaphysique*. For Bergson and Eliot the effect of any arrangement of images must be to evoke a nonverbal moment—an intuition—which can only be achieved if the individual "parts" of the poem function not as "component parts, but [as] partial expressions" (*IM*, 29). For both Eliot and Bergson "the novelty of [the artist's] form has rather been forced upon him by his material than deliberately sought" (*ASG*, 25). And for both, that novel form must be organic to be authentic, must grow from seed and contain in every cell the genetic code of its mature expression: the whole poem.

The poet's target is our spirit; he tries to bring us back into the moment. But he cannot simply bang away at that objective with a hammer, or what he pins down will be rendered lifeless and ineffectual. Therefore, he is really forced more and more into "indirection." He holds up an image to our inner eye, but his real object lies just off to the side; it is a trick of seeing, like that we use on a moonless night. If his poem is crafted well, he brings us into an unnamed— because ineffable—experience. We thus justifiably call him a catalyst, for he is in himself unimportant, merely the means of our reawakening. Eliot likened the poet to a platinum filament. Bergson called him a "reagent" like that used in developing film (*CM*, 159). The logic is the same: The poet brings out latent energy in an apparently static scheme. His strategy must always catch us off guard, but it is anything but illogical.

The poet's logic is simply other than the scientist's. Any apparent irrelevancies in his work are "due to the fact that terms are used with more or other than their normal meaning." It is certainly not true that "the ideas of a great poet are in any sense arbitrary; certainly in the sense in which imagination is capricious, the ideas of a lunatic or an imbecile are more 'imaginative' than those of a poet. In really great imaginative work the connections are felt to be bound by necessity as logical as any connections to be found anywhere"

(*KE*, 75). They are connections felt, however, not seen. The scientist conducts his raid on a material world spread out upon a table—
simply there. But for the poet there is another, richer world, a
"knowing and being in one," as Bradley puts it.[68] Great art works
upon this ground of knowledge not with the scalpel, but with the
intuition, the faculty that claims the ability to know without dis-
secting the unit we can "never analyse away" (*KE*, 30).

Finally, in Eliot's poetic there is a *dédoublement* that parallels
Bergson's: He places the poet in both the passive role of "vehicle"
and the active one of prophet. In *On Poetry and Poets* he writes that
the true poet "does not know what he has to say until he has said
it" (*OPP*, 108). And he defines inspiration as this very discovery of
meaning: "If the word 'inspiration' is to have any meaning, it must
mean just this, that the speaker or writer is uttering something
which he does not wholly understand. . . . This is certainly true of
poetic inspiration" (*OPP*, 137). Since "creation" would also be rendered meaningless without this affirmation of genuine novelty in the
world, the poet is elevated to a level of participation in the great
creative current running through all life. What is most significant
about him is therefore least explainable: "If either on the basis of
what poets try to tell you, or by biographical research, with or without the tools of the psychologist, you attempt to explain a poem,
you will probably be getting further and further away from the poem
without arriving at any other destination" (*OPP*, 108). Thus, both
Eliot and Bergson believe that the poet's creation must, if it is genuine, always contain an element that remains "unaccountable, however complete our knowledge of the poet, and . . . that is what matters most." The poem is absolutely novel, and "cannot be wholly
explained by anything that went before. That, I believe, is what we
mean by 'creation'" (*OPP*, 124).

Life is change; but also development into the genuinely new.
And art must exhibit these features also. The legacy of Bergson's
thought in Eliot's criticism is rich on this point. Eliot had echoed
some of Bergson's arguments against determinism as early as his
doctoral dissertation: "The mathematical representation of motion
is and is not the same as the motion represented." The dissertation
iterates, as well, the theory of entelechy: "The character of a science,

like the character of a man, may be said to be already present at the moment of conception, and on the other hand, to develop at every moment into something new and unforeseen" (*KE*, 26, 61). Here Eliot first formulated the critical approach needed to penetrate the principle of "inner development." The impossibility of legislating what truly lives must force us back on a strategy of simply avoiding preconditioned responses: "The true critic is a scrupulous avoider of formulae; . . . he finds fact nowhere and approximation always. His truths are truths of experience, rather than calculation" (*KE*, 164).

Literary law must be "discovered," not "laid down" (*UPUC*, 45; *TCC*, 41-42). Eliot said of Addison that he had made the "elementary error" of thinking he had "discovered as objective laws what [he had] merely imposed by private legislation" (*UPUC*, 60). As much as any scientist, the critic must guard against this failure of objectivity, especially since the very concept of inner development must contain something forever inaccessible to analysis. We are constantly grasping at smoke, carried forward so rapidly and irrevocably that we can never say precisely where we have been or are going. Indeed, inner development is nothing like a journey on land. It is "no concatenation," but a "starting point which expands itself and can neither be arrested nor analysed, for the process is not one simply of addition, but of inner development, so that you cannot say absolutely what the starting point was" (*KE*, 116-17). Caught forever in the midst of such a blooming-outward, the mind lives perpetually in a state of disorientation: "In poetry, as in life, our business is to make the best of a bad job" (*UPUC*, 45).

That is Eliot's characteristically pessimistic view, one that seems to divide him irrevocably from the philosopher who saw the history of life on this planet as a great unfolding progress. For Eliot, the "forces of deterioration are a large crawling mass, and the forces of development half a dozen men."[69] For Eliot, man and nature are "radically imperfect," while for Bergson they are only incomplete (*SE*, 437; *ASG*, 45-46). And yet, when Eliot formulates his theory of language and the artist, he is forced to posit something on which human knowledge will be grounded, and that ground is immediate experience. He is also forced to draw from this ground the principle of the free act, however exceptional, and to define it as Bergson does: "The free act may be termed a synthesis of feelings and ideas" (*MM*, 243). Eliot is then driven to see the parallel between free action and artistry in Bergsonian terms as well: We act freely when our acts "spring from our whole personality . . . when they have that indefinable resemblance to it which one sometimes finds between the artist and his work" (*TFW*, 172). And he is thus brought to conclude that good art performs a liberating office by returning us to the consciousness of that "unity of life" which cannot be analysed away (*ME*, 225). Born of the intuition of this unity, the poem carries some spark of its fire to us, or else fails. Thus, for Eliot, poetry should bring a "satisfaction of the whole being" (*SE*, 368).

Like Bergson, Eliot believed poetry and philosophy had taken a wrong turn sometime in the seventeenth century, when thought and feeling appeared to fall more and more apart. That change was felt in verse as an unfortunate hostility to intellectuality: "From Donne to Tennyson, something happened to the Mind of England. . . . It is the difference between the intellectual poet and the reflective poet. Tennyson and Browning are poets, and they think; but they do not feel their thought as immediately as the odour of a rose. A thought to Donne *was an experience*" (*SE*, 247; my italics). In effect, Eliot wants to restore to "thought" the quality of *erlebnis* which poets had denied it, the *emotion* that became their truth and that was their private territory. Bergson also, though he spends as much energy as Bradley in trying to destroy the common concept of the intellect, wishes to restore this unity to mental life, this interpenetration of instinct and intellectuality: "I smell a rose and immediately confused recollections of childhood come back to my memory. In truth, these recollections have not been called up by the perfume of the rose: *I breathe them in with the very scent*" (*TFW*, 161; my italics). Poetry and philosophy's slipping away from this unity of the sensual and intellective functions is, for both Eliot and Bergson, symptomatic of a disintegration of personality. Eliot saw "in the history of English poetry . . . the splitting up of personality. . . . What we have to do is re-integrate it" (*UPUC*, 84-85). And for Bergson, of course, free acts can spring only from a "whole personality." If F.O. Matthiessen is right that Eliot's most fundamental tenet as an artist and critic is the necessity for this reintegration of thought and feeling, then surely Bergson's *intuition philosophique* is an indispensable tool for our understanding Eliot.[70] Intuition was an idea that rankled him; but he could not escape it in his own "practical" view of art.

In that view, the poet emerges finally as a risk-taker who cares to submit himself to the "fire of an original and unique emotion born of the identification of an author with his subject, that is to say, of intuition" (*TS*, 38). Seen in the broader context of Eliot's Christian orthodoxy, this Promethean risk is also part of the pattern God has conceived and which He determines. But the risk is the closest thing to freedom that we have, and even if it is a kind of fate to take it, still, it is better to act ill than to act not at all. A consciousness of man's inherent incompleteness does not invalidate this imperative. And the artist champions this aspiration. In him, the vitality of immediate experience must gleam. This, as Eliot says, is the first criterion for any critical judgment: Is it a living performance, a free act born of a whole personality? One distinguishes "a great dancer and a merely competent dancer" by pointing to that something intangible that melds mere sequence into organic whole. It is the dancer's intuitive contact with creative fire, "a vital flame, that impersonal, and, if you like, inhuman force which transpires between each of the dancer's movements" (*SE*, 95).

The great dancer's performance may be recognized by what Bergson calls its "true continuity, real mobility, reciprocal penetration—in a word, that creative evolution which is life" (*CE*, 162). Eliot's critical thought has to reckon with this force—inhuman whether we like it or not. To see its primacy in his criticism is to recognize the importance of his early philosophical training in the phrasing of those profound tensions, so often characterized as mere "contradictions," that are the hallmark of his work.

FOUR

Time, Intuition, and Self-Knowledge in Eliot's Poetry

> For most of us, there is only the unattended
> Moment, the moment in and out of time . . .
> —T.S. Eliot, *Four Quartets*

≈ "The essence of mystical contemplation," wrote Evelyn Un-derhill in *Practical Mysticism,* is dualistic: "union with the flux of life, and union with the whole in which all lesser realities are re-sumed." To achieve these different sorts of union, you must first let "intuition have its way with you."[1] This challenge encapsulates the struggle of Eliot's career as a poet, for in positing "immediate ex-perience" as the ground of poetic knowledge, yet still subscribing to an Absolute in which that experience must be resumed as a "lesser reality," Eliot assumes a highly ambivalent posture toward "intuition." Intuition is not "thought"; indeed, it is associated with instinctive behavior, raising for Eliot the spectre of atavistic "ape-neck" elements in men. But if intuition involves a disturbing sort of giving up, it is still essential to art, and even finally to the mystic.

In his preface for *Thoughts for Meditation: A Way to Recovery from Within* (1952), Eliot wrote of "emotions and states of the soul, which are found, so to speak, only beyond the limit of the visible spectrum of human feeling, and which can be experienced only in moments of illumination, or by the development of another organ of perception than *everyday vision.*" To penetrate to this level—and he expressly uses the language of the ineffable and of nonvisualizable form—he admits we must abandon "our usual motives . . . abandon even the Love of Knowledge."[2] This dispassionate aban-donment bears obvious similarity to Bergson's intuition, achievable only when intentionality collapses. By this date, Eliot had found a way to talk about his view of immediate experience and intuition—a way that gives "abandonment" sanctification. But earlier in his career, he associated it with embracing the carnality and decay of the world. In coming to admit that one "must not deny the body" (*CPP*, 111) Eliot also seems to have come to find in intuition the "principle of its own self-transcendence" (*KE*, 166).

Over the course of his career as a poet, then, he moves from a painful dilemma to a conviction that intuitive experience can be—must be—included. Ultimately, he comes to identify it with God's love, love that wove an "intolerable shirt of flame." This image from *Four Quartets* acknowledges a place for Vitalism in his art, just as the mystics described by Evelyn Underhill sought *both* Absolutism and Vitalism in a "genuine life process and not [merely] an intellec-tual speculation."[3] It is part of a vision of human existence de-scribed by Eliot's friend, Joseph Chiari, that is "Platonic [but also] essentially Christian. There is no possible contradiction between the Bergsonian stress on duration as a means to reach an awareness of existence and continuous becoming, and the Christian stress on the instant of grace and illumination as a means to reach Eternity. Christian thought . . . is above all existential."[4] But is *Four Quartets* really consistent with Eliot's earliest poetic impulses? And are those impulses really consistent with Bergson's emphasis on *durée*? That would involve some rather dramatic changes, it would seem. The changes, I shall argue, are gradual, the result of a long meditation begun with Eliot's first work in philosophy.

Eliot's Earlier Poetry

At Smith Academy, St. Louis, in 1905, Eliot wrote a graduation poem that proposed the school's motto should be "Progress!"[5] He had been brought up in a household in which "Herbert Spencer's generalized theory of evolution [was] regarded as the key to the mystery of the universe."[6] As late as 1917 Eliot quotes J.B. Yeats (approvingly) that "in every great poet there is a Herbert Spencer."[7] It had become abundantly clear by this time, however, that Eliot would not abide progressivism. "There never was a time," he wrote later, "so completely parochial, so shut off from the past" as those years immediately following the war (*SE*, 352).

Eliot's early verse is preoccupied with the role of art in a world gone mad over "progress." That is one explanation for his repeated attempts to propose the "study of history—including language and literature," for the good of the "collective mind."[8] There is a knot of themes one notices in the *Prufrock* volume, for example: automatism, regression, powerlessness. Things swim along in a haze or dream, predetermined, so that characters "are acted" rather than act themselves:

> And I have known the eyes already, known them all—
> The eyes that fix you with a formulated phrase,
> And when I am pinned and wriggling on the wall,
> Then how should I begin . . . ?

Admittedly, the issues are many: feminine wiles, the dead end of the salon world, the *déjà vu* of the guillotined man "dying with a dying fall / Beneath music from a farther room." But there is also plainly an *angst* about the possibility of freedom.

Eliot's playing the role of the sensitive plant may seem strange, but there is an element of that in his early work. Action and business he rejects—the "short square fingers stuffing pipes / And evening newspapers, and eyes / Assured of certain certainties" (*CPP*, 13). Instead, he tells us, he is "moved by fancies that are curled / Around these images and cling: / The notion of some infinitely gentle / Infinitely suffering thing." The bits of paper used to curl a woman's hair; the *notion* of something (with its wistful air)—these are the "things" Eliot opposes to the male world of the clock, money, business. What good is poetry? "There's nothing in it," says the materialistic Mr. Nixon of Pound's "Mauberley." But Eliot manages to pack into these verses ominous tones suggesting there will be a reckoning, a rude awakening: The readers of the "Boston Evening Transcript" sway in the wind "like a ripe field of corn" ready for the Grim Reaper.

There has been an inversion of values, so that the age advances, as Eliot will later say in "The Rock," "progressively backwards" (*CPP*, 108). Backwards equals degeneration. It also means a primordial automatism. The street-lamp of "Rhapsody on a Windy Night" beats "like a fatalistic drum." The world yields up the "secret of its skeleton, stiff and white," a form "hard and curled and ready to snap." Crabs scuttle across the ocean bottom in "Prufrock." Another crab grips automatically a stick held out in "Rhapsody." The moon herself has "lost her memory." She twists a paper rose.

Some read the poems of this period as part of an argument Eliot was carrying on with himself about the true relation of memory to experience. According to such a reading, Eliot arrives at a conclusion that Bergson's intuition is simply not adequate to explain the problem of experience; he then stops writing such poetry. But I think we see in these early poems a problem Eliot was having with the nature of poetic creation itself, to which he was obviously deeply drawn, but which raised certain unpleasant difficulties. If a poet does anything at all, he clearly deals in rhythms that (as post-Darwinian thought and research were making clear) come with the genetic code of the human being. "The greatest poetry, like the greatest prose," he wrote, has a doubleness; the poet is talking to you on two planes at once."[9] Here again is the tension of Bergson's aesthetics. Ideas and images constitute its first term: Here the issues of purpose, time, the age's lack of memory and sensitivity, its automatic behavior, come forth. The second term is that drumbeat.

In a 1923 article, Eliot specifically connects "drumbeat" to an evolutionary mechanism essential to poetry, saying that drama and verse have their source in this primordial rhythm and lamenting the fact that "we have lost the drum."[10] One might have expected a different sort of proposition from the classicizing thinker who located the flower of Western Civilization in Dante's Italy, rather than Cro-Magnon's cave. The value of unconscious processes to poetic creation is no small source of puzzlement in Eliot's criticism. In a characteristic response to inquiries about his "night-mind," he claimed to find it "quite uninteresting."[11] But without some contact with a primitive ground of being, Eliot's other beliefs about poetic creation make no sense.

A struggle was clearly going on in his thinking after he returned to Harvard to do graduate work in philosophy. And that struggle did not end with his decision not to complete his Ph.D. Ronald Bush has said, and I completely agree, that Eliot's work in philosophy was part of an attempt to set the vocabulary of rationalism, particularly of Spencer, at odds with itself: "Eliot's drift toward philosophy, striking even before the subject became the serious study of his postgraduate years, was precisely an attempt to justify the value of the affections." [12] And yet Eliot's verse expresses revulsion at the carnal world out of which the affections grow, so that the "protozoic slime," "summer sweat," "rank feline smells," and "bees / With hairy bellies" trouble the poems of 1920 (*CPP*, 24, 33-34).

It has been enough for some to see Eliot in this period as already feeling the pull of the Church, since his commitments seem so divided. He seeks an art of primordial rhythms, and yet he seems to feel a revulsion toward human sexuality (hardly separable from the drumbeat itself). But that will not explain much, especially if a commitment to the Church is seen as a rejection of carnal impulses on theological grounds. The vocabulary may become more subdued, after 1927, but the issue seems to have remained the same: Eliot's stance as a poet and critic was to make a rationale for the life of the heart. It is precisely here that the "new vocabulary" of Hulme and Bergson came to hand. But Bergson was the heir of Spencer's evolutionism, and Eliot had become convinced that in some matters there was no such thing as "progress." "We have the right to take human value as the standard for natural evolution, but what standard have we for religion or society?" [13] He had not achieved, yet, a standpoint from which the change, carnality, growth, decay of which poetic creation is a part could be made sense of. He had been trying, through verse and prose, and through the very study of history, language, and literature he recommended to all.

In the process, he was constructing, bit by bit, a vocabulary of symbols peculiar to himself, yet drawn from the times he saw as needing to be rescued. One may think of his poetry and criticism taken together as a vast, sometimes self-contradictory attempt at performing for culture what "analytic psychology attempts to do for the individual mind." [14] Eliot brings before the reader images of things discovered in reading, discovered also in something that must have been a kind of "night-mind." Many have noted the quality of courage in Eliot's writing. It impresses one over and over: his stamina and fortitude. "By this moment, and this only, we have existed / Which is not to be found in our obituaries," Eliot wrote in *The Waste Land*, speaking of a moment of risk, daring. One finds him daring to risk a great deal at every point in his career, and it would be hard to think of anything more daring than attempting to bring into the twentieth-century poetic vocabulary what Bergson brought into its philosophic one: Christian mysticism.

Eliot's early work brings the creative act to the table, looks at it lying there, "etherized," and seeks ways to breathe life back into the body. "Prufrock" images the danger of bringing unconscious processes to consciousness: "Human voices wake us, and we drown." And *The Waste Land* shows us a world subject to atavism. The nymphs have become bored typists, smoothing hair "with automatic hand" and setting a record on the gramophone. The world these poems examine is a "Rat's Alley," a *cul de sac*. "The Hollow Men" shows the final crackup, rendered in Thomistic vocabulary, but with a pathology of creativity that is pure Bergson:

> Between the desire
> And the spasm
> Between the potency
> And the existence
> Between the essence
> And the descent
> Falls the Shadow
>
> > *For thine is the Kingdom*
>
> For thine is
> Life is
> For thine is the

To fill in the blanks, compare this with the description of free consciousness Bergson provides: "Between the idea and the action, some hardly perceptible intermediate processes come in ... the feeling of effort. And from the idea to the effort, from the effort to the act, the progress has been so continuous that we cannot say where the idea and the effort end, and where the act begins" (*TFW*,

211). If the world was engendered in a vital "spasm," then the trans-mission of energy is "breaking up" (in the parlance of the aviator) and revealing horrifying gaps, "gesture without motion." Life be-comes "death's *other* kingdom" (my italics).

Eliot admitted in an interview in 1953 that he had thought his poetry was over after "The Hollow Men."[15] But forcing the moment to its crisis did leave, after all, something else to say, the possibility of a place to begin again. As I chart Eliot's poetic career, "The Hol-low Men" represents the nadir of his reaction to the loss of possi-bilities for poetry, a loss being sustained on two fronts: first, the lack of value placed upon cultural heritage—the loss of memory—within Eliot's own culture; second, the lack of a standpoint from which to make sense of the chaos and difficulty of moral and intel-lectual growth. Was such growth possible at all? The answer was not encouraging. And it was particularly not encouraging so long as the role of *durée* (experienced time) in poetic creation remained unclear.

But through adopting a vocabulary of mystical awareness, Eliot began to bring to the center of his poetic activity the intuitive act, the knowledge made available in fits of forgetting. Thus, he began to create verse that turned more and more toward the values of openendedness and primary experience. He finally finds a point of view from which chaotic and contradictory experiences can be or-ganized, and one that has the "doublesided" awareness by which alone one can fix value.

The crucial point in the development of this vocabulary and this point of view was reached when Eliot became a communicant member of the Anglican Church in 1927. But as A.D. Moody and other biographers have noted, the change was a gradual one, and the results in Eliot's life and work were not felt with cataclysmic swiftness. Indeed, one might fairly say that Eliot's "drift toward phi-losophy" begun around 1910 in Paris was completed in his coming fully into possession of the tradition of Christian mysticism. (Recall that he identifies Bergsonism as "mysticism" even then.) Very early on, when reviewing Russell's *Mysticism and Logic*, he had decided that philosophy was not a matter of stating laws, but rather of "in-sight" and "vision."[16] And in 1952 he looked back on this period

as one in which the philosopher went off the track in trying to com-
pensate for "a feeling of inferiority to the exact scientist." As it
turned out, he went on, the *root cause* for his "dissatisfaction with
philosophy as a *profession*—I now believe to lie in the divorce of
philosophy from theology."[17] Hindsight is often inaccurate, but
contradiction of Eliot's self-evaluation would involve a great deal of
dichotomizing of his career, the kind that so many have unjustifia-
bly performed before.

Rather than a reactionary stance toward human failings and carnality in general and poetic creation in particular, Eliot's move into
the Church appears to have sanctified a troubling drive he had been
writing about for years. The "soul of Man must quicken to creation," as he wrote in "The Rock":

> Out of the formless stone, when the artist united himself with
>   stone,
> Spring always new forms of life, from the soul of the man that
>   is joined to the soul of stone;
> Out of the meaningless practical shapes of all that is living or
>   lifeless
> Joined with the artist's eye, new life, new form, new colour.
> Out of the sea of sound the life of music,
> Out of the slimy mud of words, out of the sleet and hail of
>   verbal imprecisions,
> Approximate thoughts and feelings, words that have taken the
>   place of thoughts and feelings,
> There spring the perfect order of speech, and the beauty of
>   incantation.
>
>   [*CPP*, 111-12].

Here the equations have changed. Intuition and evolution take their
place in a *human* order that is part of the divine: "The LORD who
created must wish us to create" (ibid.). This represents an acceptance that poetry is, as Heidegger says, the *primal* language, not just
"one tool which man possesses along with many others; it is only
language that makes possible our standing within openness to what
is."[18] The meaningless practical shapes are remade to a purpose,
and speech is evolved out of the sea's coma, carnality's mud. Here

also is the Bergsonian imperative that God undertook to "create creators" (*TS*, 243).

There is a reconciliation underway, here, between temporal life and that "final" standpoint from which alone progress may be said to be occurring at all. "If the progress of mankind is to continue as long as man survives on this earth," Eliot wrote in 1932, "progress becomes merely change; for the values of man will change, and a world of changed values is valueless to us—just as we, being a part of the past, will be valueless to it." But that is not his last word: "We must believe, first, that the human race can, if it will, improve indefinitely; that it can improve both its material well-being and its spiritual capacities. We must also have a conception of a perfect society attainable on earth."[19] The Choruses from *The Rock* affirm this. "What life have you if you have not life together?" they ask. And they assert: "You must not deny the body" (*CPP*, 101, 111). Eliot will have it both ways, that man exists in a tension, at "an infinite remove from perfection," but also knowing that "perfection is as nearly attainable for man here and now as it ever will be."[20]

The reconciliation taking place around the time of Eliot's conversion has not been seen clearly for what it is, completion of a *synthesizing* of two competing symbolic systems and conceptual frameworks: on the one hand, that of *durée*, evolution, and intuition; on the other, that of the Absolute, finality, Greek fate. This synthesis was attempted, as I have shown, as early as his 1913-14 paper on Bergson. In the later twenties, the synthesis begins to come about in clear terms. Eliot's move into the Church coincides with his increasing reliance on the vocabulary of *intuition*, which he now allows to have its way with him.

Four Quartets and Mysticism

In his study of Eliot and Bradley, Hugo Roeffaers concluded that, for Eliot, the ultimate goal of our understanding must be the "transcendence of immediate experience," but that this analysis cannot depart finally from what it transcends.[21] Roeffaers's view simply conforms to Eliot's that "we cannot banish *becoming* any more than we can banish *being.*"[22] But that has not stopped a small but powerful lobby in American criticism from calling Eliot's career a retreat from experience that concludes with a poem which revolts against the very human genius that made it. I am speaking of Leavis, Ishak, Bergsten, Vendler, and Nuttall, who find that Eliot's conversion was a reactionarist movement adversely affecting his poetry—turning it into preaching. "[It] is not faith but the peculiar combination of a covert reliance on faith with an ostentatious (and censorious) rationalism" that bothers Nuttall.[23] Helen Vendler characterizes *Four Quartets* as Eliot's *Ecclesiastical Sonnets*.[24] And Floyd Watkins, in *The Flesh and the Word*, says that Eliot simply reversed all his poetic values, becoming abstract, talky, and intrusive.[25] Even A.D. Moody finds Eliot "dwindles" to a man of letters, his poetry pursuing "the ideal at the expense of the actual."[26]

This view of Eliot's career, though not universal, has still been very powerful in shaping attitudes and critical intentions. Thus, we have a plethora of books on Eliot's early career; not nearly so much on the late, when it is assumed that metaphysics simply swamped the boat. But it is the *mystical* and not the metaphysical that Eliot finds closely allied to his theory of poetry.[27] "A Poet who is also a metaphysician," he had written in 1924, "is conceivable as a unicorn or a wyvern is conceivable [for] such a poet would be a monster."[28] Eliot's later poetry does not codify his "seduction" by the Church away from his earlier poetic values. To invoke the idea of a whole new aesthetic stance to explain the sublimation of experience in *Four Quartets* is to go badly wrong in reading his whole *oeuvre*.

Bergson wrote to William James in 1909 that he would have to make a large place in his philosophy for the unconscious, "for there is a certain consoling emotion drawn [from there]."[29] For Eliot, from the beginning, this consolation had to be drawn out, but it had to be reached somehow, and this is the work of many poems and essays up to and including *Four Quartets*. If some find the poem less a consolation than a consolation prize, that is perhaps because they have misunderstood the mystical language as having metaphysical intentions. Perhaps it would have been wiser for Eliot to stay with the original epigraph he had planned for "Burnt Norton," taken from *Pickwick Papers*: "What a rum thing time is, ain't it Neddy?"[30] That tone might have won a larger audience, though not made a better poem.

The epigraphs from Heraclitus on which Eliot settled, and the metaphysical vocabulary of the opening stanzas, with their illusion of syllogistic reasoning, do set a tone of scholasticism, but it will rapidly be broken:

> Time present and time past
> Are perhaps present in time future
> And time future contained in time past.
> If all time is eternally present
> All time is unredeemable.
> What might have been is an abstraction
> Remaining a perpetual possibility
> Only in a world of speculation.

If the past never ceases to exist, every future state will "contain" the past—and the present moment (which will then be past, as well). If time is not chaos, the seeds of the future were contained in the past. But if we take these interdependent propositions to heart, we confront a world in which nothing can change, in which everything is eternally present. As Bergson says, if we give to the concatenation of memories the "obligation of *containing* and *being contained,* which only applies to the collection of bodies instantaneously perceived in space," we falsify our experience of *durée* (*MM*, 193).

But there is change. Turning abruptly from this dead end, "Burnt Norton" admits frankly that we are on the wrong track trying to "think" time. It must be intuited. The poem does not pretend to be "final": "My words echo / Thus in your mind. / But to what purpose?" This admission is followed by an equally frank invitation: "Other echoes / Inhabit the garden. Shall we follow?" The bird-voice evokes a siren-song, as in "Marina," or with Philomel in *The Waste Land.* It is an open deception, then, this "deception of the thrush . . . our first world." In "Animula" our "first world" was a sensuous one close to nature, but blind to its meaning. The bird will claim to show us blinding truth: "Go, go, go, said the bird: human kind / Cannot bear very much reality." But there is another truth behind the sensuous one associated with transgression in the

Garden, an echo which Bergson says is "the earliest thing in the memory of each of us, as it is in the memory of mankind" (*TS*, 1). "Burnt Norton," then, stirs up the dust of history, memory, desire, guilt—and lets it settle.

A second sort of truth emerges. In the scene following the bird's invitations, a suprasensible and paradoxical vision is described, full of unseen presences and "unheard music." This latter is a riddle "Dry Salvages" unravels for us. Unheard music is music intuited, "heard so deeply / That it is not heard at all, but you are the music / While the music lasts" (*CPP*, 136). "Burnt Norton" presents this flash:

> Dry the pool, dry concrete, brown-edged,
> And the pool was filled with water out of sunlight,
> And the lotos rose, quietly, quietly,
> And the surface glittered out of the heart of light,
> And they were behind us, reflected in the pool.
> Then a cloud passed, and the pool was empty.

This creative heart is the same Absolute to which Eliot appealed in his 1910 paper—the "*menue Monnaie* ad infinitum." But here it expresses what could not be expressed then, a feeling for its creative vitality, a making of its truth more fully real to us. The thrush's order to depart translates this moment into a decided sense of loss. When lines echoing parts of the opening lines make their appearance ("Time past and time future . . . "), the affirmation that they point to one end "always present" is tempered. Earlier, that end seemed likely to be Death. Now, paradoxically, it is Life as well.

But why the Garden, the thrush? Who are "they"? The thrush is one of those carefully chosen symbols that resonate with Eliot's earlier work (like "Marina"). He hoped to tie together the poetic vocabulary of his work in this way. In 1931 he had written about Harry Crosby that he was most interested in Crosby's "search for a personal symbolism of imagery . . . a set of symbols which should relate each of his poems to the others, to himself." But, Eliot says, "even to speak of a 'set of symbols' is clumsy; for such a phrase suggests a lifeless, not a living and developing scheme." Eliot was seeking for himself that continuous development of personality he associated with Shakespeare's career, and he pursued it through symbolism because "symbolism is that to which the word tends both in religion and poetry; the *incarnation of meaning in fact*."[31] He hoped to create a poetry that evolved, organically, and he based his theory on the Bergsonian idea that poetry furnishes "consciousness with an immaterial body in which to incarnate itself" (*CE*, 265).

There are, of course, personal experiences behind the poem. It grew out of lines discarded from *Murder in the Cathedral* and *The Rock*. Written in 1935, it was published as the last poem in *Collected Poems*, April 1936. "Burnt Norton"'s beginning coincides with the inception of a project Eliot gave considerable thought to over the next six years, *Old Possum's Book of Practical Cats*, which I have elsewhere defended against charges of "preachery."[32] Eliot's fascination with the children he heard in the garden at Burnt Norton and the empty concrete pools becomes a major symbol of thirst for renewal; and in his children's poems he labored at more than merely "practising his technique behind the mask of the comic versifier."[33] What happened in the garden obviously touched him and offered him a symbol for the kind of rejuvenating experience for which he said he was longing, one that would renew him *as a poet*.

In his foreword to Chiari's book on Symbolism, Eliot remarked that the poetic movements culminating in what he calls "modern writing" led to a "peculiar development of *self-consciousness*."[34] I take it Eliot had in mind here both a profound artistic self-knowledge and an open acknowledgement of artificiality ("my words echo thus in your mind") in the poem itself. There is a dialogue going on—one might almost say it is simply a dialectical procedure—in *Four Quartets* about modes of knowing and the poem's status in regard to "knowing." (Recall that in his early essay on Bergson Eliot speaks of seeking truth as like trying to catch a glimpse of yourself with your eyes closed.) "Burnt Norton" enacts, insofar as it can, a process of awakening to the meaning of an intuitive experience. And that process is reflective ("my intuition is reflection, not feeling," says Bergson). The second section of the poem distances us as far as possible, in subject matter, diction, and rhythm, from the experience that has posed the paradoxical vision

of permanent change. We look at things cosmically, as they are "fig-
ured in the drift of stars." But still, we are looking at "circulation,"
the "trilling wire in the blood," the rhythm of the drum. This is one
aspect of history—reconciled in the long view, a pattern repeating
"as before."

That is the view *out* of time; but we live in time:

> Time past and time future
> Allow but a little consciousness.
> To be conscious is not to be in time
> But only in time can the moment in the rose-garden . . .
> Be remembered; involved with past and future.
> Only through time time is conquered.

To be *in* time is to intuit duration: "We do not think real time, but
we live it" (*CE*, 46). In this, Eliot's poem attempts to make more
fully real the teachings of the Christian mystics, like St. John of the
Cross, a significant figure in both *Four Quartets* and *The Two
Sources of Morality and Religion*. But when one is *in* time one is
not rationally conscious of it (to be conscious is not to be in time).
It *is* like trying to catch a glimpse of yourself with your eyes closed.

Evelyn Underhill wrote about the parallel between Bergsonian
intuition and mystical experience: "Bergson . . . comes as a media-
tor between these inarticulate explorers of the Infinite and the map-
loving human mind [and] brings their principles and their practices
into immediate relation with philosophy: telling us, in almost Augustinian language, how great and valid may be the results of that
new direction of mental movement."[35] Underhill explains the mystical experience as a "dilitation of the whole personality; which,
normally screwed down by action, expands," and as an act of immersion—a conscious letting go in which, as Bergson says "will
and vision become one." "Shaken to its depths by the current which
is about to sweep it forward," Bergson explains, "the soul ceases to
revolve around itself" (*TS*, 218). It thus achieves a vision of Now
so much richer than the "now" of ordinary consciousness, that the
mystic "can only describe it as 'partaking of the character of Eternity'" (Underhill). In this vision, the soul realizes itself as a micro-

cosm of the universe, ever-moving, never-resting. It can only describe the sensation as like that produced "when we, and the object
on which our attention is fixed, are moving at the same pace." Thus
the paradoxical vocabulary of stillness and immobility: "Hence
comes a persistently static element in the highest of man's apprehen-
sions of God." And the mystic's contemplation is precisely a "disci-
plined and developed intuition."[36]

Some doubt that such intuition has anything to do with *Four
Quartets*. They see in the poem Bradley's Absolute, and they point
to Eliot's mordant skepticism. But compare *Four Quartets* to Underhill's work, including her little books of poems, *Immanence*
(1912) and *Theophanies* (1916), which try to get the mystic experience into verse. The first speaks of the "friendship of the happy
dead," whose message comes in "whispers" while clouds sweep
across the sky; it speaks of "the changeless pivot of the passing
years," of the prophets' song after which we run like "an enchanted
child that hastes to catch the sun." It also speaks of the transcendental journey along "starry paths to the utmost verge of sky," and home
again.[37] The parallels are not accidental. They stem from a common
vocabulary and goal.

Theophanies contains more such parallels. Tree leaves are likened to children, branches give a rush of joy in "high summer,"
which "sings" in its cells, its "rhythmical cycle of life." In a garden
we hear "wordless whispers" symbolized by a bird, "the silent min-
strel of reality." In its synesthetic verbiage, Miss Underhill's verse
stands in rather startling relation to Eliot's. Clearly, they share a vision; but where Eliot manages to give his thrush sensuality and
ethereality, Underhill only manages the bald claim, "I think the
thrush's voice is more like God's."[38] Through a traditional symbolism, Underhill sought to make the mystic way more fully real to her
readers. She failed as a poet, but certainly succeeded with her popular books, *Mysticism* and *Practical Mysticism* (1915).

Four Quartets, on the other hand, succeeds. In fact, one might
think Eliot is speaking, in his mode, to the same audience Underhill addresses in *Practical Mysticism*: "It is to you, practical man,
reading these pages as you rush through the tube to the practical

work of rearranging unimportant fragments of your universe, that this message so needed by your time—or rather by your want of time—is addressed. . . . Though it is likely that the accusation will annoy you, you are already in fact a potential contemplative."[39] "Burnt Norton"'s third and fourth sections bring home the lesson to such an audience, that "time and the bell have buried the day." Dig it up, drop out of circulation, the poem seems to say, and don't go riding the tube straight down.

The final section of the poem sounds a note of despair of finding a language adequate to this altered sense of time—the mystic's. Eliot seems to be looking for something very like the gold coin Bergson describes:

> only by the form, the pattern,
> Can words or music reach
> The stillness, as a Chinese jar still
> Moves perpetually in its stillness.

In architecture, Bergson says, "in the midst of this startling immobility [there are] effects analogous to rhythm" (*TFW*, 15-16). In language, where are such durable shapes to be had? The problem is not really different. Words, like stones, "crack and break. . . . Decay with imprecision, will not stay in place, will not stay still." The poet's problem of construction does not change the facts, however. And if his form fails, that suggests only the limit of the individual and his language.

The experience on which the entire sequence of *Four Quartets* has been built is as elusive as it is absolute. It leaves us with a profoundly unsettled vision—one might call it "bicameral," in the sense that it legislates two seemingly contradictory sorts of language that determine what sorts of experience are available, for one is open, the other very definitely closed:

> The detail of the pattern is movement,
> As in the figure of the ten stairs.
> Desire itself is movement
> Not in itself desirable;
> Love is itself unmoving,
> Only the cause and end of movement,

Timeless, and undesiring
Except in the aspect of time . . .

This passage has a flatness of rhythm (as of someone tiredly climb-
ing stairs) reinforced by recurrence of forms of "move" that do
not—they sway, perhaps. The riddles here are incantatory and traditional. The rhythm is deadening.

But with the return of the image from the garden scene the verse
itself becomes more lively:

Sudden in a shaft of sunlight
Even while the dust moves
There rises the hidden laughter
Of children in the foliage
Quick now, here, now, always—
Ridiculous the waste sad time
Stretching before and after.

"Burnt Norton" has invited us to open the doors of perception. The
task of the three subsequent Quartets is to turn us back to the door
by which we entered. The world we see at "Little Gidding"'s conclusion is a transfigured one in which history may be defined not
as a nightmare, a chaos, but rather as an unending process of self-
discovery, full of suffering, certainly, but also full of growth and divine love.

That the world should finally be one of growth and evolution is
the lesson these poems try to embody; the very fact that the poet
conceives of his task as one of "embodiment" should strike chords
in our memory of Eliot's contact with Bergsonian thought. And the
techniques of oxymoron and paradox to communicate the intuition
of the ineffable fit as well. Negation is used in the first two sections
of "Dry Salvages," for example, to assert the blending of ideas which
(as Bergson has said) "when once dissociated, seem to exclude one
another as *logically* contradictory terms" (*TFW*, 136; my italics).
The future is "futureless." The wailing "soundless." "Unprayable"
prayers are sent up. And these coinages are part of the poetry of
God.

In "Dry Salvages" too we find what seems to be a direct reference to Bergsonian philosophy:

> It seems, as one becomes older,
> That the past has another pattern, and ceases to be mere
>   sequence
> Or even development; the latter a partial fallacy,
> Encouraged by superficial notions of evolution,
> Which becomes, in the popular mind, a means of disowning
>   the past.

Notice that the idea of "development" is a "partial fallacy" promulgated in the "popular mind." Evolutionism has been used as an excuse to ignore the past (what's done is done). Those who know better are nevertheless also being stripped, like Glaucus; they are exorcising, not abandoning the past. Age brings detachment, detachment a revelation of the past no longer covered over by "currents of action." Strong currents deceive. The argument parallels Bergson's: What serves our practical ends covers over truth. What the organism wants—survival, pleasure—dictates a covering of the world and the self, a regression.

That is precisely why Eliot points out at this moment in the poem that when we review the past we tend to think of the "very good dinner," the moment of happiness. We have forgotten the crude, primordial self, threatening to break through: "Behind the assurance / Of recorded history" lies always the "primitive terror." This should teach us to fear the recrudescence of Apeneck Sweeney:

> (The lengthened shadow of a man
> Is history, said Emerson
> Who had not seen the silhouette
> Of Sweeney straddled in the sun.)   [CPP, 26].

This is to say, as Bergson did, that underneath, modern man is essentially the same as his "remotest ancestors" (*TS*, 262). The only thing, clearly, that can stand between us and this reversion to type is our knowledge of the past.

The fifth section of "Dry Salvages" reiterates the principle of mystic intuition. It is something only given in "self-surrender." The saint gives up all hope of anything beyond Now, and gains understanding. What have we? "Hints and guesses, / Hints followed by guesses," the poet says. But the "hint half-guessed, the gift half understood, is Incarnation." Not the *doctrine* of incarnation, but incarnation itself. This is the life that leaves us with what Harry, in *The Family Reunion*, calls the "partial observation of one's own automatism" and the "partial anesthesia of suffering without feeling" (*CPP*, 235). We only half guess the meaning of incarnation because we only rarely penetrate to the level of being where we can sense our confluence with the divine. When we can hold still—and for most of us this involves a "distraction fit"—we commit the "possible, but exceptional" mystical act (*TS*, 7). It is a passive conquering, a quiet merging with and acceptance of the tides and currents.

The *Four Quartets* insist on a particular *mode* of perception. If we try to "converse with spirits . . . release omens / By sortilege, or tea leaves," we get nowhere. We cannot "riddle the inevitable with playing cards." But there is something we can do in the experience, even if there is nothing exactly to be done *with* it:

> right action is freedom
> From past and future also
> For most of us, this is the aim
> Never here to be realized;
> We are only undefeated
> Because we have gone on trying.

Right action is freedom—it has that openness that springs from the "whole personality." It is wise action.

And "wisdom," Eliot wrote in "Goethe as Sage," is a "native gift of intuition, ripened and given application by experience." If language is generally inadequate to communicating anything, still "the language of poetry is the language most capable of communicating wisdom" (*OPP*, 257, 264). That is because poetry communicates on two levels at once; like music, it touches a substratum in our being. The final poem of *Four Quartets* offers what it can of wisdom about past and future and Now.

Eliot had visited the chapel at Little Gidding in May 1936. The town had been the site of a religious colony formed in 1625 by Nicholas Ferrar, an Anglican priest and an acquaintance of George

Herbert.[40] The colony sought escape from the war. It survived until Charles I's rout at Naseby in 1647. Charles is said to have prayed at the chapel afterwards. Ruined by fire, like Burnt Norton, the chapel was restored in the nineteenth century. Eliot's choice of this place, a failed community where a doomed king once stopped, has been cited as evidence that he believes in seeking out lost causes for the sake of joining ranks with the "undefeated."[41] But the choice of place is not perverse. The very point is that here and now are not important in themselves. The poem wishes to establish how, in Bergson's words, "detachment from each particular thing becomes attachment to life in general" (*TS*, 201).

At the same time, the choice of Little Gidding is not meaning-less. It is a place nearest to death, to consecrated ground and his-tory. Suspending our animation, we enter the world of the dead: "What the dead had no speech for, when living, / They can tell you, being dead: the communication / Of the dead is tongued with fire beyond the language of the living." Poetry itself, in the sense that it speaks for what lies buried in each of us, is a tongue of the dead. The poem's second section plays on the alchemist's quadrapartite cosmogony to give a litany: "death of air . . . death of earth . . . the death of water and fire." In the terza rima section based on *Inferno*, 15, the poet meets a loiterer who looks like "some dead master / Whom I had known, forgotten, half recalled / Both one and many." Thus, the "compound ghost" represents a colony of the not-living who reflect us, in passing: "So I assumed a double part, and cried / And heard another's voice cry: "What! are *you* here?' / Although we were not. I was still the same, / Knowing myself yet being some-one other."

This *dédoublement* is at the heart of the intuition, the revelation. The words themselves have engendered the world in which they are heard. They hold up a mirror, in which we see a "face still forming," yet the words suffice "to compel the recognition they preceded." This conundrum of linguistic creation acknowledges a fundamental fact: There is a sense in which the moment *creates itself*. In renew-ing language, the poet performs the office of renewing contact with experience and offering the protection of "aftersight and foresight." If one assumes that the object of the poem is to reveal to us *ourselves* (the Bergsonian assumption) then the "face still forming" is ours. We are perpetually Becoming. As the poem concludes, it explicitly tells us that "history may be servitude, / History may be freedom." It depends upon the mode of grasping it. The actors in even the most vicious conflicts are eventually "folded in a single party" to become "united in the strife which divided them."

What we receive from the dead, finally, is a "symbol perfected in death." Here Eliot presses home the idea that the symbol incarnates "meaning in fact." Helen Gardner's reproduction of the "Little Gidding" manuscript shows that at this point Eliot cancelled lines dealing with Shakespeare's *Richard III*, and specifically with Richard's defeat, when his enemies discover his crown in a thornbush.[42] This would have made the point, but too negatively, perhaps: There are no victors. Instead, Eliot chose to leave the specific mention of the "spectre of a Rose" in lines above to hover until the poem's last line, when it would be united with the fire. That fire, the subject of the poem's penultimate section, is matter using itself up: We can choose only "pyre or pyre." If we are literally fired matter—energy using itself up—we still hope for a redemption from passion. We wear an intolerable shirt of flame. Eliot refers apparently to the poisoned robe given by Nessus to the wife of Heracles, which she in turn gave to her husband, believing it would increase his love for her. Heracles, however, killed himself because of the pain.[43] The contrast is drawn between human and divine passion. But the death toward which these symbols point is not a punctuation mark. It is a mode of being, a seeing and feeling that transfigures. We can choose, that is, only our kinds of fire; but the choice is everything.

"Little Gidding"'s conclusion adopts a self-consciousness about endings and beginnings that reconciles the poet and his language to a world in which the only finality is a continuous Becoming:

> to make an end is to make a beginning.
> The end is where we start from. And every phrase
> And sentence that is right (where every word is at home,
> Taking its place to support the others,
> The word neither diffident nor ostentatious,
> An easy commerce of the old and new,
> The common word exact without vulgarity,

> The formal word precise but not pedantic,
> The complete consort dancing together)
> Every phrase and every sentence is an end and a beginning,
> Every poem an epitaph. And any action
> Is a step to the block, to the fire, down the sea's throat
> Or to an illegible stone: and that is where we start.

Think on your end (*memento mori*, always present), and move in measure to the rhythm of creation, the complete consort, dancing together. The poet takes his place with those who accept, not deny life, knowing that every vital action is a leap to a fall but nevertheless part of the creative impulse of the universe.

The mystic who "dies" to this world is born to it again in a union with God: "We die with the dying . . . we are born with the dead." This rebirth, for Eliot, is symbolized in the return of the past to vital presence: "See, they return, and bring us with them." The past, as Bergson says, is not really dead; it has only ceased to be useful to us. But "Little Gidding" establishes that use—"liberation." Real history, like myth, is immanent. To intuit this life is to bring past and present into a timeless act of thought: "So, while the light fails / On a winter's afternoon, in a secluded chapel / History is now and England." Strangely, we return to this world, knowing that our outward explorations lead to a revelation of self, and that the self "vanishes" as it merges with creation.

This is the key to the equilibrium which Being and Becoming finally strike in Eliot's late work, an acceptance of the mystical consciousness described by Underhill and others: "The struggle of the self to disentangle itself from illusion and attain the Absolute is a life-struggle. Hence, it will and must exhibit the freedom and originality of life; will, as a process, obey artistic rather than scientific laws. [The] self, always changing, moving, struggling—always, in fact, *becoming*—alive in every fibre, related at once to the unreal and to the real [is] with its growth in true being, ever more conscious of the contrast between them."[44] The self we see in *Four Quartets* is one of dual consciousness, a self both in and out of time, and a self conscious of the tension between what is true in time on earth and what must be true outside this time and above this earth. The poem represents the exploration and resolution of the crucial

issue of Eliot's career as a poet. That issue is of continuous importance to him over a period spanning the two World Wars. Its
conclusion allowed Eliot to set down, for practical purposes, the
poet's pen.

FIVE

Eliot, Bergson, and the Southern Critics

> *[The past] will find strength to cross the threshold of consciousness in all cases where we renounce the interests of effective action to replace ourselves, so to speak, in the life of dreams. . . . The body, always turned towards action, has for its essential function to limit, with a view to action, the life of the spirit.*
>
> —Henri Bergson, *Matter and Memory*

❧   In *Reactionary Essays on Poetry and Ideas* (1936), Allen Tate defends T.S. Eliot; Tate rails against the "modern desire to judge an art scientifically, practically, industrially," and claims poetry is not to be judged as a "pragmatic instrument." He goes on to deny that *The Waste Land* is "a satire on the unscientific values of the past." Rather, in Tate's view, the poem satirizes the idea that man has finally found truth in science. Tate praises (in the same volume) the way in which "Ash Wednesday" "succeeds in creating the effect of immediate experience by means of a broken and distracted rhythm." (He refers to the passage beginning "If the word is lost . . .") He also says that "poetry finds its true usefulness in its perfect *inutility*, a focus of repose for the *well-driven intellect* that constantly shakes the *equilibrium* of persons and societies with its unrelieved imposition of *partial formulas* upon the world."[1]

These patently Bergsonian terms had gotten into the vocabulary of Tate, Warren, and Ransom, each of whom defended T.S. Eliot at some length during the late thirties and early forties. That is no coincidence. We know how enormous was Eliot's direct influence on the Southern New Critics generally (despite the original bafflement and lack of appreciation for Eliot among the Fugitives of the twenties), and on a number of critics who wrote for the *Kenyon Review*, like Empson, Warren, Tate, and Brooks, in particular. Many of them, like Ransom, had been reading Bergson themselves. William Handy noted two decades ago the Kantian heritage of the Southern New Critics and their adaptation of Bergsonian aesthetic vocabulary.[2] They clearly use that vocabulary to argue the validity of aesthetic experience as a mode of knowing.[3] In this, they follow in Eliot's footsteps, disseminating Bergsonian principles of critical and literary theory among American writers of the thirties and forties.

Ransom's *The New Criticism* (1941) also defends Eliot. The one complaint he has about Eliot's work, which he praises for recognizing the "gnomic truths" of poetry, is that Eliot does not go far enough in the direction of defending poetic knowing as another mode of cognition. He makes it clear that he does not wish to denigrate scientific knowing; only to establish the legitimacy of a different mode.[4] The argument was one he had already elaborated in *The World's Body* (1938):

The aesthetic moment appears as a curious moment of suspension; between the Platonism in us, which is militant, always sciencing and devouring, and a starved inhibited aspiration towards innocence which, if it could only be free, would like to know the object as it might of its own accord reveal itself. The poetic impulse is not free, yet it holds out stubbornly against science for the enjoyment of its images. It means to reconstitute the world of perceptions. Finally, there is suggested some such formula as the following:

> Science gratifies a rational or practical impulse and exhibits the minimum of perception. Art gratifies a perceptual impulse and exhibits the minimum of reason.

The heritage of Ransom's approach is clear. He speaks about a "formula." He argues for two modes of mental life, one practical (that is, intentional) and scientific, the other *perceptual*. He uses the term "Platonism" to refer to the ratiocinative side of this dichotomy, and suggests that there is another "logic" (poetry is not free) not the logic of Platonism. Thus, the volume is filled with the argument that "scientific predication concludes an act of attention, but miraculism initiates one," and that "the predication of Metaphysical poetry is true enough. It is not true like history." And that aesthetic attitudes "make an opposition to the utilitarian and scientific atti- tudes and, I think, to the moral ones."[5] (The last phrase rehearses Eliot's and Bergson's position that art must not practice in the moral sphere.)

That is as much as to say that truth can be represented in two ways; your representation depends upon your mode. One can look (intuit) or grasp (analyze). Poetry is based on the former mode. If there were any doubt that Ransom's perceptualism bases itself on a Bergsonian intuition of the object, he clears the matter up: Poetry returns us to a state in which we are "looking, marvelling, and rev- elling in the thick *dinglich* substance that has just received strange representation." In sentiment, we move close to the object in a "non- utilitarian way." It is not "useful, nor moral, nor even disciplinary; it is simply aesthetic" and seeks only to *know its object*: "Sentiment is aesthetic, aesthetic is cognitive, and the cognition is of the object as an individual."[6]

Ransom and the contemporaries he gathered together through the *Kenyon Review* were engaged in the struggle to justify art as "specially brilliant but detached fragments of knowledge."[7] They clearly sensed their kinship with Eliot, and not particularly with that other American expatriate, Ezra Pound. That is because Eliot spoke so directly to their issue, and on so many occasions provided the leading review, set up the targets, identified those who were coming closest to the mark. *The Kenyon Review* in its inception (1939) simply codified what was already a clear pattern in the crit- icism of a number of American writers, many of them members of the then-dispersed Agrarian movement. Like Tate, Ransom had moved by 1938 far in the direction of accepting a technological society. *The World's Body* does not contain a single essay that ad- dresses Agrarian principles for living a balanced life. Eliot himself had exhibited an inchoate preference for agrarianism. One finds it still lingering in passages of *Notes Towards the Definition of Culture* (1948), and this may have been one of the elements that drew Ran- som and other Agrarians, like Davidson and Warren, in his direc- tion. But by the late thirties the Southern New Critics (and through the *Kenyon Review* a number of others) had already gone beyond

Eliot in asserting the argument for a poetic "knowing" with its own rigor and formulations.

Tate, particularly, had worked closely with Ransom in the latter part of the twenties, and had published a dogmatic and shrill article against the New Humanists in Eliot's *Criterion* that showed the degree to which Ransom's ideas were shaping his own (the essay appeared in July 1929 and was reprinted not long after in *Hound and Horn*). What Ransom had to say to Tate at that point in their careers is best indicated by John L. Stewart's definitive study of the Fugitive and Agrarian movements, *The Burden of Time*. Stewart talked to Ransom in 1946, and asked him what was the earliest and most consistent guiding principle behind his criticism and poetry: "[It was] that modern man is crippled by a dissociation of reason and sensibility which results in an imbalance whereby the reason, armed with abstract principles which have been spectacularly successful in supplying the material needs of the body, tyrannizes over the sensibility and restricts its innocent, profitless delight in the vividness and variety of the world. With this conviction went a 'fury against abstractions and a desire to restore the sensibility to its proper eminence in man.'"[8] This idea, which Ransom remembers as all his own, was confirmed in his reading of Kant, Schopenhauer, and Bergson. It clearly influences Tate in *Reactionary Essays*: "Poetry is one test of ideas; it is ideas tested by experience, by the act of direct apprehension."[9]

Tate's "Three Types of Poetry," like Empson's *Seven Types of Ambiguity*, performs an analysis of poetry along new lines indicated by its status as a mode of prehension. He divides poetry into types reflecting "three attitudes of the modern world":

First: Poetry of "the spirit of the practical will."
Second: Poetry in revolt against the domination of science.
Third: Poetry of the "creative spirit"; a synthesis of the first two types, "nameless because it is perfect."

A dialectical process leads to the third sort of poetry. There is science providing abstractions on which the first house of poetry is built. Along comes the romantic impulse to flee outdoors; the second type of poetry produces, then, "romantic irony." The third type of poetry exhibits the hallmarks of the Bergsonian aesthetic, and is aptly called the poetry of "creative spirit." It is interested in "the quality of experience, the total revelation—not explanation for the purpose of external control by the will." [10]

For Tate, the term "will" is loaded with much the same baggage as "Platonism" is for Ransom. Tate puts forth a concept of poetry as seeing, in which (as Bergson says) "will and vision become one" (*TS*, 218). In putting science opposite romanticism Tate claims to have isolated two opposing sorts of "will," both stemming from the same basic wilfulness, and hence both erring. Romanticism is just "science without the systematic method of asserting the will." The validity of poetry, then, lies in the kind of "objectivity" described so ably by Bergson, one that has abandoned intentionality and seeks nothing, except to let the object reveal itself as it would, and then to formulate that experience in a linguistic artifice that avoids the sort of Adamic "naming" associated with control ("will," again). The upshot of Tate's theory is a sharp attack on I.A. Richards. Tate will not accept Richards's distinction between "certified" and "pseudo" statements. He sees Richards as coming back once more to the well of utilitarianism, defining poetry in terms that make it no different from any linguistic system used for purposes of "immediate action." It ought to be clear, Tate says, that Richards's approach is the one society has developed instinctively toward the arts, since we live in a scientific age. [11]

William Empson makes the identical attack on Richards, with his usual acerbic wit. He says Richards's vocabulary opens up all sorts of inconsistencies, and that the fundamental one rests on a doubt about how to define "truth." Empson argues for the reality of a truth unaddressed by Richards, one that touches upon realms of belief but lies finally in a complete entanglement of practical with aesthetic impulses. And the consequence of this, for Empson, is that one cannot adopt Richards's view, essentially a refashioning of the old one that poets tell "excellent lies." [12] One finds here the foundation for a theory of poetic truth based on modes of knowing and speaking that humanist psychology cannot address because it does not recognize the primacy of *insight*.

Robert Penn Warren wants to argue in a similar way for a literature of illuminations. His 1942 Princeton lecture on "Pure and Impure Poetry," printed in the *Kenyon Review*, praises Eliot and Faulkner for having adhered faithfully to experience and defends their work against charges of adulteration and "impurity." He argues for the heterodoxy of all "pure poetry." Pure poetry, he says, cannot be poetry whose language is composed entirely of the "poetic" effect, for to be true attar-of-poetry it must distil the spectrum of language available in the poet's society. Its heterodoxy declares its purity precisely because it resists a final analysis.

In this essay, Warren declares his debt to the Bergsonian heritage in a number of ways—for example, when he figures the analytical exercise graphically as *abschnitten*, the "cuttings" of Bergson's *Time and Free Will*:

[The] poem is like the monstrous Orillo in Boiardo's *Orlando Innamorato*. When the sword lops off any member of the monster, that member is immediately rejoined to the body, and the monster is as formidable as ever. But the poem is even more formidable than the monster, for Orillo's adversary finally gained a victory by an astonishing feat of dexterity: he slashed off both the monster's arms and quick as a wink seized them and flung them into the river. The critic who vaingloriously trusts his method to account for the poem, to exhaust the poem, is trying to emulate his dexterity. . . . But he is doomed to failure.

The reason the critic is thus doomed seems clear: The poem is a living thing, and the critic can deal only with dead concepts. He can hack off a piece here or there, but the whole remains unconquered, miraculously still whole.

To this monstrous defiant organism Warren opposes a bogus "pure poetry" which "tries to be pure by excluding, more or less rigidly, certain elements which might qualify or contradict its original impulse." But such poetry emasculates itself: "Nothing that is available in human experience can be legislated out of poetry. [Even] a chemical formula, for instance, might appear functionally in a poem." Part of Warren's intention is to defend *The Waste Land*, but his larger intention is a defense of all poetry, adapting the antilegislative jargon Eliot used to advantage in his own criticism. Warren describes Eliot's masterpiece as "elliptical" (borrowing the term from Frederick Pottle). The "elliptical" poem is so for "purposes of inclusion, not exclusion." It makes nonsense of Poe's suggestion that the long poem is a contradiction in terms. Warren's "pure poetry" inheres in the "set of relationships" created by the poem's parts and is not dependent upon any feature or quality that can be sliced off for inspection.

We thus find in the criticism of Warren, Ransom, and Tate a full flowering of the Modernist organicism whose aesthetical roots lie in Bergson's *Creative Evolution* and William James's *Principles of Psychology* (1890). This criticism defends a long poem, "elliptical" in structure, which founds itself on what Bergson, Hulme, and Warren alike call "tensions." Warren explains the "resistances" such a poem offers:

There is the tension between the rhythm of the poem and the rhythm of speech . . . between the formality of the rhythm and the informality of language; between the particular and the general, the concrete and the abstract; between the elements of even the simplest metaphor; between the beautiful and the ugly. . . . This list is not intended to be exhaustive; it is intended to be merely suggestive. But it may be taken to imply that the poet is like the jiujitsu expert; he wins by *utilizing the resistance of his opponent—the materials of the poem.* In other words, a poem, to be good, must earn itself. *It is a motion toward a point of rest, but if it is not a resisted motion, it is a motion of no consequence.*[13]

The poem Warren describes is vital and complete in the Bergsonian sense, a human "creation" in which all particular manifestations of life accept their mobility "reluctantly"; "a reality making itself across a reality unmaking itself" (*CE*, 178, 128, 251).

Pure poetry, as Warren defines it, resides in the complete moving consort—the *action* of the parts together. Thus, the "ellipses" suggest and also *call up* an experience that cannot otherwise be reached. They turn the resistances of language back on language itself, bending words to their "will." Warren's argument is simply Bergson's: that the poem summons its idea to the reader's mind through tensions between its parts, thus *demonstrating* that idea—not in the sense of logical proof, but through experience.

Ransom, Tate, Empson, and Warren show that in American criticism in the thirties an argument begun twenty years earlier in Europe was still being carried forward and developed. The influence of Eliot's habits of mind and vocabulary on Ransom and Tate, particularly, seems undeniably to have been substantial in the long run, even though each man felt independently the importance of the particular issues and the terminology early on. Ransom was headed down this road even when he was still resistant to the sort of poetry being written by Eliot, Pound, and Hulme. Still, the parallels with Eliot's thinking are so striking that there must have been a very conscious pattern of selection and rejection on Ransom's part, a moment of decision about commitment to particular approaches and ideas and not to others. The same seems to have been true of certain other *Kenyon Review* critics.

One finds throughout Tate's work, for example, signs of Eliot's having been there before. When Tate evaluates the case for and against the American Humanists, he makes essentially Eliot's point: The doctrines of Humanism are sound in themselves, but because they are not *complete*, they are rendered false. That is, Tate admits that "the rightful concern of man is his humanity," but still says Humanists end in the same moral and philosophical plight as Naturalists, since they can appeal to no higher authority, discover no "absolutes." Finally, Tate says, if you deny religion, you expect it of literature and end up with neither.[14] It is as much in these broad generalizations, their technique, their discriminations of the critical and philosophical issues that count from those that do not—as much in these generalizations as in the specific aesthetic judgments made by the Southern New Critics (and their compatriots in the *Review*), that one sees Eliot's influence.

It is difficult to decide whether Eliot's influence is merely contributory, and not determining. There is, naturally, the larger ground of the philosophical convictions of Ransom, Tate, Empson, and Warren. They were conscious of an important comradeship with Eliot, but the standards they consistently applied may have been shared because of a similarity in origin: philosophical and aesthetic study. The climate of opinion and belief surrounding these writers was also created by them. Their heritage is Kant, Schopenhauer, Coleridge, James, and Bergson. The specific judgments, however, are colored heavily by the aesthetic stance, the Defense of Poetry, enabled by Bergson and offered in the interpretations of Hulme and Eliot. Bergson is seldom held up for praise, for reasons that have already been discussed, but perhaps bear brief review.

There was, first, the fact that Bergson had been denigrated, in acid language, by the representatives of the New Classicism. Ransom and Tate stood in uneasy relationship to this movement, and were careful always to point out their differences—especially with Eliot, for example. But finally, they were steeped in the dispositions of Eliot and Santayana. They took their stand in the late thirties as the Fugitives had in the twenties, but this time the rhetoric of Agrarianism had been replaced by one of anti-Humanism. They became, for the most part, spokesmen for values that are only to be *fixed* through some final term not available to Humanism. And they saw that in this fight Bergson had been labelled the enemy.

At the same time, they had already experienced some of the excitement over creative evolution and "psychology" generated by James and Bergson. The language of aesthetic discussion had already by 1930 been thoroughly invaded by the terminology of Bergson's *intuition philosophique*. Perhaps its roots lay as much at home as across the Atlantic. But the acceptance and nurturance of those shoots was evidenced dramatically by a gradually increasing enthusiasm for particular aspects of Eliot's work, which spoke to the need Ransom and others felt: to establish a beachhead for the role of the artist in American culture and thought. The Great Depression made the need for such a victory seem, if anything, more urgent to those in the South.

Adoption and adaptation of Bergsonian philosophical and aesthetic ideas fostered literary innovation. That innovation fathered another parallel growth in the critical enterprise, which resulted, finally, in the establishment of the *Kenyon Review*. In 1937, Ransom had decided, "I see so much future for critical studies that my own are just beginning; it's the biggest field that could possibly be found for systematic study [and] I want to wade right into it."[15] Ransom's sense of excitement, and his willingness to restrict the *Review* to arts and letters when he had for so long argued against the separation of the work and the life, represents more than just the discovery of a new career goal. It shows that the prospects for and the importance of a systematic and separate literary criticism had dawned on him.

Since Ransom had decided to accept, with Eliot, the fact that modern man's dissociations were here to stay, the next question became the systematization of literary study along particular lines. And it was to that task that Ransom bent himself in the *Review*. The approach, beyond any doubt, is an outgrowth of the philosophical attempt to justify and explain the importance of art and sensibility in the culture, and to do so in a forum and on grounds that would make literature the equal—the twin, or *doppelgänger*—of science. This agenda lay behind the *Review's* variegated entries. If no single number of the publication quite measured up—as Ransom lamented in 1951—to the expectations of "perfection," that does not mean there was no such goal in mind.

Ransom's chagrin is balanced, then, by a sense of "pride in the achieved body of criticism however long that may have taken to accrue," a body of criticism which has "functional integrity, perhaps bearing a national importance." Ransom's high estimation of the importance of the critic is not mere aggrandizement of the accomplishments of writers among whom he numbered himself in the *Review's* pages. Rather, it is the consequence of his having perceived the importance of the issue of art in society, its need for strong defense:

We have lost our faculty, and to some extent we have lost our taste, for the rule of action which is positive and life-giving. And why not accept the confident voices of ancient authority? It is becoming better and better established that the one authority which is still universally reputable is literature. But literature is cryptic, it is Delphic. . . . It is the critic who must teach us to find the thing truly authoritative but hidden; the critic trying and judging the literary work which has a content that is visible and *another content which is not so visible.*[16]

The role of the literary critic, as Ransom defined it, was to master the substance behind the outward form, to interpret and to bring forth the truth there to an age in desperate need of art's resources. In this way, Ransom thinks of the job he has been performing as a rescue operation, something positive and valuable in an age of darkness and chaos: a reading of the oracle.

Such high expectations verge toward the demands Richards put on art, and away from those of Eliot, who carefully excludes litera-ture from having such powers to rescue culture. But these expecta-tions are nonetheless an extension of Eliot's own views. He would have said, perhaps, that they were true, but had been pushed to the point where they became false. What Ransom did not apparently see was that the New Critical approaches, and particularly the *pro-fessionalization* of literary criticism, would lead to a polarization of art, on the one hand, and on the other to an increasingly hermetic critical vocabulary. Few trained literary critics now play the impor-tant social role Ransom predicted for them. And few would agree with him that literature is the one authority still "reputable."

What has been lost is precisely what Hazard Adams finds he cannot rescue in *The Philosophy of the Literary Symbolic*: the elite art object. Since the magic sign has been banished from discussion by the dogma of deconstructionism, there can be no place for such objects, and thus no place for such criticism. The temple topples. In *Arts on the Level*, Murray Krieger, a student of Eliseo Vivas (once a contributor to the *Kenyon Review*) considers the outcome of these historical trends:

I feel, obviously, that many of the demythologizing tendencies in our recent theory may be healthy, provided they do not end by taking dis-criminations in value—or worse, the objects themselves—from us. . . . [thus] I would hardly recommend that we try to return to the unquestioning confidence we once had in the critical enterprise before we had to respond to the awareness aroused by recent antagonistic theory. The recognition by critics of their own fictions, together with the limits of the aesthetic fictions they at once create and uncover for us, gives them self-deconstructive shrewdness that can only increase our confidence in their more grandiose claims.

But Krieger ends on a note of frustration with the enervation of the critical enterprise. Finally, "it is the critics' power to lift that art ob-ject off the level and to reconstruct it at its full height that sustains us as it sustains their culture and the uneven arts themselves."[17] We see, as we trace the fallout of the Bergsonian debate in the twenties and thirties, the emergence of a critical approach that apparently contained the seeds of its own demise.

The Bergsonian aesthetic promoted by Southern New Critics had profound effect on the acceptance of innovative poetry and fiction. Their embracing of such an aesthetic, and later their defense of Eliot and justification of *The Waste Land*'s innovative techniques had influence on most young writers coming to maturity during the two decades following World War I, including, naturally, William Faulkner.

SIX

Deciphering Faulkner's Uninterrupted Sentence

Well, I believe that our whole psychical existence is
something like a single sentence, continued since the first
awakening of consciousness, interspersed with commas,
but never broken by full stops.

—Henri Bergson, *Mind-Energy*

Any discussion of Bergson and American literature must deal with Faulkner. My object is, however, not only to explain Faulkner's relationship to Bergson. I wish to show how Bergsonian philosophy and aesthetics illuminate American literature. I have demonstrated that Eliot and the New Critics owe a debt to Bergson that is little-recognized because Bergson has not been reread for so long. If Faulkner can be profitably discussed in relation to Bergson, he is not alone, and in my final chapter I will suggest how other American writers might be approached along similar lines. I remind the reader simply that this volume does not attempt to be comprehensive, but rather to restore Bergson's dualism to the discussion of American literature.

Let us first dismiss the weak claims some have put forth that Faulkner was directly influenced by Bergson's thought. In dismissing the claims, I do not pretend to settle the issue of how thoroughly Faulkner may have known Bergson's work. Rather, I mean to make it clear that no one can be sure of the answer, any more than of other puzzling issues in the writer's life. Faulkner once said he agreed with Bergson on the nature of God and Time (*LIG*, 70). He made this statement to Loïc Bouvard, a French graduate student, in 1952. Millgate and Meriwether attach considerable importance to Bouvard's interview, saying Faulkner seems to have revealed himself candidly to questioning. Perhaps so. But is this a basis on which we can speak of the "influence" of Bergson?

When Faulkner says he was influenced "by Bergson, obviously," we must interpret cautiously. Faulkner may only have meant that most writers of his time, including Eliot, were so influenced. But many critics have tried to go beyond this, and build a case for Faulkner's own study of Bergson. Joseph Blotner guesses in his *Biography* that Faulkner had "read his Henry Bergson" long before 1946—possibly while still of college age. Faulkner apparently later gave an aspiring young writer, Joan Williams, a copy of *Man's Fate* and encouraged her to read *Creative Evolution*, saying, "It helped me."[1] Could *Creative Evolution* have helped Faulkner become a writer? Encouraged by the implications here, Richard Adams suggested that Faulkner "probably read *Creative Evolution* and *Laughter*, which was translated in 1911, and very possibly also *Introduction to Metaphysics*. . . . It seems reasonably certain that Faulkner learned to do his share of the work partly by studying Bergson's theories."[2] And by "his share of the work," Adams clearly means writing. Conder has assumed the same, and speaks of "the influence of Bergson on Faulkner."[3]

But no available evidence supports or refutes Blotner's and Adams's claims about Faulkner's reading. Virtually no philosophical works—classical or popular—were contained in Faulkner's private library, which included over 1,200 volumes from more than two dozen countries at the time of Faulkner's death, but no work of Bergson's.[4] A personal letter to Professor Blotner brought the reply that "there seemed to be nothing concrete to go on apart from WF's recommending Bergson to people and his comments with the French graduate student in *Lion in the Garden* . . . but I think it is not unlikely that he read some Bergson."[5] Cleanth Brooks may be right when he says that Faulkner never "read Bergson very deeply or thoroughly." Brooks finds that "the influence of Bergson has been generally overestimated and that its importance has been occasionally pushed to absurd lengths."[6] It is not clear exactly what Brooks means by "the influence of Bergson," but he is right that in Faulkner's case assertions of direct influence should be viewed with polite skepticism.

But then we must explain some remarkably convincing expositions of Faulkner's work in Bergsonian terms—the latest of which is Conder's in *Naturalism in American Fiction*. The relation between Faulkner and Eliot has been explored on several occasions, and it is clear that Faulkner made use of "Prufrock," *The Waste Land*, and others of Eliot's works.[7] I contend that Faulkner studied Eliot thoroughly enough to have picked up critical judgments and aesthetic values just as much as specific literary devices. Knowing the impact Eliot had on Faulkner, and seeing that impact in the criticism of other Southern writers, particularly Ransom and Tate, we see why we find in Faulkner a deep, rich vein reflecting Bergsonian values. This is a vein everyone, including Brooks, is forced under some guise to admit.

Faulkner and the Durée Réelle

More is involved than just Bergson's thorough identification with experienced time. But that is where we must start: with Faulkner's obsession with fluidity, change, and the related concepts of "enduring" and "outrage."[8] Over and over Faulkner identifies life with "constant flux . . . constant change" (*FIU*, 151). In this "fluidity which is human life," the only "alternative to change and progress is death" (*FIU*, 239, 190). Faulkner speculated more than once in his classes at the University of Virginia that man is by nature "incapable of peace . . . the only peace man knows—he says, 'Why good gracious, yesterday I was happy'" (*FIU*, 65). He characterized himself as a "man in motion who happens to be a writer," and declared that "what is important is that man continues to create" (*FIU*, 197-98; *LIG*, 364). Like anyone else, writers must cope and compromise with change if they hope to accomplish anything (*FIU*, 37). The writer tries "to arrest motion, which is life, by artificial means and hold it fixed so that 100 years later when a stranger looks at it, it moves again, since it is life. Since man is mortal, the only immortality possible for him is to leave something behind him that is immortal since it will always move" (*LIG*, 253). The paradox here is that the most immortal art is that which is most "living" and hence "mortal." The artist tries to "catch this fluidity, which is life," but must ask "compassion, understanding, that change must alter, must happen. . . . That no matter how fine anything seems . . . once it stops, abandons motion, it is dead" (*FIU*, 277).

But Faulkner also views other matters after the Bergsonian fash-ion. He claimed to see the life-force as "the mind that spawns . . . a force, a blind force, that by its standards is neither good nor bad."[9] The essential amorality of that life-force is often forgotten in discus-sions of Faulkner's characters, who must deal with the hunger for permanence in a world that is "not interested in good and evil" (*LIG*, 252). The hunger for permanence is often tied to moral im-peratives, and becomes confused with morality when it is consid-ered as life-denying. Don Quixote, notes Faulkner, "entered reality only when he was so busy trying to cope with people that he had no time to distinguish between good and evil" (*LIG*, 253). If Faulkner valued this "coping" above a denial of life, that does not necessarily mean he thought mere coping intrinsically moral or mo-rality intrinsically opposed to life. Like Eliot and Bergson, Faulkner saw art's business as simply other than that of morality.

Faulkner also believed that good art is an "incarnation" of con-sciousness. Like consciousness itself, a novel must have the fluidity of life. Conrad Aiken was the first to see in this a key to Faulkner's prose style. In a 1939 article Aiken focused on two important fea-tures of the prose. First, Faulkner works on the reader by a "process of immersion." Second, his formal aesthetic requires that the sen-tence, and even the novel, stay psychologically "unfinished, still in motion, as it were, until the dropping into place of the very last syllable."[10] The result was what Clifton Fadiman later called the "non-stop or Life-sentence," a sentence that tries to be a microcosm of an expanding universe.[11] Aiken's article assumes that Faulkner believed, like Bergson, that all life—psychic or material—is a mat-ter of self-creation "that draws much from little, something from nothing" (*CM*, 31). "Life, like conscious activity," Bergson said, is this sort of "unceasing creation" (*CE*, 25). Since life has this continuity, the writer's prose must strain, in Faulkner's words, to "cram everything, all experience, into each paragraph."[12] The sentence must try to put "the whole history of the human heart on the head of a pin," and "the long sentence is an attempt to get [a character's] past and possibly his future into the instant in which he does something" (*FIU*, 144, 84). Precisely because consciousness is "like a single sentence," the "whole past still exists" (*CM*, 56). A good novel, then, pushes us into the river and lets us sink or swim, according to Aiken, who does not raise questions of overall design, of final form.

Several critics have assessed Faulkner's characters by the degree of their alienation from the flowing of consciousness, and in the fifties they began to recur to Bergson. Perrin Lowrey, in a 1954 essay, argues that *The Sound and the Fury* presents three dissociated awarenesses of time in Benjy, Quentin, and Jason, integrating them in Dilsey.[13] Peter Swiggart also defines Faulkner's characters in this way. Bergson's real duration, Swiggart says, is a standard toward which the dissociated consciousnesses of time may be thought to point.[14] Karl Zink makes a similar claim, saying Faulkner's images of stasis increase the reader's awareness of tension between "experience" and "simple clock or calendar time."[15] The article implies that Faulkner thought calendar time illusory, real time "flux."

Darrel Abel's "Frozen Movement in *Light in August*" (1957) was the first attempt to relate Bergson's terminology to Faulkner's characters and style, and it suggests a number of intriguing parallels.[16] Abel says the artist may be thought of as making "cuttings" out of his intuitions of becoming, and he also suggests that Joe Christmas's problem is mainly one of self-"realization"—that is, he cannot establish what Bergson calls the one thing "we all seize from within, by intuition . . . our personality in its flowing through time—our self which endures" (*IM*, 3). Finally, Abel sees Hightower's vision of the wheel as a triumphant moment condensing "a long history" in a "quasi-instantaneous vision" (see *CM*, 105). Curiously, the article sees Hightower's wheel as no different from Joe's entrapping circle; both are "intuitions of duration."

Durée *Versus the Durable Form*

At this point, we have come to the crux of the problem. Faulkner has, like Bergson, been labeled an irrationalist, and while that may help us in understanding how his characters hunger to be "sloshing around in Bergsonian *durée*," as Estella Schoenberg puts it, it creates grave problems when we try to understand Faulkner as crafting "that single urn or shape" of the novel—as a conscious pattern-maker (*FIU*, 65).[17] Encouraged by Faulkner's public statements, some critics have been drawn to view his fiction as part of a statement against rational mind, against conceptualizing or abstracting, and in favor of immediate experience. "I don't have much confidence in the mind," Faulkner claimed (*FIU*, 6). "I don't know anything about rational and logical processes of thought at all," he said while in Japan, and explained further that he thought of rationality as "the processes of the mind which must follow a reasonable, I mean, a mathematically reasonable pattern."[18] Like Bergson's attack on the narrow rationalism of his time, Faulkner's skepticism of what is "mathematically reasonable" was construed as a more general rejection of the intellect. The mistake of taking Faulkner at his word, compounded by the mistake in pigeonholing Bergson, has never stopped troubling the issue.

Walter Slatoff's *Quest for Failure* (1960) drew a logical conclusion from the assumption that Faulkner is an irrationalist. Noting that Faulkner's vision is often "accordant to Bergson," Slatoff finds that Faulkner believes in intuition and not intellect.[19] Since the intuition is irrational, the novels are too—Faulkner's prose deliberately emphasizes its own flaws.[20] Slatoff's logic is valid, but his conclusion is untrue. If Faulkner believed flux to be shapeless, it would not be amiss to see self-destructive tendencies in his sentences and narratives. But he does not.

Several interesting dissertations were written on Faulkner and Bergson after Abel's and Slatoff's work appeared. Shirley Parker Callen's "Bergsonian Dynamism in the Writings of William Faulkner" (1962) interprets Faulkner's novels as, at base, a rejection of conceptualization. She divides the characters into those who endure by maintaining contact with real duration and those (the great

mass) who are guilty of using "adopted concepts."[21] Another dissertation, by Agnes Pollock (1965), also attempts to discriminate
characters on the basis of their time-awarenesses: intuitive or conceptualized.[22] Unaware, for the most part, of the aesthetic dilemma
Bergson was creating, the studies concentrate on what characters
say and do and think, a defect also found in Margaret Church's
otherwise sensitive essay on Faulkner and Bergson in *Time and
Reality* (1963). According to Church, Joe Christmas, because he
achieves a moment of insight into Bergson's transcendent flux,
comes to represent "the highest achievement of man."[23]

If Joe Christmas's death represents the highest achievement of
man, then perhaps it is not surprising that that vindictive corpse,
Addie Bundren, has found the meaning of life. Such is the conten-
tion of Robert Nadeau, for whom Bergson's dynamism is a skeleton
key to *As I Lay Dying*. Nadeau actually believes that *As I Lay
Dying* ends on a triumphant note, as the life-force is seen to perpet-
uate itself in Anse's marrying.[24] Jesse Gatlin performs a similar au-
topsy on *The Sound and the Fury*, ending on the puzzling note that
Faulkner's *durée*, unlike Bergson's, runs in a circular track.[25]

Such are the peculiarities and superficialities generated by the
use of Bergson to analyze Faulkner's characters and values independent of his narrative structures. These arguments don't do justice to
the dual vision of the novelist; they attribute to his characters a view
of time antithetical, in a sense, to the very writing of a novel. That
is because they do not begin with that "uninterrupted sentence"
that is the ground of our understanding Faulkner's values and his
characters' behavior. And here Bergson can be of real help, if we are
willing to admit the nature of language into the discussion, and to
see that Faulkner, like Eliot, looks on final form as the goal as well
as potentially the "enemy."

The problem of an aesthetic "immersion" first raised by Aiken
finally reemerges with Eric Larson's "The Barrier of Language"
(1967).[26] Larson seems to agree with Slatoff that Faulkner intentionally builds up "tensions of irresolution" at the level of phrase,
sentence, chapter, and presumably even the novel's whole fabric.
But where Slatoff sees failure, Larson sees success. By breaking up
the familiar forms, Faulkner gets the reader to supply the lack, be-

come a participant, help create the "nonverbal or experiential truth or motion." In this, he agrees with Richard Adams, whose *Faulkner: Myth and Motion* (1968) shows what a rich relationship exists between Faulkner's use of myth and the use of myth by Eliot, Joyce, Pound, Fitzgerald, and Hemingway.[27] Adams sees Faulkner's use of myth as only one element in a carefully planned program to create in the reader a "startling sense of temporal dislocation."[28] This technique keeps us from "feeling time as a thin, straight string with events marked off at measured intervals; instead, we feel it as a heavy knot, cluster, or tangle, with all the ends lost in the middle. Motion is lost, or stopped; and time is held still for aesthetic contemplation." Yet Faulkner, like Bergson, "is primarily interested in motion." It is only that the motion of life's stream is never truly perceived until "some object, or better, some person, can be made to stand still against its flow." Thus, the function of Faulkner's static images is "to make motion emphatically apparent" at the same time that it fixes it "for aesthetic contemplation."[29] How these two functions can be consonant Adams never explains.

Adams's study must, then, return to the question of language raised by Larson. If Faulkner agrees with Bergson that "*perception signifie immobiliser*" and that nothing immobilizes like the word, how can the novels believe in their chance at communicating this unspeakable flux of becoming? Susan Parr attempts to confront the problem of what Faulkner called "the impossibility—or at least the tremendous difficulty—of communication" (*LIG*, 72). According to her, Faulkner purposely created confusions in order to blow apart the illusion of his fiction.[30] Faulkner constantly undercuts his narrator's veracity, rendering all "fact" ambiguous and forcing the reader back onto his intuition.[31] Like Slatoff, Parr has developed Larson's "tensions" with a Bergsonian approach. But what about the problem that Stephen Dedalus points out in *Portrait of the Artist* plagues all "esthetic discussion": We must know "whether words are being used according to the literary tradition or according to the tradition of the marketplace."[32] Is all language really "by its very nature doomed to failure," as Parr asserts?[33] Does successful art do nothing more than spin the reader in the confusions of the ineffable, to end in holding up a fractured mirror to the self?

In this, Bergson has been dragged in to verify Faulkner's pose of failure, his "anti-intellectualism" and contradictions of style, image, plotting. It is generally recognized that *durée* is a positive value in both Faulkner and Bergson, but the consequences of accepting this god continue to be negative. Donald Kartiganer describes Faulkner's narratives as "dislocating the possibilities of form" and exhibiting a Bergsonian drive toward "an act of self-destruction."[34] And André Bleikasten sees Faulkner's fiction as a reaction against history and intellect.[35] The reasoning here is at base aesthetic and not "thematic": All "forms" are seen as life-denying, and the artist (in Kartiganer's words) is caught in "a tragic dynamic of opposed commitments—one to motion and the other to form."[36] As Bleikasten puts it, "immersion in 'real' time only means further disarray and dislocation."[37] Form and experience are irrevocably alienated and Bergson is said to give his benediction to this "tragic" opposition.

Some deny that Faulkner's metaphysic is one of "tragic time." In *The Abstract and the Actual* (1974), Panthea Reid Broughton makes the crucial distinction between language in the marketplace, which has lost its contact with vital experience, and language in literature, which has had its connection to experience renewed. "Faulkner's heroic characters," Broughton argues convincingly, "have seen how ultimately inaccessible to reason is existence; yet they are not paralyzed by the sight."[38] Language is no more culpable than action in the alienation many of Faulkner's characters experience from life; but language offers an unparalleled opportunity. Faulkner, Broughton makes us see, knew "the difference between an inert and a vital abstraction. . . . His entire canon, in fact, stands as a *caveat* against the fixed abstraction." Faulkner writes mostly about people who use abstractions to "evade reality, not to embrace it," but the fact remains that a constantly revitalized language is not "immobile, inert, life-denying."[39]

Faulkner pursues, according to Broughton, a consistent technique in vitalizing his own abstractions. He weds them to the actual. One problem remains, however: How can nonverbal "actuality" be gotten into words? Though Broughton does touch on Faulkner's "sonorous, almost hypnotic" prose, which creates a mood that is "itself a level of meaning," she does not make the connection between this level of "communication" and the semantic. Bergson is still seen as supplying the concept of a "living and fluid *irrational* world" and must then offer no possibilities for transcendence in language; Whitehead, "unlike Bergson" (why "unlike"?), finds in "vital abstraction a means to transcending" the merely material and static, and is therefore more applicable to Faulkner.[40] The static images are somehow more vital than the prose's sonority.

But Faulkner has a dual vision, and it is only our conventional image of Bergson that has prevented us from seeing how really useful he is in unlocking some of Faulkner's secrets. Cleanth Brooks summarizes the problem neatly in *Toward Yoknapatawpha and Beyond* (1978): "In spite of Faulkner's acceptance of Bergson's conception of time as fluid and continuous . . . it is hard to think of a novelist who exceeds Faulkner in his careful attention to the details of clock time and calendar time. . . . Faulkner's characters clearly lived their lives and underwent their passions in Bergson's *temps durée*, but this fact does not absolve them from living through a time that could be ticked off by the clock and measured by the calendar. . . . I find little in Faulkner's narrative treatment that can be certainly attributed to Bergson's influence."[41]

Eschewing the proposition of influence per se, I will argue that Bergson offers plenty of insight into Faulkner's narrative forms, beginning with the all-important building block of voice. The confusion comes from the assumption that Bergson rejects clock-time as "unreal" and therefore unimportant. Bergson does not, as these critics suppose, believe only in an amorphous Present and reject all possibilities for the mind to know—that is, to give form to—that Present.[42]

Bergson's Present is never amorphous, though it may be confused. The point is—and this is as true for James, Whitehead, and even Sartre, as for Bergson—it cannot be a *visible* Present. It is a hyphen: that which is being made. That is why it is so inaccessible to consciousness, which tries to give it visible form, only to find itself falling into past or future "states." What is being made is not, however, lawless. If life is pure mobility, it is nevertheless true that "wherever anything lives, there is open somewhere a register in which time is being inscribed" (*CE*, 16). Pure memory itself, when we let it "cross the threshhold" into consciousness, "retains and ranges alongside each other all our states in the order in which occur, leaving to each fact its place and consequently marking its date" (*MM*, 195; see also 199). Why should we suppose that Bergson's philosophy, rigidly adhered to, would "absolve" Faulkner's characters from the exigencies of clock and calendar? Why should we expect, as Brooks seems to do, that if Faulkner had really taken Bergson to heart, he would have written as though calendar time were "something with which man did not need to concern himself because it was 'unreal'"?[43]

No; for Faulkner as for Bergson, there are two kinds of knowing. One we call "perception," but it is actually "memory," for as soon as we have visualized the present state, it is gone. Memory offers to consciousness, then, a reconstruction. And it necessarily concentrates on information that is "useful": "The past has not ceased to exist; it has only ceased to be useful" (*MM*, 193). The other kind of knowing cannot be rendered in visualized states. It lies in the very feel of consciousness. The healthy mind knows in both modes, not one only. Bergson would no more approve a Gail Hightower, who lives "dissociated from mechanical time," than a Joe Christmas, caught in the circle of his "fence picket days" (*LA*, 272, 246). He would have agreed with Faulkner that Joe and Hightower are opposites.[44] And Faulkner would have agreed with Bergson that the truly enriching consciousness incorporates an ordered past in a developing present that proceeds in a "reasonable evolution" (*MM*, 243). The reasonableness of consciousness fits no mathematical formula, it is true—but it may fit a verbal one.

The Shape of a Voice

A fact little noticed in discussions of Faulkner's style is his virtuosity in blending voices. Many novelists have excelled in creating voices, but few have succeeded as Faulkner in making those voices sound with the resonance of one keyboard, one harp of sympathetic strings. If we are to discover the "reasonableness" of Faulkner's narratives, I believe we must listen attentively to his many voices. Joseph Reed is right when he says that you can only explain Faulkner's work if you accept his self-definition as a "story-teller," an orchestrator of voices, a master of shifting levels of diction and coherence.[45] Charles Anderson has said that Faulkner was steeped in the "Ciceronian tradition of the Old South and the Senecan tradition of Elizabethan England," and surely this is Faulkner's rhetorical heritage, whether or not it is his "moral center" as Anderson contends.[46] A first confrontation with *Absalom, Absalom!*'s prose is like stepping into a senate chamber, where rhetoric rolls in echoing and sonorous waves from wall to wall. The mesmerizing qualities of this prose are a level of meaning in themselves; but what is that meaning and how is it given to us?

Before answering this question, let me emphasize that there is no one Faulknerian style. *As I Lay Dying* and *The Sound and the Fury* are handbooks of style. They render everything from crude dialect to symbolist imagery. Moving between the poles of inner- and outer-directed language, Faulkner has kept well in mind the important distinction between the language of the marketplace and that of literature. He has excluded neither. Yet a case can be made for considering the style of *Absalom, Absalom!*—a novel which manages to let many voices sound without losing a sense that they all echo in the same chamber—as a goal toward which the experiments of Faulkner's most productive period (1929-36) point.

The Sound and the Fury offers us four distinct narrative personalities, *As I Lay Dying* fifteen. But the styles are clearly less numerous than the characters. There are gradations, but in Quentin's section of *Sound and the Fury*, and in every section of *As I Lay Dying*, we hear variations on three distinct styles. There is a public voice, rendered in speech, Quentin's dialect. Then there is a more private voice, rendered in diction more formal than speech, the voice in which Quentin consciously recollects. Finally, there is a voice that is as close to consciousness itself as Faulkner can bring it—the vocabulary is often not the character's at all, and the texture is remarkably uniform, from character to character. Quentin speaks in his own dialect: "I reckon the police won't get me for wearing my new suit one time" (*SF*, 63). He recounts memories consciously in a less colloquial voice: "If it had been cloudy I could have looked at the window, thinking what he said about idle habits" (*SF*, 60). Most of what Quentin tells us, even in the italicized or unpunctuated sections of his monologue, is rendered in one or the other of these voices: the public one, or the voice of controlled thought.

Yet there are moments, scattered throughout the section, when the control breaks up, and these moments are almost always those that touch on the sensitive subject of Caddy's sexuality: "'No,' Shreve said. *running the beast with two backs and she blurred in the winking oars running the swine of Euboeleus running coupled within how many Caddy*" (*SF*, 115). Anacoluthon, not italics, is the most likely sign of Quentin's consciousness bubbling to the surface, and Faulkner plays the game of showing us in what tension Quentin constantly keeps himself as he tries to avoid the flow of conscious-ness leading constantly back to the issue: "That Christ was not cru-cified: he was worn away by a minute clicking of little wheels. That had no sister" (*SF*, 60).

Neither Jason nor Benjy communicates to us on this level in *The Sound and the Fury*. In *As I Lay Dying*, by contrast, every character does. Here is an example of Vardaman's shifts in diction: "'Durn him. I showed him. Durn him.' I am not crying now. I am not anything. . . . 'Then hit want. Hit hadn't happened then . . .' It is dark. I can hear wood, silence; I know them. But not living sounds, not even him. It is as though the dark were resolving him out of his integrity, into an unrelated scattering of components—snuffings and stampings . . . " (*ALD*, 36). Here the fragmentariness of pure memories and the grammatical fragmentariness of images that we saw in Quentin's section have already begun to be amalgamated in a peculiarly recognizable voice. Vardaman will never utter the words "integrity" or "components" in his everyday speech, nor in his con-scious thinking, which stays always at the level of "is": "It is dark . . . " But as Faulkner takes us deeper into the psychological being, the higher style we associate with *Absalom, Absalom!* comes more into play: "It is as though the dark were resolving . . . . " Here we have a foretaste of the endless subordination that is the hallmark of the later novel.

Light in August and *Sanctuary*, both written entirely in the third person, make further use of this particular voice whenever a char-acter's inner life is opened to our gaze, and one sees Faulkner consistently adding to the repertoire, incorporating more and more fragmentary perceptions and memories in a stream of thought rolling on. After finding herself in Miss Reba's care, and suffering through the doctor's examination, Temple Drake lies in bed, listening, as Quentin did in *The Sound and the Fury*, to the sound of clocks striking the hour and half-hour. She watches the light fade: "She watched the final light condense into the clock face, and the dial change from a round orifice in the darkness to a disc suspended in nothingness, the original chaos, and change in turn to a crystal ball holding in its still and cryptic depths the ordered chaos of the intricate and shadowy world upon whose scarred flanks the old wounds whirl onward at dizzy speed into darkness lurking with new disasters. She was thinking about half-past-ten-o'clock. The hour for dressing for a dance" (*S*, 130). This passage poises its poetry carefully between the consciousness of the narrator and that of Temple. But by distinguishing carefully Temple's conscious thought about the clock's ringing, the narrator more than implies that what immediately precedes is a rendering—no doubt it would be unrecognizable to Temple herself, but to us it must ring true—of Temple's inner consciousness of the world's "ordered chaos."

In *Light in August* Faulkner clearly makes the long-winded style we associate with *Absalom, Absalom!* a tag for deeper psychic states. As Lena waits for one of the many wagons that will carry her along, she becomes absorbed in its slow progress toward her: ". . . the sound of it seems to come slow and terrific and without meaning, as though it were a ghost travelling a half mile ahead of its own shape. 'That far within my hearing before my seeing,' Lena thinks" (*LA*, 5). Lena intuits the wagon's arrival and departure in a single "perception." We notice now that Faulkner is using not only the same subordinator, but some of the same vocabulary repeatedly, like the word "ghost," which underscores the insistent provisionality of "as though." When Hightower has his moment of vision toward the end of the novel, "It is as though they had merely waited . . . to be reaffirmed . . . then they sweep into sight, borne now upon a cloud of phantom dust" (*LA*, 366). His ancestors were merely waiting in the wings of memory, to be released into consciousness like a tide.

The high style of *Absalom, Absalom!* aims at attaining that al-

most hypnotically suggestive prose with which Faulkner has exper-
imented continuously to that point, that mesmerizing language
which Bergson suggests must catch us up in the movement of a
mind, making our minds "fall into step" (*CM*, 143, 102). Here
must be the first level of meaning in Faulkner's prose, the one we
arrive at before we have even begun to think, in which we unconsciously merge with the artist: "Before intellection properly so-
called, there is the perception of structure and movement," Bergson
notes. "There is on the page one reads punctuation and rhythm"
(*CM*, 102). When we turn to *Absalom, Absalom!*, we have already
got a pretty good idea of how Faulkner tries to achieve the effect:
He writes longer and longer sentences, uses lots of conjunctions,
especially subordinators, and prepares for us a virtual musical score
of lexical repetition. The finishing touch on this style he added in
Absalom: a forest of personal pronouns.

Even the longest sentences in *The Sound and the Fury, As I Lay
Dying, Sanctuary*, and *Light in August* would probably not prepare
the reader for what he finds in *Absalom, Absalom!* There is nothing
(except perhaps in Proust) like the first chapter of *Absalom* when it
comes to sheer length of sentences. Kucera and Francis found in
the million-word corpus of their *Computational Analysis of Present-
Day American English* only nine sentences exceeding 100 words in
length. Indeed, of the fifteen discourse types surveyed by them,
none, including journalism and fiction, had an average sentence
length greater than 25 words. In the whole corpus, only one sentence exceeded 160 words.[47] The first chapter of *Absalom*, which
is about 8,400 words long, has twenty-four sentences of 100 words
or more. Four of them exceed 200 words. The average sentence is
40 words long. Yet that is a little misleading. Almost a quarter of
the sentences in this chapter are 5 words or less. You can't easily
define a Faulkner sentence, since most of the long ones are probably
a series of shorter sentences connected by semicolons or commas
that ought to be periods. At the same time, there are instances of
four or five substantial sentence fragments in a row, fragments
which would, if connected by commas, colons, dashes, or semicolons, make a grammatically complete sentence. The more one
looks at the interjections and ellipses, the less certain the bounda-

ries of the sentences seem. The only certainty is that at moments a breath is taken.

A major tool Faulkner uses to blur the boundaries between sentences is the conjunction. In *Absalom's* first chapter he has employed an astonishing number of them at the beginnings of sentences. Fully forty percent of his sentences begin with conjunctions, and most are not the "continuatives" we normally use in speech, like "well," "oh," or "say." Faulkner's continuatives are those uttered by people talking to themselves: "yes" and "no" almost exclusively. The subordinators "as if" and "as though" are his meat and potatoes; adversatives like "yet" and "but," and causal/ temporals like "then," "because," "since," and "so" account for some eighty-three items in the first chapter, but "as if" and "as though" occur forty times themselves, giving to the longer sentences that characteristic feeling of twining, turning, never-settling; the sheer frequency of this formula also creates an intentional effect of *déjà vu* for the reader.

Faulkner also uses semantic strings throughout the first chapter of *Absalom* in order to move its prose nearer a poetical high style with hypnotic power. In this one short chapter the possibilities for lexical "echo" seem huge, and a thorough, but not exhaustive listing of lexically related items turns up at least four major strings: time-related terms, words associated with death (like "dust"), words directly or indirectly related to "voice," and family-role names. One example of Faulkner's conscious patterning seems particularly instructive. The item "now" appears occasionally throughout the chapter, but occurs only seven times from page 7 to page 22. Then, on pages 23 and 24, it occurs twelve times, and on pages 27 and 28 it turns up eleven times. The reader will recall that these pages describe Judith and Henry's rides in the Sutpen carriage to church. Proper names are also potentially very instructive in this first chapter. The items "Judith," "Thomas," "Henry," and "Ellen" appear infrequently until the last page of the chapter, when they occur with a vengeance: twenty-six times.

The infrequency with which characters are actually named in the early part of the chapter is, of course, intentional, a part of Faulkner's attempt to mesmerize. The reader realizes soon after beginning the novel that he is participating in a kind of pronoun game, though there are so many other games going on simultaneously that he may not see immediately that this one has fairly simple rules. Faulkner has followed four techniques here. First, he interjects references, signalling that other references may not be so easy to figure out as they appear. Second, he uses colloquialized pronouns wherever possible, and sometimes even where they seem unlikely. Third, he simply plays around with pronouns, the way grammar school kids sometimes do ("you know I know you know I know"). Finally, he creates some moments of genuine ambiguity, heightening them by the use of demonstratives that signal a general sense of "what I just said" or "everything just mentioned."

While he doesn't supply many proper nouns early on, preferring to use pronouns, Faulkner often adds a possible referent or referents in parentheses: " . . . as if she (Miss Coldfield) had never seen . . ." (*AA*, 14); "It (the talking, the telling) seemed (to him, to Quentin) . . ." (*AA*, 22). The overabundance of reference is almost as puzzling as lack of information would have been. The implication is, too, that perhaps there are other reference items which need, but have not received clarification; the use of colloquialized reference helps to stir our fears here. Taking full advantage of his characters' dialects, Faulkner has them substitute person-pronouns for things and vice versa: ". . . it mused (mused, thought, seemed to possess sentience) as if, though dispossessed of the peace—who was impervious anyhow to fatigue—which she declined to give it . . ." (*AA*, 13); "I saw that man—the evil's source and head which had outlasted all its victims—who had created two children . . . a man that anyone could look at and see . . ." (*AA*, 18-19). Faulkner draws attention to the tortured thought of Rosa Coldfield by rendering alternative constructions in practically the same line: "a man who . . . a man that . . ." (*AA*, 19). In the example from page 13 of the novel, we see the parenthetical qualifier piling on more information, but switching from thing ("it") to person ("who") to thing again ("it") in a process so rapid that one has to go back and read the phrases again to convince oneself that the pronouns all refer to the same man/thing: Thomas Sutpen. The example from pages 18 and 19 performs the same trick.

Sometimes, Faulkner engages in exuberant childlike play with permutations of pronouns—and Rosa is herself childlike in this: "our father knew who his father was in Tennessee and who his grandfather had been in Virginia and our neighbors and the people we lived among knew that we knew and we knew they knew we knew and we knew that they would have believed us about whom and where he came from even if we had lied . . ." (*AA*, 17). Note the use of "about whom"; in the next line, we get "about who" (*AA*, 17). This game need not cause real confusion, if one is willing to be patient, but there are moments in *Absalom*'s first chapter when it is very difficult to tell who is "whom." Rosa calls Henry "the son who had repudiated the very roof under which he had been born and to which he would return . . . and that as a murderer and fratricide; and he, fiend, blackguard, devil . . ." (*AA*, 15). Here only the triplet "fiend, blackguard, devil" alerts the reader to the fact that reference has switched from "he" (son) to "he" (father). This simple sleight of hand becomes more complex when Faulkner uses demonstratives: "Ellen knew that . . . that was not it. She accepted that—not reconciled: accepted—as though there is a breathing-point in outrage where you can accept it almost with gratitude since you can say to yourself, *thank God, this is all; at least I now know all of it*—thinking that, clinging to that . . ." (*AA*, 29). "That" and "it" go through so many changes here that one can't be certain about the references. The first "that" refers to Sutpen's proclivity for naked wrestling with his negro slaves. The next "that" refers either to the same thing or to Ellen's knowing of it. The third "that" probably refers only to the fighting. "You can accept *it*" may refer us to the thing that caused the outrage, or the outrage itself, and so on. A few such ambiguities are not so hard to absorb, but when they are piled on—and with a grammatically puzzling interjection ("not reconciled: accepted")—the difficulty increases. Significantly, we have moved from third- to second- to first-person narrative, deeper into the character.

Through blurring the boundaries of the sentence, employing many conjunctions in sentence-initial position, establishing chains of lexical "echo," and complicating pronoun references, Faulkner creates a prose style in the first chapter of *Absalom, Absalom!* that imitates the flow of consciousness. That prose shifts the ground of verbal truth from denotation and frozen (grammatically clear) relationship to connotation, rhythm, and emerging relationship. If that is the case, then what is to rescue Faulkner from the arbitrariness of any single word? No single word can be "right" independent of its context, and we have tried to show how that context began, for all its profuseness and verbosity here, in the simple one of voice. When words are isolated from the stream of that voice they seem suddenly drained of meaning, and it would be well to pause for a moment to look at what Faulkner's characters themselves have to tell us about that experience of the isolated word which seems somehow to rise up in hostility against the very stream that gave it birth.

For Faulkner's characters, the word isolated is like a black hole in space; the heart of creation, it seems entirely vacant. Reality is, Bergson tells us, a reality which is making itself in a reality which is unmaking itself (*CE*, 251), and to turn from the stream of consciousness to the individual avatar of the word is to see things suddenly come to a standstill, the blood draining out of creation's face. Every time we try to match our intuition and the word, we find ourselves reduced to a visual form that rapidly slumps into conventionality. The correspondence between word and thing is arbitrary, and by itself hostile to meaning, for it tends to evoke stock responses. Jason epitomizes this mentality. When he is rescued from the attack of the wasp-like little man he has offended in his vindictive pursuit of Caddy's daughter, Quentin, we find Faulkner's prose neatly encapsulating his compartmentalized consciousness. The rescuer leads " . . . Jason on around the corner of the station, to the empty platform where an express truck stood, where grass grew rigidly in a plot bordered with rigid flowers and a sign in electric lights: Keep your ⬛👁 on Mottson, the gap filled by a human eye with an electric 👁 pupil" (*SF*, 242). The environment reflects Jason's personality, and the eye is an ironic comment on Jason's blindness. But the brief rebus of the penciled eye is a further comment on the nature of the word. For Jason, words are things: An eye is merely a conventional sign. Like Jason's stock response, it is as automated as electricity.

When Tull describes Cash's work on the coffin in *As I Lay Dying*, he draws a similar picture for the reader:

Cash made it clock-shape like this   with every joint and seam bevelled and scrubbed   with the plane, tight as a drum . . . [*ALD*, 56-57].

The innocent inclusion of this sketch takes on much deeper tone when we reach the sole section awarded to Addie in the book.

Addie thinks about Anse's name, having realized at last that Anse is "dead," a life-denier: "Anse. Why Anse. Why are you Anse. I would think about his name until after a while I could see the word as a shape, a vessel, and I would watch him liquefy and flow into it like cold molasses . . . until the jar stood full and motionless: a significant shape profoundly without life like an empty door frame; and then I would find that I had forgotten the name of the jar. I would think: the shape of my body where I used to be a virgin is in the shape of a   and I couldn't think *Anse* . . ." (*ALD*, 116-17). Here, no sketch provides the "shape to fill a lack" (*ALD*, 116). The pupil of the eye, the coffin in the shape of a clock (of course!) are merely those shapes, vacant like doorways. Addie's sense of loss comes to her only in the unmentioned shape of the uterine urn. What has Anse done to earn her undying hatred? He has "stopped" her motion with his dead weight, and thereby he has drained language of meaning—one thinks of the phrase from *Soldier's Pay*: "Women know more about words than men ever will. And they know how little they can ever possibly mean."[48] Here is the leverage for Addie's revenge: By extracting from Anse his "word" that he will take her body to Jefferson for burial, Addie thinks to turn the tables on him, to inflict damage for the emptiness his obtuse rigidity has inflicted on her.

But, as the gap in the line before "and I couldn't think Anse" suggests, Addie cannot get words and reality together any more. The words she sees going up "in a thin line, quick and harmless," while "doing goes along the earth, clinging to it, so that after a while the two lines are too far apart for the same person to straddle from one to the other" (*ALD*, 117). Addie remembers that she had once heard the dark land talking to her in a "dark voicelessness in which the words are the deeds," and she remembers having felt that she had somehow a "duty to the alive, to the terrible blood." But finally she feels isolated. For those around her, like Cora Tull, sin and salvation are a matter of mere words (*ALD*, 119). Faulkner must have shared Addie's rejection of bloodless verbiage. But her note of despair is only one in his scale.

There may be an "immitigable chasm between all life and all print," as Faulkner speculated in *The Unvanquished*, a book whose stories seem obsessed with printed requisitions, letters, and money, and with their deceptions.[49] In a 1931 review of Erich Maria Remarque's *The Road Back*, Faulkner mused that the experience seems sometimes to expire before it gets to the page: "Perhaps the word kills it."[50] But only perhaps. Dawson Fairchild makes a different claim in *Mosquitoes*: While words have no "life in themselves," still "words brought into a happy conjunction produce something that lives."[51] The life of words is a matter, then, of the voice that brings them into conjunction. One reflects here on the fact that so many of Faulkner's characters who despair over language also despair over the vacancy and isolation of the self. And the development of the voice speaking to us in *Absalom* must be thought of as the development of a consciousness capable of maintaining contact with the sinuosity of the real—for there is no other source that can give meaning to words.

But how does that consciousness confront history without disintegrating like Quentin's or despairing like Addie's? Bergson has said that in order to maintain contact with the real, a consciousness "has to do violence to itself," has to reverse the direction of the operation by which it habitually thinks, has perpetually to revise, or rather to recast, all its categories. Kartiganer, like most, misinterprets this statement when he reads it as claiming that the mind must "engage in an act of self-destruction."[52] Bergson clearly means not destruction but reconstruction. To realize this self-renewing process of consciousness in print, the writer must coin new terms, create new ideas, though this would, of course, "no longer be communicating something, it would not be writing" by our old standards. The artist remolds language, venturing out of the realm of "expression," in which language is nothing more than a medium of exchange, into the realm of "impression" and intuition (*TFW*, 16). In doing so, he reverses the usual flow of things, and the conversion of the personality's flowing into public property becomes the conversion of public property (readymade language) into mobile private experience (*TFW*, 129).

As Francis Leaver has noted, Faulkner's prose pushes constantly on this door, using an abundance of abstract nouns, coinages, and intensives to try to dislocate everyday language back into experience.[53] Faulkner, as no other American novelist, has "recast" the common coin of speech for his purposes. Though one finds him doing it everywhere, *Pylon* and *Absalom, Absalom!* are perhaps the most dramatic examples of his power as a re-molder. He turns adjectives into verbs: Sutpen "abrupts" upon the scene in *Absalom* (*AA*, 8). He piles on the adjectives mercilessly, sometimes violating our instinct for their proper order: Quentin thinks of Rosa's "female old flesh" (*AA*, 8), then six pages later thinks of her "old female flesh" (*AA*, 14), leaving us to ponder the implications of the shift. Rosa tosses off phrases like "looking out upon the whatever ogreworld of that quiet village street" (*AA*, 21). And in *Pylon* the fountain flows even more freely, giving us "curbchanneled spindrift of tortured and draggled serpentine and trodden confetti pending the dawn's whitewings—spent tinseldung of Momus' Nilebarge clatterfalque."[54] Faulkner claimed he was a failed poet. But he also said, "My prose is really poetry" (*LIG*, 56). One sees here how seriously he has sought the immediacy, compactness, and freshness of verse in his novels. As seriously as he has pursued the continual elaboration of novelty, he has just as intently worked on the counterforces that give a shape to the seeming chaos and anarchy.

The Life-Sentence and the Book

To read Bergson in conjunction with Faulkner is to realize that Adams was right: The imagery of stasis, which would seem antithetical to the flowing of a voice, is actually its complement. It provides the necessary next step from the individual "notes" of lexical repetition ("ghost," "demon," "outrage," and "furious") to the chords of memory. Here is the tool that takes the endlessly elaborating voice toward an overall design, a "face still forming," in Eliot's words (*CPP*, 141). Faulkner creates the uninterrupted sentence that emu-lates the flux of consciousness, and at the same time never lets us forget the inexorable ticking of the clock. This profoundly Bergson-ian tension gives shape and pathos to the narratives. It renders a world in a Bergsonian conflict: These selves create themselves in a medium that is continually unmaking itself. So, for the reader, the story transpires not as a mere chain of events, but as a dawning in the consciousness chained to those events.

Finally, consciousness is itself a tension: "It (the talking, the tell-ing) seemed (to him, to Quentin) to partake of that logic- and reason-flouting quality of a dream which the sleeper knows must have occurred, stillborn and complete, in a second, yet the very quality upon which it must depend to move the dreamer (verisimil-itude) to credulity—horror or pleasure or amazement—depends as completely upon a formal recognition of and acceptance of elapsed and yet-elapsing time as music or printed tale" (*AA*, 22). Here is the "curious strain" Hugh Kenner notes lies at the heart of every Faulkner reader's experience: One must take notes, keep track of the clock and calendar, and yet simultaneously "pretend that we need do none of this, need only listen to a voice we ourselves sup-ply."[55] And here precisely is that grasp of the "two-sided character of things" that Bergson admired in Lucretius.[56]

In trying to explain what sort of "truth" Faulkner aims at, criti-cism has too often been driven to despair over this dual vision. Does Faulkner believe in the concrete and not the abstract . . . vice versa? Does he use the frozen only to suggest the mobile, or elevate the static above the chaos of experience's maelstrom? Does he believe life is essentially free or determined? For both Bergson and Faulk-ner, what the mind believes is largely a matter of predisposition, and so competing views of experience do in a sense coexist. "Man's free will," says Faulkner, "functions against a Greek background of fate" (*FIU*, 38). The healthy consciousness moves between the poles of this awareness.

If Faulkner seems to have delighted in the confusions about dates and events in both his biography and his fiction, it is not really a delight in chaos he expresses, but a delight in the process of creation. Each attempt to define a person, place, feeling, idea, or event is a new approximation that must eventually be scrapped for a better. Faulkner's is not a record of man's inability to comprehend, but rather an evocation of consciousness's self-renewing vocabulary. For him, the characters in his novels seem to be "still in motion, still talking, and still acting" (*FIU*, 197-98). And that is why he still thinks he can get to know them better, can provide us with updated information; he gives this explanation for the inconsistencies between *The Sound and the Fury* and the appendix he wrote for Cowley's *Indispensable Faulkner*: "The inconsistencies in the appendix prove that to me the book is still alive after fifteen years, and being still alive, is still growing, changing. . . . so it is the book itself which is inconsistent: not the appendix. . . . I was even wrong now and then in the very conclusions I drew . . . and the information in which I once believed."[57] The experience of the novel is, likewise, one of discovery and revaluation, vision and revision.

Faulkner's prose reifies this shifting perspective, between the making and the unmaking of truth, the poles of intellect and intuition, the concrete and the abstract, fatalism and freedom. It approaches the rendering of "experiential truth" through the bobbing and weaving of consciousness. Taking seriously the charge that an artist ought to "create his own language," Faulkner's language glories not in arbitrariness or absurdity, but in the superiority of intuited truth to the accidents of "fact" (see *LIG*, 267). As we look at the values that seem implicit in his narrative, we ought to keep in mind that he sees, with Wallace Stevens, a choice "not between but of," and chooses to include those things "which in each other are included."[58]

SEVEN

Faulkner and the Bergsonian Self

> *There is only one road leading from action confined in a*
> *circle to action developing in the freedom of space, from*
> *repetition to creation . . .*
> —Henri Bergson, *The Two Sources*
> *of Morality and Religion*

❧ Faulkner populates his books with characters reacting against change, refusing to accept history, as many have noted.[1] It has been less noted, however, that this rejection of change is tantamount to a rejection of self—that Faulkner, like Bergson, relates freedom directly to self-knowledge and self-acceptance. "Although we are free when we are willing to get back into ourselves," writes Bergson, "it seldom happens that we are willing" (*TFW*, 240). Rather than admit self's bubbling, unpredictable stream into consciousness, we repress it; and the tool of that repression is the spatializing intellect. Thus, as Whitehead says, we tend more and more to disdain "information about the universe obtained through visceral feelings" in order to concentrate on "visual feelings."[2] If the process goes far enough, we find "our life unfolds in space rather than time; we live for the external world rather than for ourselves. To act freely is to *recover possession of oneself*" (*TFW*, 121; my italics).

Faulkner's implicit theory of self and memory parallels Bergson's with remarkable exactness. Like Bergson, he sees life as endless creation. And like Bergson he seems convinced that, when we have healthy psyches, there is "one reality, at least, that we all seize from within, by intuition. . . . It is our own personality in its flowing through time—our self which endures" (*IM*, 3). And for Faulkner, as for Bergson, the free act which is characterized by an overflowing of the fundamental self is "exceptional" (*TFW*, 167). It isn't easy, as Addie Bundren tells us, to accept the "terrible blood, the bitter red flood" (*ALD*, 117). Addie, like many of Faulkner's characters, suffers a dissociation of talking and doing that is directly related to her stubborn resistance to the emotional world. Precisely because they live divided against themselves, many of Faulkner's characters are vulnerable to disorders of consciousness—that is to say, of re-membering.

Faulkner's characters are often in profound trouble when it comes to intuiting their inner lives. After he has been beaten by the friends of Bobbie the waitress, Joe Christmas feels literally discon-nected: "Perhaps he was conscious of somewhere within him the two severed wireends of volition and sentience lying, not touching now, waiting to touch, to knit anew, so he could move" (*LA*, 163). And when Joe goes to kill Joanna Burden, he starts off believing "with calm paradox that he was the volitionless servant of the fatal-ity in which he believed that he did not believe . . . " (*LA*, 207). Joe later finds his body seeming "to walk away from him" (*LA*, 209). Joanna herself is, of course, a "dual personality" (*LA*, 174), and Gail Hightower, Doc Hines, and Simon McEachern all find at key points that mind and body have gone savagely out of synchro-nization.

The result is that characteristic Faulknerian polarization: For Joe Christmas, perceptions hang like birds over the square in "still-winged and tremulous suspension" while his emotional life throbs with the "noise of his own blood" (*LA*, 85-86). Faulkner, like Eliot, associates this humming of life's depths with a primordial creative force, symbolized by the feminine. Faulkner's characters must deal with this principle and its expression in a carnal life that is often the stimulus of "outrage." *The Sound and the Fury* establishes a pattern for character that is developed in later novels: Confronted with the unpredictability and the shock of creative life, most characters de-cide they would rather stop growing. So Faulkner writes of dam-aged creativity. He conceives the world in profoundly Bergsonian terms. For him, there are two very different sorts of memory and two very different patterns into which they organize our lives. Those patterns determine our possibilities, for one is open, the other fatefully closed.

Caddy: The Missing Center

The problem with the Compson family, Faulkner said in an interview, is that they are "still living in the attitudes of 1859 or '60" (*FIU*, 18). The key to their lack of growth is their inability to accept Caddy. They try to escape, they act vindictively, they point the finger of blame everywhere else. And Caddy is the missing center of this novel, a female driven from her place.

Maxwell Geismar accuses Faulkner of having a "hatred of life" because so many of his characters revolt against it. More to the point in this matter, Richard Chase says it is the men who revolt, that Faulkner has created a "gynecological demonology."[3] Irving Malin agrees here, telling us that intuitive, earthy women in Faulkner's canon are never "motivated by the abstract notions which perplex the daily routines of men," and that Faulkner's women are thus, unfortunately, rather "superficial" creations.[4] There is, without a doubt, something like a gynecological demonology in Faulkner's novels. According to Gavin Stevens, women deal with men in perfect assurance of having their way because "all they need is the instinct, the intuition before it became battered and dulled."[5] But of course the women in Faulkner's world are not all "so wise," just because "they have learned to live unconfused by reality."[6]

"Women don't care whether they are facts or not," Eula Varner Snopes asserts in *The Town*, "just so they fit . . . men don't care whether they fit or not just so they are facts."[7] If we take Eula to be speaking for Faulkner, then men would certainly have to be the less practical creatures. This is what Uncle Ephraim tells Chick Mallison. Men don't know how to listen: "They ain't got time. They're too busy with facks. . . . If you ever needs to get anything done outside the common run, don't waste yo time on the men-folks; get the womens and the children to working at it." Chick thinks over his father's "outrage, his almost furious repudiations."[8] The more we think of it, the more we remember those males in Faulkner who refuse to accommodate to a changing world: Sutpen, Simon Mc-Eachern, Quentin Compson, and Mr. Nightingale of *The Mansion*, who alike "set [their] intractable and contemptuous force against the juggernaut of history and science both," and are ultimately destroyed by their own "simple inflexibility." The men pursue a permanent sanctuary "fixed, forever safe from change and alteration."[9]

But Geismar is wrong: These aren't Faulkner's values. The dynamic between masculine and feminine operates in one way at the symbolic level—here there seems to be a division between intellect and intuition, idealism and realism. But Faulkner is as interested in how that symbolism operates within the lives of his characters as he is in making any one of his characters a symbol. Thus, Caddy is a symbol to Quentin, to Jason, and even to the narrator—when she is absent. But she is also a real person in whose mind the dynamic of feminine and masculine responses to life is also played out. She finds herself becoming warped in the heat of her brothers' passionate demands, and is eventually driven by her own demons. Her promiscuity stems from the same self-destructiveness infecting all the Compsons: "There was something terrible in me sometimes at night I could see it grinning at me," Quentin remembers Caddy saying, "grinning at me through their faces . . . I'm sick" (*SF*, 87). The sickness does come, admittedly, from those around her. Her daughter speaks for her when she says, "If I'm bad it's because I had to be. You made me" (*SF*, 201). Caddy has her own problems.

Caddy in the tree, peeking in at the window, sees the rituals of mourning going on after Damuddy's death. *The Sound and the Fury* moves from this scene out in many directions into the lives of its speakers. But always there is the vacant spot created by Caddy's absence—a vacancy symbolized by other losses, including Damuddy's death. Mrs. Compson is also a kind of zero, as Quentin implies when he thinks, "If I'd just had a mother" (*SF*, 134). But Caddy remains the significant lack. She is the one around whom the debate and passions swirl, the issue over which the family divides and self-destructs.

We react most violently against those things that reflect a repressed part of our personality. According to Bergson, we also regress to habits formed early in life when we are faced with true novelty—we fall back on stock responses rather than adjusting to the new. All the Compsons react in extremely repressive ways to-ward Caddy. Jason and Quentin, particularly, victimize Caddy out of their own sense of victimization. But Benjy epitomizes the Compson disease; he operates like an abstraction from the souls of Quentin, Jason, and Mrs. Compson: the primitive child in each of them. He lives in a tortured Now in which sensory stimuli auto-matically evoke memories recorded in their exact order of occur-rence and represented to consciousness with the intensity of present objects. He cannot make voluntary connections, draw parallels, or learn from experience—he still does not know, at thirty-three, that the stove will burn his hand. He sees people as volitionless objects that materialize and disappear.

Most important of all, Benjy cannot tolerate *change*. Like Jason and Quentin, Benjy hates Caddy's metamorphosis from girl to woman. Like them, too, Benjy is addicted to routine. In the final scene of the book, he bellows his outrage at Luster's having turned left instead of right around the public square. Once Jason has re-stored the usual route to the program, Benjy subsides, holding his broken narcissus, satisfied merely that each thing is once again "in its ordered place" (*SF*, 249). Benjy is, according to Faulkner, a pit-iable "animal," a device used in the telling that "serves his purpose and is gone" (*LIG*, 245-46). But we should note that Benjy's infan-tilism is at least human enough that it is without animal instinct. And he does have memories.

The workings of Benjy's memory are thoroughly Bergsonian. There are two kinds of memory, according to Bergson, which ideally function in tandem with a flexible organizing personality (or consciousness). The scheme appears in a drawing from *Matter and Memory*. Cone ABS is the whole of memory. At its base, AB, lies pure memory, where images and sense-impressions are stored "in the order in which they occur, leaving to each fact its place and consequently marking its date" (*MM*, 195). Most of what is in this area of memory is naturally not permitted to become conscious. Instead, the brain selects the memories applicable to present situa-tions and possible future states. If we let consciousness float, we

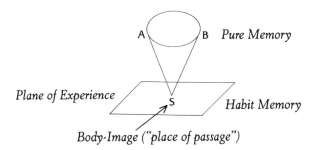

may explore our pure memory by haphazard contact; that memory is a complete cosmos, in which nothing of our past life has been lost. We clearly drag a heavier and heavier load with us through time, and "the point of the cone is ever driven into the future by the weight of the past" (*MM*, 324-25).

We need some protection against the access of pure memory, and the brain provides it; but we need further some means of acting without getting lost in the dream of the past, and so we require habitual memory, which, "fixed in the organism, is nothing but the complete set of intelligently constructed mechanisms which ensure the appropriate response to the various possible demands." This memory "acts our past experience, but does not call up its image" (*MM*, 195). The image of the body is a correlative of the self, and extends upward from the plane of immediate experience like an axis, the one stable element in all memory. Here are the things Benjy lacks: an active brain to select from pure memory's banquet and a developing set of habitual responses to help him function in the world. He is a being without self-consciousness: When he sees himself in the mirror, he cries (*SF*, 56). His castration, too, is a further damaging of "self."

Benjy's is an infant's consciousness in an adult's body, a consciousness of astounding immaturity, whose images have been translated by Faulkner into calculatedly transparent verbiage. He is tossed randomly among the flotsam and jetsam of his past, unaware of the "unreality" of those memories, unable to do anything with them as they are simply inflicted on him, helter skelter. The one habitual response he makes—the moan or howl—is too undifferentiated to be interpretable except by a patient Caddy, who finally discovers that her perfume has upset him (*SF*, 31-32).

Benjy doesn't want Caddy to change, and when he finds she no longer smells like trees, he begins to cry. When he encounters Charles and Caddy on the front porch swing, he keeps up the fuss until she finally has to walk away with him: "'I wont.' she said. 'I wont anymore, ever, Benjy. Benjy.' Then she was crying, and I cried, and we held each other. 'Hush.' she said. 'Hush. I wont anymore.' So I hushed and Caddy got up and we went into the kitchen and turned the light on and Caddy took the kitchen soap and washed her mouth at the sink, hard. Caddy smelled like trees" (*SF*, 36). All Benjy "knows" is that he's happy when Caddy smells the way she always has. She must remain pure with the pureness that is constantly associated with water and trees throughout Benjy's section. Caddy is the creative center, as Faulkner's vocabulary emphasizes. Here's an image reminiscent of one from *The Waste Land*: "Caddy's head was on Father's shoulder. Her hair was like fire, and little points of fire were in her eyes. . . . She smelled like trees. *She smelled like trees*" (*SF*, 55).

Benjy's resistance grieves Caddy, and so do the more sophisticated childishnesses of Quentin and Jason. "There are too many Jasons in the South who can be successful," Faulkner remarked in an interview, "just as there are too many Quentins in the South who are too sensitive to face its reality" (*FIU*, 17). Jason's is a mean response: "You think you're grown up, dont you. You think you're better than anybody else, don't you. Prissy" (*SF*, 30). Quentin, on the other hand, cannot "get past" his sister's sexuality, just as in *Absalom, Absalom!* he cannot "get past" the account of the moment when Henry kills Bon. Indeed, the two books resonate beautifully with each other. Miss Rosa tells Quentin that "there are some things which happen to us which the intelligence and the senses refuse just as the stomach sometimes refuses what the palate has accepted . . . occurrences which stop us dead . . . leaving us immobile, impotent, helpless; fixed, until we die" (*AA*, 151-52).

Like Benjy, Quentin wants Caddy to exist only for him: "Can you imagine *the curtains leaning in on the twilight upon the odour of the apple tree her head against the twilight her arms behind her head kimono-winged the voice that breathed o'er eden clothes upon the bed by the nose seen above the apple*" (*SF*, 82). Pure and purely tempting, Caddy must remain the immutable Eve of Quentin's childhood. In this, and in this synesthetic consciousness ("by the nose seen"), Quentin is different from Benjy only in degree, not kind. Like Benjy, he tries to get himself between Caddy and her lovers. Though he comes off as an ineffectual figure in his confron-tation with Dalton Ames, he still succeeds, like Benjy, in fouling up their meeting, and thus probably in ruining his sister's life, for there is no evidence that Caddy ever sees Ames again after Quentin pre-vents her from going back to apologize to him (*SF*, 127).

Like Benjy, Quentin associates Caddy with tree smells; unlike Benjy, he is both attracted and repulsed by Caddy's fertility. In the long flashback to the Dalton Ames fight, the smell of honeysuckle keeps "coming up in damp waves" to overpower Quentin with the sickening thought of Caddy's lovemaking (*SF*, 120). When Quen-tin opens the gasoline to clean his vest in his room at Harvard, other potent memories happen to him—that is, they are not so much recalled as let through: "I found the gasoline in Shreve's room and spread the vest on the table, where it would be flat, and opened the gasoline. *the first car in town a girl a Girl that's what Jason couldn't bear smell of gasoline making him sick then got madder than ever because a girl Girl had no sister but Benjamin . . .*" (*SF*, 134). Such memories, Bergson specifically notes, are not really "associationist." They are a deeper, fused state one "breathes in with the very scent" (*TFW*, 161, 164-65). Quentin's memories hover always in the same territory, converting one story into a hundred variations. Trying to scrub the spot from his vest, Quentin is demanding somehow that Caddy the girl not become a Girl.

In fact, Quentin's response to the "perfume" of flowers is just Benjy's with a more sophisticated consciousness, a visceral reaction, or rather, a reaction against the visceral: "Because women so deli-cate so mysterious Father said. Delicate equilibrium of periodical filth between two moons balanced. Moons he said full and yellow as harvest moons her hips thighs. . . . all that inside of them shapes an outward suavity waiting for a touch to. Liquid putrefaction like drowned things floating like pale rubber flabbily filled getting the odour of honeysuckle all mixed up" (*SF*, 100). At one point, Quentin thinks about the cedars he associates with his grandfather, trying "not to think of the swing" that reminds him (just as it reminds Benjy) of Caddy. But then "all cedars came to have that vivid dead smell of perfume Benjy hated so," as though Caddy's despoilment had spoiled nature: "Just by imagining the clump it seemed to me that I could hear whispers secret surges smell the beating of hot blood under wild unsecret flesh watching against red eyelids the swine untethered in pairs rushing coupled into the sea" (*SF*, 137). Quentin's revulsion is strongly associated with these whispers he recalls from the porch swing, just as it is symbolized by mud on Caddy's drawers.

But it is more strongly associated with blood. When Quentin asks Caddy whether she loves Dalton, her answer is to place Quentin's hand against her throat and say "Dalton Ames": "I felt the first surge of blood there it surged in strong accelerating beats say it again her face looked off into the trees where the sun slanted and where the bird say it again Dalton Ames the blood surged steadily beating and beating against my hand . . ." (*SF*, 128). Quentin rejects this, but finds, when he closes his eyes, the very redness of his eyelids a testimony to what in her is also in him.

In Quentin's final monologue, stimuli bring into consciousness whole sections of the past which reel off before our eyes. Yet Quentin can do something with these memories, as Benjy could not. He amalgamates them with other memories and impressions. But his creative powers have been turned against the very stream of his own life. Like Benjy, Quentin rejects the part of Caddy that is changing; like Benjy, too, Quentin is dependent on order and routine. His habit memory helps him avoid, through most of the day on which he kills himself, thinking about what he is actually doing. To the end, he goes through with a routine of dressing; his last thought is that he had forgotten to brush his hat, but Shreve had a brush, so he wouldn't "have to open the bag any more" (*SF*, 139). Sealing up the past as best he can, so he won't have to deal with it, Quentin exits through the one door left.

Quentin struggles with his fear of the "blood" by turning it into a quest for permanence. Though Mr. Compson is obtuse about Quentin's dilemma, he is at least right that Quentin seeks "an apotheosis in which a temporary state of mind will become symmetrical above the flesh" (*SF*, 138). That is, Quentin seems to think he can "arrange" life in some pattern that will last, and in an act of self-immolation, blow the flame of life "cleanly out along the cool eternal dark instead of lying there trying not to think of the swing" (*SF*, 137). Finally, Quentin correctly identifies the source of flux and carnality as his own consciousness, and eliminates it, just as in *Absalom, Absalom!* he will project himself into two characters, Bon and Henry, one of whom kills the other to prevent his sleeping with the sister, Judith.

The river, in which "drowned things" float, is Quentin's Little Sister Death. Time the river is death and disease, yet life is "created by disease" (*SF*, 33). Clock time is the death of real time, yet Quentin finds he can think of nothing else, though he has torn the hands off his watch. As a child, he recalls, he tried to match the clicking of the clock in the classroom by counting with his fingers, always disappointed when he could not make his counting come out even with the clock's (*SF*, 68-69). He knows his impulse to control is killing, but cannot stop himself. Caddy is the incarnation of that force he fears, the unpredictability he cannot accept, yet cannot reject entirely (see *SF*, 138). The only way he can deal with his ambivalency is to turn Caddy into Little Sister Death so that he can enter her at the very moment he dies. Yet he agonizes: "Did you ever have a sister? Did you? Did you?" (*SF*, 61). Substitute tones of disgust for those of despair, and the sentence could be Jason's.

Mr. Compson says that in trying to escape unpredictability men will try any expedient, "from violence to petty chicanery" (*SF*, 138). Jason tries both. He is so busy saving time that he never has any, and so convinced that "time is money" that he has little cash, either. Like Quentin, Jason wants control. He turns his repression away from himself, however, and onto Caddy and her daughter, Quentin.

Jason does not see the absurdity of his routinized responses: "Once a bitch, always a bitch, what I say," he begins (*SF*, 140). He is bigoted, claiming to have nothing "against the jews as an individual" without hearing the self-contradiction (*SF*, 149). He has no respect for his mother. He just agrees with Mrs. Compson that his father made a mistake in thinking his children "didn't need controlling": "I always told your father," says Mrs. Compson, "that they were allowed too much freedom." Quentin, she adds, "could have controlled Caddy" if he had tried—showing how unaware of Quentin's relationship to Caddy she really is. Jason, agreeing that Quentin could have controlled Caddy through her respect for him, muses: "Too bad it wasn't me instead of him. You'd be a lot better off" (*SF*, 202-3).

Jason's general response to people is to threaten them; he threatens to beat Quentin with his belt (*SF*, 144). He is constantly warning her: "You do a thing like that again and I'll make you sorry you ever drew breath" (*SF*, 146). To his girl friend, Lorraine, who lives in Memphis, he claims he says, "If you ever try to call me up on the telephone, Memphis won't hold you" (*SF*, 151). Faced with a female, threatening is the only response Jason practices, the only way he can find to "manage them": "Always keep them guessing. If you can't think of any other way to surprise them, give them a bust in the jaw" (*SF*, 150). He encourages Mrs. Compson to burn the checks Caddy sends for Quentin's welfare, just as he cut up the paper dolls Caddy and Benjy made together.

Jason bullies everyone, but he is indeed a man "so smart he cant even keep up wid hisself" (*SF*, 194). He can't stand the thought that he has become a fool who has "been robbed by Quentin, his niece, a bitch" (*SF*, 240). He defines himself in the same terms he does others, by social appearances and prejudices. Bergson notes that there exists

below the self with well-defined states, a self in which *succeeding each other* means *melting into one another* and forming an organic whole. But we are generally content with the first, i.e., with the shadow of the self projected into homogeneous space. Consciousness, goaded by an insatiable desire to separate, substitutes the symbol for the reality, or perceives the reality only through the symbol. As the self thus re-

fracted, or broken into pieces, is much better adapted to the requirements of social life in general and language in particular, consciousness
prefers it, and gradually loses sight of the fundamental self. [*TFW*,
128-29]

This social adaptation becomes ineffective when it loses contact
with the inner self, for "the mechanism by which we only meant at
first to explain our conduct will end by also controlling it," and "automatism will cover over freedom" (*TFW*, 237). Jason is out of control precisely because he obsessively seeks it.

Thus his wrath bounces right back at him. Stung by the loss of
the money—he thinks nothing, naturally, of the money he has sto-
len from Quentin herself—he thinks he pursues with "cunning";
actually, he "blunders on," confronting an old man. Finding he has
released the old man's fury, he can't extricate himself. Finally, he has
to hit the man, knocking him down, but not out, with a "clumsy,
hurried blow." Having flubbed his chance to find out whether
Quentin is in the circus train area, he runs from the railroad car:
"His breath made a hah hah hah sound and he stood there trying
to repress it" (*SF*, 241). This twisted vitality has its last laugh, however, The puny old man clubs Jason from behind with a hatchet.
"What were you trying to do?" asks the man who has rescued Jason
from the old man, "Commit suicide?" And Jason is, in a way, as
suicidal as Quentin. Inflexible and full of anger at life, he becomes
the victim of his own life-denying mentality. His last words are to
Luster: "If you ever cross that gate with [Benjy] again, I'll kill you"
(*SF*, 249).

Corpses and Copers

The Bundrens of *As I Lay Dying* do not sense disaster any better
than the Compsons, though they too are confronted literally with a
corpse. They end up replacing it with a woman who has the distinction of owning a graphophone. Like *The Sound and the Fury*,
the novel gives us a glimpse into the lives of three older brothers
who have no sympathy for their pregnant sister; and one of these is
a supersensitive young man with important affinities to his sister
and to his youngest brother. *As I Lay Dying* also lets individual

voices speak to us of the conflict between the visceral and the visual, the blood and the patterning that seeks to become "symmetrical above the flesh."

The monologue technique has expanded, however, to become a virtuoso performance. There are fifty-nine short sections, delivered by fifteen different narrators. The effect on the reader of visiting so many separate cells is a great feeling of loneliness and isolation. The character who most often speaks, Darl, symbolizes that feeling. Darl ends in being shipped off to the mental hospital at Jackson, estranged both from his family and himself.[10] Repeated acts of selfishness and insensitivity emphasize the agony of this isolation. The novel's world is one of "doing," we seem to be told, which has insulated itself from the creative imagination that alone has power to make doing signify. Darl's mutable consciousness is unable to cope with the world, which becomes the property of "copers," who, like Cash, cut things always on the bevel. Dewey Dell, a sort of halfway point between Caddy and Lena Grove, hasn't much chance of sympathetic treatment in this world of hard corners, but she is not, like Caddy, destroyed by her mistreatment; we are led to believe that her refusal to give up in some way guarantees her survival.

Just as Quentin and Benjy exhibit varieties of the Compsons' childish response to Caddy's growing up, so Vardaman and Darl offer a crucial touchstone in the array of the Bundren family's responses to Addie's death. Of the fifty-nine short monologues, Vardaman delivers ten, Darl nineteen. The only other characters with more than three sections are Tull (six) and Cash (five). Toward the end of the book, Darl and Vardaman have a sequence of seven alternating sections, and, indeed, seven of Vardaman's ten sections come directly before or after one of Darl's. Together, Darl and Vardaman account for ten of the last sixteen sections of the book. To Darl we constantly recur, and the conjunction of Darl and Vardaman makes the novel's readers aware that the childish response is playing itself out in most of the characters. Darl and Vardaman are specifically placed side by side and made continuous in their last sections of the book, when Darl carries on Vardaman's monologue, using childish diction. First, Vardaman has been thinking about Darl's being taken away: "*He had to get on the train to go to Jackson.*

I have not been on the train, but Darl has been on the train. Darl. Darl is my brother. Darl. Darl (*ALD*, 175). Turning the page, we read the title of the next section as though it were still Vardaman's voice: "DARL." And then Darl himself picks up the thread: "Darl has gone to Jackson. They put him on the train laughing. . . . Darl is our brother, our brother Darl" (*ALD*, 176-77).

Darl is ultimately brought to a child's level of functioning, uttering a Benjy-like babble which he separates from himself as another's voice. He "foams. Yes yes yes yes yes yes yes" (*ALD*, 177). We recall that Jason would have sent Benjy to Jackson if he could (*SF*, 204). Indeed, Jason's very name lacks only a sound to become "Jackson," where brothers become zoo keepers.

Addie is a more problematic and enigmatic character than Mrs. Compson; she has only one section to herself, quite late in the book. But she is still more obviously the family's "albatross." Addie is the author of this "journey" to Jefferson, and seems to have been motivated by revenge (*ALD*, 116). She is, then, one of those who tries to impose a pattern—though one should immediately admit her loyalties are divided. The pattern she imposes does not, one would think, work out quite as she had imagined. She misjudges the invulnerability of Anse, who has "eyes like pieces of burnt-out cinder" and shoes that "look as though they had been hacked with a blunt axe out of pig-iron" (*ALD*, 20, 8). Addie, the precursor of Joanna Burden, glories in her relationship with Tull, but ends in seeing it as the fulfillment of a pattern her father had programmed for her in childhood: "The reason for living is getting ready to stay dead" (*ALD*, 114, 118).

Addie ends, then, not in sticking with her responsibility to the living, but rather in trying to "shape and coerce the blood to the forlorn echo of the dead word high in the air" (*ALD*, 118). Her offspring have the same problems she does in getting thought and action, feeling and doing, together. Like the Compsons, they are a self-destructive lot; yet their problems are not holdovers from a previous age, but new ones symbolized by the town itself toward which they wend. In Tull's words, they are going to town more out of an instinctive selfishness than because they must fulfill the obligation laid on them by Addie: "They would risk the fire and earth and the

water and all just to eat a sack of bananas" (*ALD*, 92). That primitive appetite is a big part of what appalled Addie during her life-
time.

Addie is presented as many quantities in *As I Lay Dying*. For
Cash, she is "animal magnetism in a wooden box" (*ALD*, 53). Vardaman deals with her death by turning her into a fish—he cannot
otherwise come to grips with her carnality (not spirit, but meat).
Darl tells us that Jewel's horse was his mother, implying that he has
no love for his real mother. To Anse, Addie is simply part of the
household furniture. He is married again within a couple of days of
the family's arrival in Jefferson. Vardaman, despite his anguish over
his mother's death, is already metamorphosing in the direction of
his father, is "almost old enough now to be selfish and stonehearted
like the rest of them" (*ALD*, 14). He has a model train on his mind
the whole way to Jefferson. Only Darl, as Cora Tull notes, has any
of the feminine qualities that one presumes experience hammered
out of Addie herself: "I always said he was the only one of them
that had his mother's nature, had any natural affection" (*ALD*, 13).
Cora may be mistaken in thinking Darl the inheritor of a feminine
nature, just as she seems to have been mistaken in her evaluation of
Addie's character; but there can be no doubt that Darl represents
what Anse and his kin are driving away, just as Caddy was driven
from the Compson household.

Darl goes mad in the end. Why? First, there is the gap between
the appearance of this journey and its reality. As the sacrilege deep-
ens, and Addie's body—like her memory—grows corrupt, Darl revolts. He sets fire to the barn in which the coffin lies. Vardaman
sees him do it. The furious Jewel rescues the corpse that has become an excuse for a selfish journey. (The family tries to ignore the
stench that everyone else finds evidently appalling.) Anse takes
away Dewey's money, which she desperately needs for an abortion.
He and the others almost cause Cash to lose his broken leg when
they pour cement over it to hold it rigid—and here's another symbol
for the materialism of the Bundrens. The whole family turns on
Darl in the end. Vardaman has told Dewey of Darl's arson, a crime
Cash admits he thought of committing himself. We know that
Dewey probably betrayed Darl to Gillespie, the barn's owner, even

after admonishing Vardaman to keep the secret. And when the men come to take Darl away, she leaps on him furiously, and has to be held back. Cash finds this puzzling, commenting that he had thought Dewey and Darl "kind of knowed things betwixt them" (*ALD*, 163).

Here lies the second reasons for Darl's madness. He has an intuition of Dewey's love. Darl and Dewey are psychically close. So when Dewey makes love to Lafe, Darl knows all about it: "I saw Darl and he knew. He said he knew without the words like he told me that ma is going to die without words, and I knew he knew because if he had said he knew with the words I would not have believed that he had been there and saw us. But he said he did know and I said 'Are you going to tell pa are you going to kill him?' without words I said it and he said 'Why?' without the words. And that's why I can talk to him with knowing and hating because he knows" (*ALD*, 16-17). Darl later confirms: "I knew about Dewey Dell on that day" (*ALD*, 89). He seems to accept Dewey's making love to Lafe—we cannot know exactly what he is thinking about this, but he gives Dewey no sign that he will hold the knowledge over her head as a threat or otherwise try to come between her and her lover. Yet Dewey expects Darl not to like it: "Are you going to kill him?" She hates him not for what he knows, but for what he feels, and we find out later on that Darl has after all, like Quentin and Benjy, come between his sister and her lover: "Darl came between me and Lafe," Dewey Dell tells us, but does not elaborate (*ALD*, 37). Dewey believes her brother has this incestuous love, and senses his eyes as "swimming to pinpoints. They begin at my feet and rise along my body to my face, and then my dress is gone" (*ALD*, 78).

When Darl is finally loaded on the train, he recurs to this incestuous desire: "Two men put him on the train . . . the state's money has a face to each backside and a backside to each face, and they are riding on the state's money which is incest. A nickel has a woman on one side and a buffalo on the other; two faces and no back. I don't know what that is. Darl had a little spy-glass he got in France at the war. On it it had a woman and a pig with two backs and no face. I know what that is. Is that why you are laughing Darl?

'Yes yes yes yes yes yes'" (*ALD*, 176). For Darl, as for Quentin, the beast with two backs is a terrible revelation. This inability to cope with repressed sexual desires connects directly to a more general inability to accept "the womb of time: the agony and the despair of spreading bones, the hard girdle in which lie the outraged entrails of events" (*ALD*, 78). Cash and Darl lie at opposite ends of the spectrum, symbols of a deeply divided self. Cash: "I made it on the bevel. . . . It makes a neater job." Darl: "It is as though the space between us were time: an irrevocable quality" (*ALD*, 53, 96).

John T. Irwin has discussed Darl's ambivalency toward Dewey Dell in *Doubling and Incest* (1975).[11] He concentrates on the split within Darl, however. I think we cannot see the profundity of the division between inner and outer life with the sort of reading Irwin proposes, nor can we easily explain the particular pathologies of these characters. Faulkner announces himself, with *As I Lay Dying* and the Jason section of *The Sound and the Fury*, as the transcriber of automatism's black comedy: "Automatism covers over freedom" could be the motto here. Characters in subsequent novels tread ever more bizarre territory.

In *Sanctuary*, for example, Popeye's cruelty and impotence seem to electrify Temple Drake and turn her from a silly and unpredict-able brat into a sexual robot. Twisted, malnourished, and impotent, Popeye mutilates the world, cutting up birds and kitten with scis-sors as though they were pieces of paper (*S*, 244). Brought up in Simon McEachern's closed system of life, Joe Christmas also devel-ops perverse allegiances: He learns to prefer the dead but predict-able male world to the frighteningly unpredictable female—and he associates the female world with the primitivism of the "niggers." After attacking the negro slut in the shed, Joe stops to think "how he and the man could always count upon one another, depend upon one another; that it was woman alone who was unpredictable" (*LA*, 117). This war on unpredictability does have its comic side. (Berg-son's theory of comedy seems as though it were written with Faulk-ner in mind.) But finally, the disjunctions and meanness of Jason, the dimwittedness and literalness of Cash, however absurd, have dark consequence.

The Mechanisms of Memory

Joe and McEachern have strong sensations of inevitability because their system excludes the unpredictable by *fiat*. Free choice cannot whelm them with responsibility, for they live an authoritarian, mechanical, routinized, and objectified life centered on ritual and dogma. They are cold to each other. The threat of pollution from without, however, unites them against the feminine and the black. For Joe, this is a life-struggle, for he finds he must kill the very part of himself that might have been free. When McEachern is about to punish him, Joe wishes Mrs. McEachern would not interfere: "She would try to get herself between him and the punishment which, deserved or not, just or unjust, was impersonal, both the man and the boy accepting it as natural and inescapable fact until she, getting in the way, must give it an odor, an attenuation, and aftertaste" (*LA*, 123). Joe's violence to the slut is only understandable in terms of his need for certainty; in her he fears he recognizes a part of himself he cannot accept. Faulkner suggested this is Joe's tragedy: that he cannot know who he is (*FIU*, 72). And Regina Fadiman discovered that, in revising *Light in August*, Faulkner carefully "increased the ambiguity about Christmas's Negro blood," not because he wanted to confuse his readers, but because he wanted to focus attention on Christmas's self-doubt, which overrode everything in his life and ended in self-destruction.[12]

Joe's self-destruction is directly involved in his rigidifying, spatializing consciousness, the one that makes closed patterns, banishing all indeterminacy in an apotheosis of framing. A closed system, may be thought of as "action confined in a circle," according to Bergson (*TS*, 56). And *Light in August* carefully distinguishes between the entrapment of Joe and the linear journey of Lena, the only character who seems to be getting somewhere. The circle is not used in the book exclusively as a symbol for the closed self refusing to grow, nor as the only symbol of life-denying closure. Only when circles are considered as flat patterns—as, in other words, geometric figures—do they play this role in the thought of Joe, Doc Hines, McEachern, and other characters of madness and frustration. When Joe finally arrives at the moment "something" is going to happen (he will kill Joanna Burden), he has a feeling that events are profoundly out of his hands: " . . . the dark was filled with the voices, myriad, out of all time he had known, as though the past was a flat pattern. And going on: tomorrow night, all the tomorrows, to be part of that flat pattern, going on. He thought of that with quiet astonishment: going on, myriad, familiar, since all that he had ever been was the same as all that was to be, since tomorrow to-be and had-bcen would be the same. Then it was time" (*LA*, 208). Here is the self-fulfilling nihilism of "sound and fury," the never-ending pattern of tomorrow and tomorrow and tomorrow in which Joe is caught. His is the sort of time that has given up its birthright of freedom, the kind that Sartre described as "decapitated" because it removes the possibility for "free choice and act."[13]

Joe resists unsuccessfully this view of time in which nothing can be murdered or created and which builds a prison through spatializing the "feel" of reality. He senses it as a street which "ran for thirty years. . . . It has made a circle and he is still inside it" (*LA*, 252). The undeviating corridor becomes a circle, for it leads back on itself; it is a solipsistic universe—light bending and bending until there is nothing visible outside the narrow scope of the eye's beam. Joe is doomed to run the same loop of film through the projector; but he has chosen the film. Though it isn't completely his fault, he must pay the price for never having "broken out of the ring of what I have already done and can't even undo" (*LA*, 252).

Other characters experience something like Joe's madness without his awareness. Doc Hines and his wife are dramatic examples of the "decapitation" Sartre reacts against. They respond completely out of their habitual memories, reeling off preprogrammed behavior without reference to the past. The healthy consciousness moves flexibly between habit and memory, but, as Bergson notes, not all consciousnesses maintain good health: "A human being who should dream his life instead of living it would no doubt keep before his eyes at each moment the infinite multitude of the details of his past history. And, on the other hand, the man who should repudiate this memory with all that it begets would continually act his life instead of consciously representing it to himself: a conscious automaton, he would follow the lead of . . . habits" (*MM*, 201). *Light in August* seems filled with the latter type. Hines and his wife have "something puppetlike about them, as if they were operated by clumsy springwork" (*LA*, 274). When Hines talks, his voice starts up in full stride, then stops "exactly like a needle is lifted from a phonograph by the hand of someone who is not listening to the record" (*LA*, 276).

The key to this madness is its tunnel-vision. The dietitian who thinks Joe may reveal she has had a man in her room is possessed by this flat-patterned mentality, which seems always to hinge on bigotry. She finds her "life seemed straight and simple as a corridor" which leads her to another madman, the janitor, who steals Christ-mas and tries to put him in an orphanage for blacks (*LA*, 93). Joanna Burden, too, seems "to see her whole past life . . . like a gray tunnel at the far and irrevocable end of which . . . her naked breast of three short years ago ached in agony, virgin and crucified" (*LA*, 196). Joanna is preparing for a foregone conclusion, the natural outcome of her bigoted background. For McEachern, too, "bigotry and clairvoyance were practically one" (*LA*, 148). The utter convic-tion of McEachern, like that of Hines, is self-fulfilling, absolving him of the need for choice and assuring him of the same self-crucifixion that prepares for Joe and Joanna. McEachern, who rides straight to the dance-hall to find Joe, though he could never have rationally deduced where Joe was, thinks of himself as suddenly being called on stage to play a role he has rehearsed for years. He is like "a martyr who has already been absolved" (*LA*, 151). He takes satisfaction in this self-created hell, in which, to use Bergson's phrase, "we speak, rather than think; we 'are acted' rather than act ourselves" (*TFW*, 231).

Joe's is a self-crucifixion, as well; the intellectual functions of this mind have caged and pilloried the intuitive human functions. The result is automatic behavior, as when he goes to see Bobbie "with-out plan or design, almost without volition, as if his feet ordered his action and not his head" (*LA*, 130, 131). Cleanth Brooks interprets Joe's mechanical "clairvoyance" as part of an intuitive conscious-ness, but Joe's foresight is not fundamentally different from Mc-Eachern's or even Percy Grimm's.[14] It is just that Joe provides the reader some access to the workings beneath the surface, to the struggles of the real self resisting its shadow, the automatic network of responses. For Joe, the only escape is directly through the pattern of transgression and punishment that originated in the McEachern household and in his mother's upbringing. In childhood, Joe had learned to dissociate his mind from his body and to take pleasure in his own unresponsiveness. When McEachern would beat him, Joe felt like a piece of "wood or stone; a post or tower upon which the sentient part of him mused like a hermit, contemplative and remote with ecstasy and self-crucifixion" (*LA*, 118). Hightower is the witness to Joe's final "ecstasy" when the responsibility for choice has finally been lifted completely. Joe finally achieves peace when the "pent black blood" rushes out of him "like a released breath" (*LA*, 346).

Gail Hightower has also reacted against life. But rather than seeking the escape of McEachern in mechanical responses, High-tower lives "dissociated from mechanical time" (*LA*, 262). His intuition dominates over his intellect, and he is like those Bergson described as "dreaming" their lives. Though he achieves a vision of sorts, he has lived a life out of balance, dwelling on and in a past that, as Bergson says, "has not ceased to exist; it has only ceased to be useful" (*MM*, 193). "Useless" memories occupy Hightower, and he loses his wife and congregation because of his escapism. Doc Hines lives in a purely unconscious state of motor responses; Hightower hovers far above the plane of experience, musing, out of touch with reality.

Faulkner suggested Hightower and Joe are opposites.[15] In an important sense, Joe's psychic position is opposite to Hightower's. Joe cannot know where he came from; Hightower cannot forget. Bergson compares the conscious mind's mediation between memory and present perception to a telephone switchboard, letting in the appropriate associations from pure memory, hooking up the right responses to everyday stimuli from habitual memory—putting the past and present in touch. The past hovers around us like *Matter and Memory*'s cone, forcing "itself upon [us] . . . under one form or another" (*MM*, 193). But how conscious of its presence, how open to its becoming present are we?

When Joe consciously seeks memory, the process is painfully mechanical. In the dark of Joanna Burden's kitchen, Joe searches his memory for the name of the food he eats, but cannot see. Joe is in the darkness of Bergson's "pure present" here, with no visual access to the visceral experience. He eats "from an invisible dish, with invisible fingers: invisible food." He asks, "What is that taste?": "*I have eaten it before, somewhere. In a minute I will* memory clicking knowing *I see I see I more than see hear I hear I see my head bent I hear the monotonous voice which I believe will never cease going on and on forever and peeping I see the indomitable bullet head the clean blunt beard they too bent and I thinking How can he be so nothungry and I smelling my mouth and tongue weeping the hot salt of waiting my eyes tasting the hot steam from the dish* 'It's peas,' he said aloud" (*LA*, 170-71). One can hardly wait for Joe's switchboard—"memory clicking knowing"—finally to make the connection. Joe is strangely a "foreigner to the very immutable laws which earth must obey" because he has learned to hold the world so profoundly at bay, to spatialize, never to touch. He is like "the unswimming sailor," whose "thought had been molded by [the country's] compulsions without his learning anything about its actual shape and feel" (*LA*, 251).

Hightower has also given up free choice; but his path lies in the opposite direction from Joe's. In a metaphor which reminds one strongly of Bergson's cone of memory, Faulkner describes Hightower's preaching—his monologue to himself—as a kind of dream: "not a nightmare, but something which went faster than the words in the Book; a sort of cyclone that did not even need to touch the actual earth" (*LA*, 44). Christmas is locked in the visual "flat pattern" world "without dimension," which I have equated with Bergson's "Plane of Experience," where habit memory operates (*LA*, 279). Hightower, in contrast, never descends out of the cloud of pure memory. There can be no doubt that Hightower's pure memory is Bergson's. It is at once detached from and yet completely organized by clock and calendar time—a visionary's amalgam of religion, personal experience, and a grandfather's fabled war exploits, but yet inherently ordered in time. "He lives dissociated from mechanical time. Yet for that reason he has never lost it. It is as though out of his subconscious he produces without volition the few crystallizations of stated instances by which his dead life in the actual world has been governed and ordered once. Without recourse to clock he could know immediately upon the thought just where, in his old life, he would be and what doing" (*LA*, 272).

Hightower's perfectly ordered memories are anything but accurate when they touch on present things. It is his old, dead life, with which he no longer has contact, that supplies the order. When he consciously seeks the past, it is as an escape. That escape is imperfect, as he discovers. Bergson has suggested that the man who seeks release through escape into the "dream" of pure memory finds that "the past to which he returns is fugitive, ever on the point of escaping him, as though his backward turning memory were thwarted by the other, more natural memory of which the forward movement bears him on into action and to life" (*MM*, 94).

Light in August describes Hightower's attempted re-entry into life, a moment of intuition when Christmas dies that makes him conscious of the futility of what he has called "living." Hightower comes to see his life was "stillborn": "I had already died one night twenty years before I saw light" (*LA*, 355). He must somehow return to contact with experience, bring the past down with him out of the clouds. As Joe must struggle to escape mechanism, Hightower must struggle to escape his dreams: "He had grown up with a ghost," his grandfather (*LA*, 357). He tries to bring together the two severed wireends of memory: "the two instants about to touch" which are first pure memory ("the sum of his life") and second habit memory, or that point at which the real body contacts real experience ("the suspended instant out of which the *soon* will presently begin") (*LA*, 362).

Hightower knows that his sin is in a way worse than that of those who have simply repressed their creative life. Hightower has failed to engage. As he comes to grips with his own guilt and responsibility, he sees a vision of life's forward push—the *élan vital*.[16] His face and the faces of all those he has known become something like Eliot's "compound ghost," both composite and recognizable; the faces are a unity, fixed on a wheel of life that finally breaks free of a backward-dragging force. Lena, her child, Byron, Christmas, even Grimm, take their places in this pattern of the free-spinning wheel.

Hightower achieves this intuition only after having reached a state of extreme detachment—again, the parallel with Bergson is clear. His body seems "empty and lighter than a *forgotten* leaf" (*LA*, 366; italics mine). He finally comes down out of the cloud, "so that it can be now   Now." The lack of punctuation and the spacing remind us of Addie's "gap," and assert an indescribability about the moment. Hightower then sees his own vision of the cavalry charge return, transfigured: "They sweep into sight, borne now upon a cloud of phantom dust. They rush past, forwardleaning in the saddles, with brandished arms, beneath whipping ribbons from slanted and eager lances . . . and the brandished arms of men like the crater of the world in explosion" (*LA*, 367). At last Hightower has seen his fantasies in their true relation to the world's volcanic energy; futile and valiant, these riders move forward on the crest of a huge wave of energy, unified by self-inflicted suffering and self-denial, but never stopping.

Hightower's vision is patently Bergsonian. In *Creative Evolution* Bergson writes: "All the living . . . yield to the same tremendous push. The animal takes its stand on the plant, man bestrides animality, and the whole of humanity, in space and time, is one immense army galloping beside and before and behind each of us in an overwhelming charge" (*CE*, 271). This is Hightower's illumination, the intuition which fixes him in his room. However short a time it lasts, it is emphatically not the denial of his previous maunderings; it is a realization he has about life's "push." It is a stirring in his consciousness of unconscious processes which will become a "dream of history" evoked in rich detail by *Absalom, Absalom!* Hightower has his moment in and out of time in the "lambent suspension of August" (*LA*, 365-66). Remarkably, he appears to read its meaning correctly and to know what by this "light" he is required to do: admit imperfection and rejoin the living.

Bergson and American Modernism

❖   For consciously "modern" writers in America during the period between the wars, technology and its muse, Science, seemed
on a path toward spiritual impoverishment and disaster. As the gap
between body and soul widened, that literature recorded the dissociations—the *dédoublement* of the self—but it also held out hope
of a path back to wholeness. This, at its simplest level, is what Bergson personified to American artists like Faulkner, William Carlos
Williams, Frost, Wolfe, Henry Miller, and Gertrude Stein. They
responded equally or more strongly than the generation of British
artists considering the same sorts of problems: Joyce, Woolf, the
later Yeats. In the end, Bergson reasserted a traditional potency for
art, and his aesthetic stands in the Kantian tradition, drawing parallels between religious and aesthetic experience, explaining the
meaning of ritual and habit, offering a means to regenerate continually decaying creative impulses.

Bergson's meaning to American writers is not really separable
from the meaning to them of Eliot's career and the emergence of
such works as *The Golden Bough* and *From Ritual to Romance*. By
attempting to go back to the roots of culture and experience, Bergson helped American writers to define their reaction against the

trend of the time. He offered the terms of an argument which critics like Ransom picked up and used. And one finds the terms appearing in the prose writings of poets whose criticism is less orthodox and more strident than Ransom's or (even) Tate's—like William Carlos Williams.

Williams published *In the American Grain* in 1925, and he clearly had been affected by the same complex of issues affecting other poets of the period:

Men are trained never to possess fully but just to SEE. This makes scientists and it makes masochists.

Deanimated, that's the word: something the sound of 'metronome,' a mechanical means; Yankee inventions. Machines were not so much to save time as to save dignity that fears the animate touch.

Our life drives us apart and forces us on science and invention—away from touch.[1]

Williams's dislike for science's visualizing and his assertion of art's visceral character—especially that it gives a wholeness—is part of the Bergsonian argument. Indeed, Williams expressed genuinely anti-intellectual, and more, genuinely anti-rational convictions at different stages of his career, in prose and verse. The position, as it turns out, is inseparable from his view of time. For Williams, "touch" restores past to present. *In the American Grain* might be thought of as a kind of rescue operation. It wants to restore the past in an imaginative act, in which living mind meets and melds with the universe of its own cultural memory.

Williams's concept of history is doublesided: It looks from one view like a dead end, always present. But history may be freedom, as well as servitude. There are two very different patterns into which "history" may be seen to organize our experience. One is closed: "That's history," says Williams. "It is concerned only with one thing: to say everything is dead." But the other is not: "History must stay open, it is all humanity." Williams insists on the Bergsonian principle that the past exists, is as durable as anything else physically present in our world. "That of the dead which exists in our imaginations has as much fact as have we ourselves. The premise that serves to fix us fixes also that part of them which we remember" (*Grain*, 188). To recognize ideas here paralleling roughly ideas in Eliot's "Little Gidding" is to recognize the confluence of apparently diverse writers. They are working on a similar problem, the origins and resources of freedom, with similar tools. Williams finds those resources accessible only through our getting back in touch with ourselves (a very Bergsonian proposition): "[History] lives in us practically day by day. . . . If it is, as it may be, tyranny over the souls of the dead—and so the imaginations of the living—where lies our greatest well of inspiration, our greatest hope of freedom (since the future is totally blank, if not black) we should guard it doubly against interlopers" (*Grain*, 189). Williams argues that history must be reclaimed for freedom. In this, he joins other American writers of the period who are convinced that life has been conceived of as pattern rather than experience.

History as memory is not deadening. Rather, it is the vital "fountain" of life: "You mean tradition. Yes, nothing there is metaphysical. It is the better part of all of us. It is the fountain! But men, never content in the malice with which they surround each living moment, must extend their illwill backward, jealous even of a freedom in the past, to maim and destroy there too" (*Grain*, 189). Like Faulkner, Miller, even like Anderson, Williams conceives of the living present as surrounded by backward-dragging forces. And as much as *Absalom, Absalom!*, *In the American Grain* has sought to get tradition (history *resartus*) into its very language. Williams's prose tries to get the vitality, immediacy of the past onto the page, to contrast it sharply with the assassination performed by analysis, chronology, and biography.

For Williams, history is not patterns—or if it is, they are patterns of *meanings*. And meanings, as Eliot wrote in his doctoral dissertation, cannot be "merely contemplated, but must be *erlebt*" (*KE*, 94). This *erlebnis* (experience) falls through the cracks of scientific inquiry. American writers like Williams and Frost saw the opportunity this presented them: to develop a different sort of "knowing," one that might heal the divisions in modern life, mitigate the alienation of American culture from even the little past it could recover, and restore some vitality to literary activity—put it back in the cultural mainstream. This, too, was the goal of Thomas Wolfe, who often failed to establish controls over the stream of his own creative force.

Wolfe's career has been judged a magnificent failure on all sorts of grounds, but clearly the most important has been lack of structure in his narratives, a lack chiefly caused, a consensus argues, by the overwhelming force of the egotistical musing that marks his style so deeply. Wolfe's world, as it is revealed in *Look Homeward, Angel*, is haunted by "the ghostly ticking of his life." He is obsessed with the Bergsonian polarity between flux and "cuttings":

And it was this that awed him—the weird combination of fixity and change, the terrible moment of immobility stamped with eternity in which, passing life at great speed, both the observer and the observed seem frozen in time. There was one moment of timeless suspension in which the land did not move, the train did not move, the slattern in the doorway did not move, he did not move. It was as if God had lifted his baton sharply above the endless orchestration of the seas, and the eternal movement had stopped, suspended in the timeless architecture of the absolute. Or like those motion-pictures that describe the movements of a swimmer making a dive, or a horse taking a hedge—movement is petrified suddenly in mid-air, the inexorable completion of an act is arrested. Then, completing its parabola, the suspended body plops down into the pool. Only, these images that burnt in him existed without beginning or ending, without the essential structure of time. Fixed in no-time, the slattern vanished, fixed, without a moment of transition.[2]

As J.B. Priestley suggested, Wolfe's writing does not "go on and on and on" so much as "hold a scene and go in and in and in."[3]

The longing, that is to say, is directly related to an intense and sometimes even maniacal clutching for the Moment. Whether exhorting us, or word-painting, Wolfe stays on this polarity between clock-time and experienced time, the ways in which we are "robbed" of our own existence. That is not to minimize the importance of Wolfe's grappling with his own past, trying to come to terms with it and incorporate it in his literary world. But his rhetoric aims constantly, as Maurice Natanson has said, at the "articulation of reality through privileged moments," an articulation whose chief imperative seems to be "Look! See!"⁴ This re-vision of American experience is obsessed not merely with the Moment, but with the sources for vitality, the means to combat "death-in-life," as Wolfe repeatedly names it.

Bergson has everything to do with the approach of Wolfe and Williams, whether they read him deeply or not. Their careers hardly make sense unless we recreate the context of American literary discussion in the twenties and thirties with Bergson in mind. The number of those participating in the discussion was large. Many were even directly influenced by their reading of Bergson in translation: Stein, Frost, and Henry Miller, for example.

Stein, of course, was in Paris, and she attended Bergson's lectures.⁵ That she was a student of William James is well known, but of her thoughts on and discussion of Bergson not a great deal has been said. Wyndham Lewis clearly identified Stein as of the school of "evolutionists"—James, Bergson, and Whitehead. And she shares with all these thinkers what Allegra Stewart has called a "sacramental view of human creativity."⁶ Stein's correspondence with Sherwood Anderson and her creation of the hermetic writings of her early career, like *Tender Buttons*, suggests that she was applying Bergsonian ideas about the renewal of language through "indirection" and the pursuit of the unique. Her influence on Anderson's career was profound, even if one sees it as a very diffuse sort of influence, because she helped him phrase to himself the sort of job an artist ought to be doing. And that job incorporates rather grand cultural ambitions.

Indeed, every American writer touched by the debate coming out of the Bergsonist phenomenon has such aspirations. The peculiarly American brand of that reaction seems to have been to do what Ransom, Stein, and Williams did: to take the issue as far as it could be taken. Some would say, for example, that in these writers, and perhaps in Wolfe and Faulkner, too, what one gets is not so much an encounter with the processes of the mind as an embrace with chaos. But while Stein's major works still receive some attention from contemporary criticism interested in philosophical and perceptual issues, Wolfe's is not seen as part of the same American literary impulse. They seem worlds apart. But they cannot be viewed in this way if one traces the roots of each back to a Vitalist trend of which Bergson is the logical symbol.

Many saw Bergson in just that way. Frost, for example, was affected deeply by *Creative Evolution*, which he had read with great excitement when the translation into English appeared in 1911.[7] It may be that Bergson helped Frost, as he had helped the Maritains and others, to sort out a religious quandary.[8] Bergson not only justified the idea of a hidden reality (in terms acceptable to Frost), but also made possible some realignment of evolutionary thought and the Bible. At least, Frost appears to have found in *Creative Evolution* an argument for the substantial value of a religious impulse, a way of viewing religion as experience rather than empty ritual. And Bergson offered new vitality to Frost as a poet, as well.

Frost's later view of freedom was clearly shaped in the period in which he read *Creative Evolution*. He was impressed, particularly, by Bergson's vision of the creatively evolving universe. The play impulse of "Birches" and "Blueberries" is perhaps the earliest expression in verse of Frost's clarity about the relative value of the openended activities against which intellect (in Bergson's terms) revolts. His poem "Accidentally on Purpose" (published in his last volume) records the lingering effect of Bergson's thinking. Here, evolution is said to have been "coded" from the beginning to produce humanity. Many poems of the twenties, like "The Grindstone," play upon the "grinding discord" of deadly habit and dull routine in opposition to the vital impulse toward freedom felt in the brain of the speaker: "I was for leaving something to the whetter." And "West-running Brook" explicitly says:

> Our life runs down in sending up the clock.
> The brook runs down in sending up our life.
> The sun runs down in sending up the brook.
> And there is something sending up the sun.
> It is this backward motion toward the source,
> Against the stream, that most we see ourselves in,
> The tribute of the current to the source.

The source for the theory behind these images has not been apparent to everyone. But it can be no other than Bergson's vision of the universe, a stream making itself across a stream unmaking itself.

Dorothy Judd Hall has said that Frost's whole career can be seen as "Bergsonian," a vision that "grew organically by freedom of association."[9] Whether we wish to go this far or not, certainly Frost responded to the "tension" inherent in Bergson's vision, the dualism in Bergson that it has been the purpose of this book to reintroduce for discussion by criticism. Frost himself knew that his discovery of Bergson in 1911 was an important moment for him as man and artist. And Henry Miller had a similar experience.

Miller, who described his early career to Lawrence Durrell as having been influenced "imponderably" by his reading of *Creative Evolution*, shares a great deal more with Faulkner than has generally been recognized.[10] He connects, for example, language and the womb to the sort of "timelessness" we associate with Bergsonian intuition. In *Tropic of Capricorn* (finally published in Paris in 1939) he writes: "The talk goes on, in that low throaty voice. No beginning, no end. I'm aware not of time nor the passing of time, but of timelessness. She's got the little womb in the throat hooked up to the big womb in the pelvis." Miller's whole *oeuvre*, with its intentionally confrontive graphicness, might be read as an assertion of the visceral over the visual, a search for the reality "in the blood and not in the stars," a reality in the voice—not seen through a telescope.[11] Like Faulkner, Miller sees human experience as a choice between acceptance and outrage. If Miller is also anxious to prove himself the picaresque hero of his own fiction, he is still, like Faulkner, promoting a view of the world in which acceptance of the self's creativity-in-decay is everything: "We can know the truth and accept it, or we can refuse knowledge of it and neither die nor be born again. In this manner it is possible to live forever, a negative life as solid and complete, or as dispersed and fragmentary, as the atom" (*Capricorn*, 334). Miller's anti-materialism, then, is both social and psychological, physical and metaphysical. Again and again he returns to the dialectic between feeling and seeing, grasping and visualizing, rebirth and atomization.

It is not possible, really, to make sense of the fragmentary and disjointed narratives reeling from the brain of his *persona* without reference to the Bergsonian aesthetic, one requiring the tension between two sorts of time, the purposeful disorientation of the reader's attention by arrangement of diverse materials pointing toward (but never naming) an ineffable experience.According to Miller's own formula, "thought and action" become one, "because swimming you are in it and of it, and it is everything you desire to be." The sensations one experiences reading *Tropic of Capricorn* are thus divided at the heart, for "you are fixed in a reality which permits the thought that nothing is fixed, that even the happiest and mightiest rock will one day be utterly dissolved and fluid as the ocean from which it was born" (*Capricorn*, 332).

In this book, Miller writes openly of the influence of Bergson upon him as an artist. He says that *Creative Evolution* helps explain both its thematic preoccupations and artistic strategy:

If [*Creative Evolution*] had not fallen into my hands at the precise moment it did, perhaps I would have gone mad. It came at a moment when another huge world was crumbling on my hands. If I had never understood a thing which was written in this book, if I have preserved only the memory of the word *creative*, it is quite sufficient. This word was my talisman. With it I was able to defy the whole world, and especially my friends. . . . The discovery of this book was equivalent to the discovery of a weapon. . . . It gave me the courage to stand alone, and it enabled me to appreciate loneliness. [*Capricorn*, 219]

What Miller had obviously found in Bergson's work was a clue to his essential divergence from the culture's mainstream. The book provided an argument from legitimate and open grounds for the importance of art, of the *open-ended* experience. And thus it really did serve Miller as a "talisman." "With *Creative Evolution* under my arm I board the elevated line at Brooklyn Bridge after work," he writes. To have this book is first of all to be accompanied on a lonely quest: "My language, my world is under my arm. I am the guardian of a great secret" (*Capricorn*, 222). The book served as a shibboleth to divide initiates in this mystery from those who, like Eliot's riders in the London tube, did not understand the nature of their own loss.

But *Creative Evolution* did after all provide the specific arguments and explanations discussed in the second chapter of this present book. And these Miller clearly absorbed. They led him, he tells us with characteristically inflated rhetoric, back to vitality, to life, to language. They offered a door that was better than just an escape; it was a means of fighting back:

[*Creative Evolution*] itself disappears from sight. . . . It is chewed alive, digested and incorporated into the system as flesh and blood which in turn creates new spirit and reshapes the world. It was a great communion feast which we shared in the reading of this book, and the outstanding feature of it was the chapter on Disorder which, having penetrated me through and through, has endowed me with such a marvellous sense of order that if a comet suddenly struck the earth and jarred everything out of place . . . I could orient myself to the new order in the twinkling of an eye. I have no fear or illusions about disorder any more than I have of death. [*Capricorn*, 221]

Miller's great secret, then, was the idea of order—that the deck was being constantly reshuffled, and that this itself was a principle of order in apparent chaos. His grasping in *Tropic of Capricorn* for an aesthetic device to render this constant reorientation of vision necessitated by experience depends upon ideas that are ubiquitous among American writers in the thirties—it is his own "dislocation of language" into his meaning.

Miller's promethean pose, his exaggeration, his taking the argument to the limit—these elements also make him part of the recognizably American reaction to Bergson's writings. Bergson summarizes thus (in the chapter to which Miller refers): "We must, by a strong recoil of our personality on itself, gather up our past which is slipping away, in order to thrust it, compact and undivided, into a present which it will create by entering" (*CE*, 200). Miller's recoil of personality creates the vision of a mad prophet wending his way deeper into the city's labyrinth of time; a saint of a different proportion, he offers a "communion" Eliot, among others, would almost certainly deny. Nonetheless, it parallels the graphic communion imaged in *Four Quartets*: "It was a great communion feast which we shared," Miller says.

Of course, one man's idea of what he shares with others is not

sufficient to prove a case. Moreover, we must finally judge for ourselves whether Faulkner was really influenced "by Bergson, obviously." But there is, as it turns out, a genuine consistency of approach, argumentation, and vocabulary among major American
writers between the wars; and that vocabulary emerges from a dialogue in which Bergson was the most important single voice. That
is why one can speak of such different writers as Miller, Eliot,
Faulkner, Williams, Frost, and Stein as sharing a Bergsonian impulse, for they are writing about his issue—about the possibility of
reasserting freedom for the human spirit in opposition to the devo-
tees of "pattern."

When Williams says "History must stay open," he means we
must conceive of the world with Miller's talisman under our arms,
conceive of it as a world not created, but creative. Stein echoes this
view when she writes "if you can *remember* it, it may be history, but
it is not historical."[12] The consciously "modern" American writer of
this century is compelled to present the results of his or her own
explorations in the labyrinth. This artist is also compelled to confront the claims of an aesthetic that requires a "pattern" of disorientation and reorientation outlined by Bergsonian philosophy. And
the consciously "modern" writer in America has a cause, a battle to
fight on two fronts: to assert the value of art, and simultaneously to
assert the value of the openended view of time and history. This is
what distinguishes Faulkner, to my mind, from the Naturalist tradition to which Conder has so ably connected him; his world is
haunted by automatism, but it points to something far beyond.

Bergson, whose career began with the attempt to defend the possibility of freedom and the reality of intuition, provides the tags—
the aesthetic and poetic. To understand American literature of the
period, one must understand him and the non-historical mode of
knowing he balanced against "clock-time." One must know of his
tremendous popularity and of the backlash against him among significant reactionary thinkers of the teens and twenties. One must
understand as well the workings of the *intuition philosophique*: an
act of will by which consciousness thrusts itself *outside itself*, so that
it can confront again the enigma of its own memory, too great to be
contained by the consciousness of which it is (supposedly) a part.

The independent life of our memories is directly connected to the Bergsonian idea of living history, and it places Bergson in the Augustinian tradition: "Yet is [memory] a power of mine, and belongs unto my nature; nor do I myself comprehend all that I am" (*Confessions*, X, 15). Intuition must avoid, then, the narrow rationalism of analysis to embrace data science dismisses as "subjective." To the rigor of science's laws, American Modernists opposed another rigor discovered in the doing. Whether they were aware of it or not—and many were not—their vocabulary lies in a direct descent from Augustine through Kant and Bergson.

Bergson also helps us to understand the cult of artistic "impersonality." According to him, the artist crafts image-patterns that do not express *him*, but call us to ourselves. The montage of *Capricorn* or *Absalom* or *The Waste Land* is aimed at this kind of impersonal effect. It asks that the reader hold in suspension his reading of the parts until the last syllable drops into place. The aesthetic effect attempted in these works tries, as Bergson says, to absorb the reader, to grab his hand and jerk him into a street dance. And yet it never loses sight of its doubleness: It, too, is a reality making itself in a materiality unmaking itself (*CE*, 251). The technique, like the vision, reminds us that creative impulses move across the backward-dragging "illwill" of *In the American Grain*, the "backward motion toward the source" of Frost's brook. We are reminded also that we are the "boats against the current" of Fitzgerald's *Gatsby*.[13] Our motion is of consequence, as Tate says, because it is a "resisted motion." Thus, the poem, like the human spirit itself, embodies a struggle against being drawn unwillingly "into the vortex of things by rigid natural laws."[14] This tension, this dual consciousness, characterizes the best of what we have come to call "modernist" writing. And Bergson played a determining role in the development of such a literature because he publicized, codified, and came personally to symbolize the new "time-awareness" of his age.

His aesthetics of intuition and tension, then, explain a great deal, often the detail as well as the broad thrust of such works. His aesthetic need not lead to an art at war with its own artificiality; instead, it suggests a way that artificiality may conduce to a victory, how art may, in a sense, keep itself open. By giving "outward expression to something of that contradiction, that interpenetration which is the very essence of the elements" of our psychic life, the artist may perform a crucial role in culture. Bergson's contribution to American literature between the wars is this key to the impor- tance of artistic creation, as much as it is a vision of creative life thrusting forward amid discouragements.

Bergson was essential to the development of American literary Modernism. That movement, as I see it, seeks to make readers con- scious of a truth of experience beyond similitudes; it actively makes us aware of the problematic nature of the text. It escapes skepticism, however, by laying emphasis upon the *process* by which we read, penetrating to and reincarnating meaning—renewing ourselves. That renewal seemed of such importance to Modernist writers that it became the subject as well as the object of their work. In tech- nique and theme, then, modern American literature is profoundly entangled with Bergson.

NOTES

Introduction

1. Leszek Kolakowski, *Bergson* (New York: Oxford Univ. Press, 1985), pp. 1-2.

2. Herman's, Gray's, Conder's, and Schwartz's books are listed in the selected bibliography. A recent example of an article in this field is Loretta Wasserman's "The Music of Time: Henri Bergson and Willa Cather," *American Literature* 57 (May 1985): 226-39.

3. Jonathan Culler, *Structuralist Poetics* (Ithaca: Cornell Univ. Press, 1975), p. 251.

4. John J. Conder, *Naturalism in American Fiction: The Classic Phase* (Univ. Press of Kentucky, 1984), p. 21.

5. T.E. Hulme, *Speculations: Essays in Humanism and the Philosophy of Art* (London: Kegan Paul, 1924), pp. 263-64, 157.

6. Frank Kermode, *Romantic Image* (New York: Macmillan, 1958), p. 130; my italics.

7. Lewis Mumford, *The Myth of the Machine: The Pentagon of Power* (New York: Harcourt Brace Jovanovich, 1970), p. 391.

Chapter One. Bergson and Bergsonism

1. Quoted in R.B. Perry, *The Thought and Character of William James* (Boston: Little, Brown, 1935), 2:622-23.

2. Anthony Pilkington, *Bergson and His Influence: A Reassessment* (New York: Cambridge Univ. Press, 1976), p. 242.

3. See Jean Hering, "Phenomenology in France," and Jean Wall, "The Present

Situation and the Present Future of French Philosophy," both in *Philosophic Thought in France and the United States: Essays Representing Major Trends in Contemporary French and American Philosophy*, ed. Marvin Farber (Buffalo: University of Buffalo Publications in Philosophy, 1950), pp. 67 and 34-35. See also Merleau-Ponty's *In Praise of Philosophy*, trans. John Wild and James M. Edie (Northwestern Univ. Press, 1963), pp. 12ff.

4. Henri Bergson, *The Philosophy of Poetry: The Genius of Lucretius* (New York: Philosophical Library, 1959), pp. 80, 82.

5. Bergson's first dissertation was translated into French in 1962. See *Les Etudes Bergsoniennes* (Paris: Albin Michel), 2 (1949):9-104. A brief summary of its conclusions may be found in François Heidsieck, *Henri Bergson et la notion d'espace* (Paris: Le Circle du Livre, 1957), pp. 29-40.

6. The inclusion of Russell's name may surprise some. See "Russell's Hidden Bergsonism," in Milič Čapek's *Bergson and Modern Physics: A Reinterpretation and Re-evaluation* (Dordrecht: D. Reidel, 1971).

7. Bertrand Russell, *Wisdom of the West: A Historical Survey of Western Philosophy in its Social and Political Setting* (Garden City, N.Y.: Doubleday, 1959), p. 287.

8. Hans Meyerhoff, *Time in Literature* (Los Angeles: Univ. of California Press, 1955), pp. 97-99.

9. See J. Hillis Miller, *Poets of Reality: Six Twentieth-Century Writers* (Cambridge: Harvard Univ. Press, 1965), p. 11. Miller's "new reality" is seen as accessible only through a search for immanent spirituality, a search prompted by a sense of alienation from Divinity; but that spirituality must be *in* the world, not beyond it.

10. Adam A. Mendilow, *Time and the Novel* (New Jersey: Humanities Press, 1965), pp. 3, 5.

11. P.A.Y. Gunter, "Bergson and Jung," *Journal of the History of Ideas* 43 (Oct./Dec. 1982): 638ff.

12. Wassily Kandinsky, *Concerning the Spiritual in Art and Painting in Particular*, trans. Francis Golffing, Michael Harrison, and Ferdinand Ostertag (New York: Wittenborn, 1970), pp. 24, 26; originally published by Kandinsky in 1912. See also Miller's *Poets of Reality*, p. 189, for a discussion of this value placed on the "infinite plenitude" of the moment of intense experience by Yeats and Eliot.

13. See, for example, Murray Krieger, *The New Apologists for Poetry* (Minneapolis: Univ. of Minnesota Press, 1956), for a description of Bergson's impact on the whole school of "new critics." Philip Le Brun has published an excellent article, "T.S. Eliot and Henri Bergson," *Review of English Studies*, n.s., 18 (May 1967): 149-61, 18 (Aug. 1967): 274-86. See also Dom Illtyd Trethowan, "Bergson and the Zeitgeist," *Downside Review* 85 (1967): 138-47, 262-73; Dorothy Judd Hall, "The Height of Feeling Free: Frost and Bergson," *Texas Quarterly* 19 (Spring 1976): 128-43; John F. Sears, "William James, Henri Bergson, and the Poetics of Robert Frost," *New England Quarterly* 48 (Sept. 1975): 341-61; Richard Adams, "The Apprenticeship of William Faulkner," *Tulane Studies in English* 12 (1962): 113-56; and Karl Zink, "Flux and Frozen Moments," *PMLA* 71(June 1956): 285-301.

14. Letter quoted in Shiv K. Kumar, *Bergson and the Stream of Consciousness Novel* (New York: New York Univ. Press, 1963), pp. 36-37.

15. Andreas Poulakidas, "Kazantzakis and Bergson: Metaphysic [*sic*] Aestheticians," *Journal of Modern Literature* 2 (1971-72): 283. Kazantzakis published a Greek translation of *Le Rire* in 1910, and in 1913 contributed an article on Bergsonian philosophy to the *Bulletin* of the Greek Educational Society.

16. For full discussion of Bergson's influence on Piaget and Riechenbach, see Čapek, *Bergson and Modern Physics*, pp. 65ff.

17. There is an openly conciliatory tone in the revised editions of Maritain's *Bergsonian Philosophy and Thomism*, trans. Mabelle L. Andison, 2d ed. (New York: Pantheon, 1955); orig. pub. 1913.

18. Letter to Mrs. Meyrick Heath, tentatively and erroneously dated 1913 by Charles Williams, editor of *The Letters of Evelyn Underhill* (New York: Longmans, Green, 1943), p. 146. Bergson also traveled to New York in 1913, where similar responses were apparently felt by his audiences, judging from the press reports in the *New York Times*.

19. T.S. Eliot, "Commentary," *Criterion* 13 (April 1934): 451-54.

20. E.J.H. Greene, *T.S. Eliot et la France* (Paris: Boivin, 1951), p. 10.

21. T.S. Eliot, "What France Means to Me," *La France Libre* 7 (June 15, 1944): 94-95; quoted in Alan Holder, *Three Voyagers in Search of Europe: A Study of Henry James, Ezra Pound, and T.S. Eliot* (Univ. of Pennsylvania Press, 1966), p. 333.

22. René Doumic, "Académie française: Réception de M. Henri Bergson: Discours de M. Bergson: Reponse de M. René Doumic," *La Petit Temps* (25 Janvier, 1918) gives an account of Bergson's appearance at the Lycee: "From your whole personality emanated a singular charm. . . . "

23. Quoted in Kumar, *Bergson and the Stream of Consciousness Novel*, p. 134.

24. Rose Marie Mosse-Bastide, *Bergson éducateur* (Paris: Presses Universitaires de France, 1955), p. 34.

25. Thomas Hanna, ed., *The Bergsonian Heritage* (New York: Columbia Univ. Press, 1962), p. 16.

26. T.S. Eliot, "Commentary," *Criterion* 12 (Oct. 1932): 74; and "The Idealism of Julien Benda," *Cambridge Review* 49:488.

27. Sir Ray Lankester, preface to *Modern Science and the Illusions of Professor Bergson*, by Hugh Samuel R. Elliott (London: Longmans, Green, 1912), pp. vii-viii, xvi, xvii.

28. Thomas John Gerrard, *Bergson: An Exposition from the Point of View of St. Thomas Aquinas* (London: Sands, 1913), p. 207.

29. George Santayana, *The Winds of Doctrine: Studies in Contemporary Opinion* (New York: Charles Scribner's Sons, 1926), pp. 106-7 and 58-109 passim; first pub. 1912.

30. Bertrand Russell, "The Philosophy of Bergson," *The Monist* 22:347.

31. See Robert J. Niess, *Julien Benda* (Ann Arbor: Univ. of Michigan Press, 1956), pp. 29, 64, 95-96, 122.

32. SueEllen Campbell, "Equal Opposites: Wyndham Lewis, Henri Bergson,

and Their Philosophies of Space and Time," *Twentieth-Century Literature* 29 (Fall 1983): 366.

33. Pierre Andreu, "Bergson et Sorel," *Les Études Bergsoniennes* 3:62.

34. Letter to Flewelling, Sept. 15, 1937, in Daniel S. Robinson, "The Bergson-Flewelling Correspondence: 1910-1940," *Coranto: Journal of the Friends of the Libraries—Univ. of Southern California* 10 (no. 2): 27, 34. Flewelling was positively embarrassed by the reissue of his *Bergson and Personal Realism* (New York: Abingdon Press, 1920), and wrote in 1932 to apologize: "I shall never forget the sportsmanlike manner, as well as the silence, in which you received my criticism . . . my own philosophical viewpoint has approached closer and closer to your own."

35. P.A.Y. Gunter, *Bergson and the Evolution of Physics* (Knoxville: Univ. of Tennessee Press, 1969), pp. 18-19.

36. Bertrand Russell, *A History of Modern Philosophy* (New York: Simon and Schuster, 1945), p. 793; and "Philosophy of Bergson," pp. 346, 334.

37. Letter to Flewelling, April 6, 1933, in Robinson, *Bergson-Flewelling Correspondence*, p. 29.

38. Gunter, *Bergson and the Evolution of Physics*, pp. v, vii.

39. Čapek, *Bergson and Modern Physics*, pp. xii, 195-201, 255, 365.

40. See, for example, Idella J. Gallagher, *Morality in Evolution: The Moral Philosophy of Henri Bergson* (The Hague: Martinus Nijhoff, 1970); Albert Thibaudet, *Le Bergsonisme* (Paris: Gallimard, 1923); and Ben-ami Scharfstein, *Roots of Bergson's Philosophy* (New York: Columbia Univ. Press, 1943).

41. Georges Poulet, "The Phenomenology of Reading," *New Literary History* 1 (Oct. 1969).

42. Maritain, *Bergsonian Philosophy and Thomism*, pp. 280, 337, 59, 345, 16, 18.

43. Quoted in Henri Gouhier, *Bergson et le Christ des Evangiles* (Paris: Le Sign, Anthem Fayard, 1961), p. 196.

44. I.W. Alexander, *Bergson: Philosopher of Reflection* (London: Bowes and Bowes, 1957), p. 158.

45. James Street Fulton, "Bergson's Religious Interpretation of Evolution," *Rice Institute Pamphlet* 43 (no. 3): pp. 16-17, 27.

46. Daniel Herman, *The Philosophy of Henri Bergson* (Washington, D.C.: Univ. Press of America, 1980), p. 98.

Chapter Two. Bergsonian Intuition and Modernist Aesthetics

1. Murray Krieger, "Ekphrasis and the Still Movement of Poetry: Or Laakoon Revisited," in *Perspectives on Poetry*, ed. James L. Calderwood and Harold E. Toliver (New York: Oxford Univ. Press, 1968), pp. 323-49; *New Apologists*, p. 34.

2. Arthur Szathmary, *The Aesthetic Theory of Bergson* (Cambridge: Harvard Univ. Press, 1937), pp. 47, 65.

3. Ludwig Wittgenstein, *Tractato Logico-Philosophicus* (London: Routledge and Kegan Paul, 1961) p. 3; orig. German ed., 1921.

4. Joseph G. Kronick, *American Poetics of History: From Emerson to the Moderns* (Baton Rouge: Louisiana State Univ. Press, 1984), pp. 6-7.

5. Frank Lentricchia, *Criticism and Social Change* (Univ. of Chicago Press, 1983), p. 51.

6. Paul de Man, *The Rhetoric of Romanticism* (New York: Columbia Univ. Press, 1984), p. 123.

7. W. Wolfgang Holdheim, *The Hermeneutic Mode: Essays on Time in Literature and Literary Theory* (Ithaca: Cornell Univ. Press, 1984), p. 270.

8. Ferdinand de Saussure, *Course in General Linguistics*, 3d ed. (Paris: Payot, 1965), pp. 43-45.

9. Hazard Adams, *Philosophy of the Literary Symbolic* (Gainesville: Univ. Presses of Florida, 1983), pp. 262, 356, 359.

10. Bruce Kawin, *The Mind of the Novel: Reflexive Fiction and the Ineffable* (Princeton Univ. Press, 1982), pp. 230-33, 322.

11. Hulme, *Speculations*, pp. 263-64, 157.

12. Kermode, *Romantic Image*, pp. 120-22, 130, 134.

13. Immanuel Kant, *Werke*, ed. Karl Vorländer et al., in the *Philosophischen Bibliothek* Vol. 4: 14ff. And see Kant's introduction to his *Logik*.

14. Hulme, *Speculations*, p. 149; my italics. Note that Bergson defines intuition in somewhat the same fashion Kant defines the categories: It exists *a priori* but is known only *a posteriori*, i.e., empirically.

15. Ibid., p. 153.

16. Harvey Gross, *The Contrived Corridor: History and Fatality in Modern Literature* (Ann Arbor: Univ. of Michigan Press, 1971), p. 19.

17. T.S. Eliot, "Experiment in Criticism," *The Bookman* 70 (1929): 226. See also *TCC*, 138: "As for Coleridge, he was rather a man of my own type."

18. Kenneth Burke, *The Rhetoric of Religion: Studies in Logology* (Boston: Beacon Press, 1961), p. 33.

19. Joel Elias Spingarn, *A History of Literary Criticism in the Renaissance*, 2d ed., rev. and augm. (New York: Columbia Univ. Press, 1924), pp. 18, 8-9, 158, 312.

20. Gross, *Contrived Corridor*, p. 44. Note the similarity of the term to Goethe's "Wechseldauer."

21. Ezra Pound, Letter to his father, 1927, in *Letters: 1907-1941*, ed. D.D. Paige (New York: Harcourt Brace, 1950), p. 210.

22. James Joyce, *Stephen Hero* (New York: New Directions, 1944), p. 213. Shiv Kumar has shown important parallels between Joyce's novels and Bergson's aesthetic: "Joyce's 'Epiphany' and Bergson's 'L'Intuition Philosophique,'" *Modern Language Quarterly* 20 (March 1959): 27-30; "Bergson and Stephen Dedalus' Aesthetic Theory," *Journal of Aesthetics and Art Criticism* 16 (1957-58): 124-27.

23. Aldous Huxley, *The Doors of Perception* and *Heaven and Hell* (London: Chatto and Windus, 1968), p. 97.

24. Joseph Frank, "Spatial Form in Modern Literature," in *The Widening Gyre: Crisis and Mastery in Modern Literature* (New Brunswick: Rutgers Univ. Press, 1963), pp. 17, 19.

25. Ezra Pound, *The Spirit of Romance* (1910 rept. New York: New Directions, 1953), pp. 7-8, 222.

26. William Harmon, *Time in Ezra Pound's Work* (Chapel Hill: Univ. of North Carolina Press, 1977), pp. 8, 54.

27. William Faulkner, *Early Prose and Poetry*, ed. Carvel Collins (Boston: Little, Brown, 1962), p. 74.

28. Pound, *Spirit of Romance*, p. 5.

29. Ernst Cassirer, *Language and Myth* (New York: Dover, 1946), p. 74. The principle is stated in MacLeish's "Ars Poetica": "A poem should be equal to: / Not true."

30. See Eliot's introduction to *Transit of Venus*, by Harry Crosby (Paris: Black Sun Press, 1931), p. viii.

31. See Eliot's introduction to his translation of *Anabasis*, by St. John Perse (New York: Harcourt Brace, 1938), p. 8.; my italics.

32. M.L. Rosenthal and Sally M. Gall, *The Modern Poetic Sequence: The Genius of Modern Poetry* (Oxford Univ. Press, 1983), pp. 6-17 passim.

33. Paul Tillich, *Dynamics of Faith* (New York: Harper, 1957), pp. 42-43.

34. Frank Doggett, *Stevens' Poetry of Thought* (Baltimore: Johns Hopkins Univ. Press, 1966), p. 213.

35. *Selected Prose of Robert Frost*, ed. Hyde Cox and Edward Connery Lathem (New York: Holt, Rinehart and Winston, 1966), p. 41. Frost's interest in Bergson began when he read the translation of *Creative Evolution* in 1911.

36. Thomas Wolfe, *Look Homeward Angel* (New York: Charles Scribner's Sons, 1929), p. 3.

37. Virginia Woolf, *To the Lighthouse* (New York: Harcourt, Brace and World, 1927), pp. 240-41.

38. Gross contends that twentieth-century writers are always this sort of "victim." The pose, at any rate, is ubiquitous. See *Contrived Corridor*, p. 19.

39. T.S. Eliot, "Eeldrop and Appleplex," *The Little Review*, May 1917, p. 10.

Chapter Three. Eliot's Unacknowledged Debt

1. Lyndall Gordon, *Eliot's Early Years* (New York: Oxford Univ. Press, 1977), p. 54.

2. Philip Le Brun, "T.S. Eliot and Henri Bergson," *Review of English Studies*, n.s., 18:149.

3. Staffan Bergsten, *Time and Eternity: A Study in the Structure and Symbolism of T.S. Eliot's Four Quartets* (William Heinemann, 1960), p. 13.

4. Piers Gray, *T.S. Eliot's Intellectual and Poetic Development, 1909-1922* (New Jersey: Humanities Press, 1982).

5. Ibid., pp. 85-86, 215, 244.

6. Hugh Kenner, *The Invisible Poet: T.S. Eliot* (New York: McDowell, Obolensky, 1959), p. 55.

7. Sean Lucy, *T.S. Eliot and the Idea of Tradition* (New York: Barnes and Noble, 1960), p. 140.

8. Eric Thompson, *T.S. Eliot: The Metaphysical Perspective* (Carbondale: South-

ern Illinois Univ. Press, 1963); and Lewis Freed, *T.S. Eliot: The Critic as Philosopher* (Indiana: Purdue Univ. Press, 1979). Freed's book was originally a dissertation completed at LaSalle Univ. in 1962.

9. Russell Kirk, *Eliot and His Age: T.S. Eliot's Moral Imagination in the Twentieth Century* (New York: Random House, 1971), pp. 42-44, 414.

10. Freed, *Critic as Philosopher*, p. 189.

11. Richard Wollheim, "Eliot and F.H. Bradley: An Account," in *Eliot in Perspective*, ed. Graham Martin (New York: Humanities Press, 1970), pp. 170, 186-89.

12. Thompson, *Metaphysical Perspective*, p. xx; Kirk, *Eliot and His Age*, p. 42.

13. Richard Wollheim, *F.H. Bradley* (Baltimore: Penguin, 1959), p. 284.

14. Bertrand Russell, *Wisdom of the West* (Garden City, N.Y.: Doubleday, 1959), p. 292.

15. William James, "Bradley or Bergson?" *Journal of Philosophy, Psychology and Scientific Methods* 7 (Jan. 20, 1910): 29.

16. Ibid., p. 32.

17. See the syllabus for this lecture, reprinted in A.D. Moody, *Thomas Stearns Eliot, Poet* (Cambridge: Cambridge Univ. Press, 1979), p. 49. A much fuller treatment and reprinting of Eliot's syllabi and notes as an extension lecturer may be found in Ronald Schuchard, "T.S. Eliot as an Extension Lecturer," *Review of English Studies* 25 (1974): 163-73, 292-304.

18. T.S. Eliot, "A Sermon Preached at Magdalene College Chapel by T.S. Eliot, O.M." (Cambridge: Cambridge Univ. Press, 1948), p. 5; and the introduction to Josef Pieper, *Leisure: The Basis of Culture* (New York: Pantheon, 1964), p. xi.

19. Quoted in Kenner, *The Invisible Poet*, p. 46.

20. T.S. Eliot, "Commentary," *Criterion* 3 (Oct. 1924): 2 (Bradley's obituary).

21. Ibid.

22. T.S. Eliot, "London Letter," *Dial* 71 (Aug. 1921): 216; T.S. Eliot, "Mr. Middleton Murry's Synthesis," *Criterion* 6 (Oct. 1927): 346-47.

23. T.S. Eliot, "Mr. Shaw and the Maid," *Criterion* 4 (April 1926): 389-90.

24. T.S. Eliot, review of *God: Being an Introduction to the Science of Metabiology*, by J. Middleton Murry, *Criterion* 9 (Jan. 1930): 335.

25. T.S. Eliot, "Commentary," *Criterion* 6 (Dec. 1927): 481.

26. T.S. Eliot, "Commentary," *Criterion* 5 (June 1927): 283.

27. Le Brun, "Eliot and Bergson," p. 150.

28. T.S. Eliot, "Commentary," *Criterion* 12 (Oct. 1932): 74.

29. A recent example of this sort of attack occurs in Maurice Friedman's *To Deny Our Nothingness: Contemporary Images of Man* (New York: Delacorte, 1967): "Understandable as a reaction against the sterile abstractions of philosophical idealism and rationalism, Bergson's vitalism falls into the trap of an identification of energy with ultimate reality and of a relativism in which all movement, of whatever nature, is equally good so long as its flow is not staunched. That Bergson himself would have been the first to be horrified by the Nazi conversion of vitalism into unlimited demonry only shows that he had other values that found no explicit place in his philosophy" (p. 72).

30. T.S. Eliot, "Commentary," *Criterion* 16 (Oct. 1936): 68.

31. In *After Strange Gods*, Eliot makes this specific: "Most of us are heretical in one way or another. . . . The essential of any important heresy is not simply that it is wrong; it is that it is partly right . . . an exceptionally acute perception, or profound insight" (*ASG*, 25-26).

32. T.S. Eliot, "Notes on Bergson's Lectures," a manuscript in the Eliot Collection, Houghton Library, Harvard Univ., pp. 18, 14.

33. Henri Bergson, *Matiére et mémoire: Essai sur la relation du corps a l'esprit*, 7th ed. (Paris: Felix Alcan, 1911), p. 232; my italics. (The pagination in this edition corresponds to that cited in the margins of Eliot's draft of an essay on Bergson. In the English edition used in the present essay, the page is 275.

34. T.S. Eliot, "Draft of a Paper on Bergson," a manuscript in the Eliot Collection, Houghton Library, Harvard Univ., pp. 18-19, 15, 8, 16(a). (There are two page sixteens, an error committed by Eliot.)

35. Ibid., pp. 21-22.

36. J.M. Murry, "Art and Philosophy," *Rhythm* 1 (Summer 1911): 9-12. Reprinted in Cyrena N. Pondrom, *The Road from Paris: French Influence on English Poetry 1900-1920* (Cambridge: Cambridge Univ. Press, 1974), pp. 54-57.

37. Eliot, "Draft of Paper on Bergson," pp. 22-26.

38. Ibid., p. 26.

39. Eliot, "Murry's Synthesis," pp. 343, 345.

40. T.S. Eliot, Notes for Philosophy 24A, given by Masaharu Anesaki in 1913-14, Houghton Library, Harvard Univ.

41. Eloise Knapp Hay, *T.S. Eliot's Negative Way* (Cambridge: Harvard Univ. Press, 1982), p. 167.

42. Elizabeth Schneider, *T.S. Eliot: The Pattern in the Carpet* (Los Angeles: Univ. of California Press, 1975), pp. 23-24.

43. See, for example, Krieger, *New Apologists*, pp. 34, 187; also A.G. George, *T.S. Eliot: His Mind and Art* (New York: Asia Publishing House, 1962), pp. 64-65; Grover Cleveland Smith, *T.S. Eliot's Poetry and Plays: A Study in Sources and Meaning*, 2d ed. (Chicago: Univ. of Chicago Press, 1974), p. 54; and Lyndall Gordon, *Eliot's Early Years* (New York: Oxford Univ. Press, 1977), pp. 38-55. See also Ann Ward, "Speculations of Eliot's Time-World," [sic] *American Literature* 21 (March 1949): 18; and Constantinos Patrides, "The Renascence of the Renaissance: T.S. Eliot and the Patterns of Time," *Michigan Quarterly Review* 21, no. 2, 172-96.

44. Eliot, introduction to *Transit of Venus*, p. v; my italics.

45. Eliot, "Draft of Paper on Bergson," p. 18.

46. T.S. Eliot, "Commentary," *Criterion* 5 (Jan. 1927): 1.

47. T.S. Eliot, "Commentary," *Criterion* 4 (Jan. 1926): 5.

48. T.S. Eliot, "A Commentary: That Poetry is Made with Words," *New English Weekly* 15 (April 27, 1939): 27.

49. T.S. Eliot, review of *The Name and Nature of Poetry*, by A.E. Housman, *Criterion* 13 (Oct. 1933): 154.

50. Ezra Pound, "Mr. Housman at Little Bethel," *Criterion* 13 (Jan. 1934): 223.

51. The contrast between mere transcript and living history is not exclusively

Bergsonian property, of course, but his vocabulary often turns up in twentieth century writers, and it is in many ways the issue he brings to greatest popularity.

52. George Bornstein, *Transformations of Romanticism in Yeats, Eliot, and Stevens* (Chicago: Univ. of Chicago Press, 1976), p. 129.

53. Ibid., pp. 154, 156, and 149.

54. Edward Lobb, *T.S. Eliot and the Romantic Critical Tradition* (Boston: Routledge and Kegan Paul, 1981).

55. T.S. Eliot, "Tarr," *The Egoist* 5 (Sept. 1918): 105-6.

56. T.S. Eliot, "Commentary," *Criterion* 4 (June 1926): 420.

57. Michael Roberts, *T.E. Hulme* (London: Faber and Faber, 1938), p. 93.

58. Samuel Taylor Coleridge, *Shakespeare, Ben Jonson, Beaumont and Fletcher: Notes and Lectures*, new ed. (Liverpool: Edward Howell, 1874), pp. 54-55.

59. T.S. Eliot, "The Method of Mr. Pound," *Athenaeum* 4669 (Oct. 24, 1919): 1065-66.

60. Ronald Schuchard, "Eliot and Hulme in 1916: Toward a Revaluation of Eliot's Critical and Spiritual Development," *PMLA* 88 (October 1973): 1083-94. See esp. p. 1091.

61. Hulme, *Speculations*, pp. 149-50, 160-66.

62. Ibid., p. 169.

63. Eliot, " Poetry Made with Words," p. 27.

64. T.S. Eliot, "Commentary," *Criterion* 3 (April 1925): 342.

65. Eliot, review of *Name and Nature of Poetry*, p. 154.

66. See *Knowledge and Experience*, pp. 21, 158, 164, 31. See also pp. 24-25: Why should I "cut off part of the total content and call it the object, reserving the rest to myself under the name of feeling? It is only in social behavior . . . that feelings and things are torn apart. And after this separation they leave dim and drifting edges, and tend to coalesce."

67. T.S. Eliot, introduction to *Le Serpent*, by Paul Valery, trans. Mark Wardle (London: R. Cobden-Sanderson, 1924), p. 14.

68. F.H. Bradley, *Essays on Truth and Reality* (Oxford: Clarendon Press, 1914), p. 159.

69. T.S. Eliot, "Observations," *The Egoist* 5 (May 1918): 69.

70. F.O. Matthiessen, *The Achievement of T.S. Eliot: An Essay on the Nature of Poetry*, 3d ed. (New York: Oxford Univ. Press, 1958), p. 149.

Chapter Four. Time, Intuition, and Self-Knowledge in Eliot's Poetry

1. Evelyn Underhill, *Practical Mysticism: A Little Book for Normal People* (New York: E.P. Dutton, 1915), pp. 30-31.

2. T.S. Eliot, preface to *Thoughts for Meditation: A Way to Recovery from Within*, assembled and arranged by N. Gangulee (Boston: Beacon Press, 1952), p. 11.

3. Evelyn Underhill, *Mysticism: A Study in the Nature and Development of*

Man's Spiritual Consciousness, 12th rev. ed. (New York: World Publishing Co., 1967), pp. 41, xiv.

4. Joseph Chiari, *Realism and Imagination* (London: Barrie and Rockliff, 1960), p. 188. In his recent *T.S. Eliot: A Memoir* (London: Enitharmon, 1982), Chiari describes Eliot's disappointment with Russell's *History of Western Philosophy*, particularly because of its "airy dismissal of [Bergson], with vague compliments about style" (p. 45).

5. T.S. Eliot, *Poems Written in Early Youth* (New York: Farrar, Straus and Giroux, 1967), p. 17.

6. Eliot, "Sermon at Magdalene College," p. 5.

7. T.S. Eliot, "Letters of J.B. Yeats," *The Egoist* 4 (July 1917): 89-90.

8. T.S. Eliot, "Commentary," *Criterion* 3 (April 1925): 342.

9. T.S. Eliot, introduction to *The Wheel of Fire: Interpretations of Shakespearian Tragedy*, 4th enlarged ed., by G. Wilson Knight (London: Methuen, 1930), p. xv.

10. T.S. Eliot, "The Beating of a Drum," *Nation* 34 (Oct. 6, 1923): 12.

11. "An Inquiry into the Spirit and Language of Night," *Transition* (Paris) 27 (April/May 1938): 236.

12. Ronald Bush, *T.S. Eliot: A Study in Character and Style* (Oxford Univ. Press, 1983), p. 9.

13. T.S. Eliot, paper given in Josiah Royce's seminar, 1913, quoted in Gray, *Eliot's Development*, p. 110.

14. T.S. Eliot, "Commentary," *Criterion* 3 (April 1925): 342.

15. John Lehman, "T.S. Eliot Talks About Himself and the Drive to Create," *New York Times Book Review* 103 (Nov. 29, 1953): 5, 44.

16. T.S. Eliot, "Style and Thought," review of *Mysticism and Logic*, by Bertrand Russell, *Nation* 22 (March 23, 1918): 768.

17. T.S. Eliot, introduction to *Leisure: The Basis of Culture*, by Joseph Pieper (New York: Pantheon, 1964) , pp. xii, xiv; orig. pub. 1952.

18. Martin Heidegger, *Erläuterung zu Hölderlin's Dichtung*, expanded ed. (Frankfurt: V. Klostermann, 1951), p. 35.

19. T.S. Eliot, "Commentary," *Criterion* 12 (Oct. 1932): 77-78.

20. Ibid.

21. Hugo Roeffaers, "Philosophy and Literary Criticism: A Case Study," *International Philosophical Quarterly* 20 (June 1980): 159.

22. T.S. Eliot, "Commentary," *Criterion* 12 (Oct. 1932): 78.

23. Anthony David Nuttall, *A Common Sky: Philosophy and the Literary Imagination* (Los Angeles: Univ. of California Press, 1974), p. 245.

24. Helen Vendler, *Part of Nature, Part of Us: Modern American Poets* (Cambridge: Harvard Univ. Press, 1980), p. 82.

25. Floyd Watkins, *The Flesh and the Word: Eliot, Hemingway, Faulkner* (Nashville: Vanderbilt Univ. Press, 1971), p. 274.

26. A.D. Moody, *Thomas Stearns Eliot, Poet* (New York: Cambridge Univ. Press, 1979), pp. 262, 249, 263, xiii. See *SE*, 343, for Eliot's phrase.

27. This is the theme of many passages, including those on Pascal and Housman (*SE*, 358, for example).

28. Eliot, introduction to *Le Serpent*, p. 13.

29. Letter of April 20, 1909, quoted in R.B. Perry, *The Thought and Character of William James* (Boston: Little, Brown, 1935), 2:630. Bergson is responding to implications of a passage in *A Pluralistic Universe* (1903).

30. From chapter 42 of *Pickwick Papers*. See Helen Gardner, *The Composition of Four Quartets* (New York: Oxford Univ. Press, 1978), p. 28.

31. Eliot, introduction to *Transit of Venus*, pp. vii-viii; my italics.

32. Paul Douglass, "Eliot's Cats: Serious Play Behind the Playful Seriousness," *Children's Literature* 11 (1983): 109-24.

33. Moody, *Thomas Stearns Eliot*, p. 182.

34. T.S. Eliot, foreword to *Symbolisme from Poe to Mallarmé: The Growth of a Myth*, by Joseph Chiari, 2d ed. (New York: Ruckliff, 1970), p. 4; orig. pub. 1956. My italics. This emphatically Christian book's assumptions are made explicit in an appendix titled "Time and Free Will."

35. Evelyn Underhill, "Bergson and the Mystics," *Littel's Living Age* 272 (March 16, 1912): pp. 668-69, 673-75.

36. Ibid, pp. 669, 673-74.

37. Evelyn Underhill, *Immanence: A Book of Verses* (London: J.M. Dent, 1912), pp. 28-29, 82-83.

38. Evelyn Underhill, *Theophanies: A Book of Verses* (London: J.M. Dent, 1916), pp. 26-28, 29, 65, 72, 94.

39. Underhill, *Practical Mysticism*, pp. 30-31.

40. Eliot likely knew of the historical novel by J.H. Shorthouse, *John Inglesant* (1880), which describes Ferrar's life and the events during Cromwell's rise. See Gardner, *Composition of Four Quartets*, pp. 60-61.

41. This is Moody's view, for example (pp. 255-56).

42. See Gardner, *Composition of Four Quartets*, p. 64. Moody has written a superb account of this section—indeed, his whole commentary on *Four Quartets* is indispensable; he probes the monotony of the *terza rima* section and the implications of Latini for Eliot's idea of "detachment." Moody finds, however, that Eliot has not maintained Dante's "healthy interest of the living" (p. 254). Here is where we disagree.

43. This is Seneca's version of the myth. It is a curious fact that Burnt Norton's owner performed an act of self-immolation after having alienated his wife and two lovers (Gardner, *Composition of Four Quartets*, p. 36).

44. Underhill, *Mysticism*, p. 229.

Chapter Five. Eliot, Bergson and the Southern Critics

1. Allen Tate, *Reactionary Essays on Poetry and Ideas* (New York: Charles Scribner's Sons, 1936), pp. 213-15, 220, 112.

2. William J. Handy, *Kant and the Southern New Critics* (Austin: Univ. of Texas Press, 1963), p. 14.

3. Ibid., p. 17.

4. John Crowe Ransom, *The New Criticism* (Norfolk, Conn.: New Directions, 1941), pp. 201-2.

5. John Crowe Ransom, *The World's Body* (New York: Charles Scribner's Sons, 1938), pp. 130, 142.

6. Ibid., pp. 215-16.

7. Ibid., p. 232.

8. John L. Stewart, *The Burden of Time: The Fugitives and the Agrarians* (Princeton: Princeton Univ. Press, 1965), p. 14.

9. Tate, *Reactionary Essays*, p. xi.

10. Ibid., pp. 83-88.

11. Ibid., pp. 94-95, 110.

12. William Empson, "Emotions in Poems," in *The Kenyon Critics: Studies in Modern Literature from the Kenyon Review*, ed. John Crowe Ransom (New York: World Publishing Co., 1951), pp. 136-37, 134-35.

13. Robert Penn Warren, "Pure and Impure Poetry," in *Kenyon Critics*, pp. 17-18, 35, 37-38; my italics.

14. Tate, *Reactionary Essays*, pp. 113-14, 128, 143.

15. Quoted in Stewart, *Burden of Time*, p. 188.

16. John Crowe Ransom, introduction to *Kenyon Critics*, p. vii.

17. Murray Krieger, *Arts on the Level: The Fall of the Elite Object* (Knoxville: Univ. of Tennessee Press, 1981), p. 71.

Chapter Six. Deciphering Faulkner's Uninterrupted Sentence

1. Joseph Blotner, *Faulkner: A Biography* (New York: Random House, 1974), 2:1219, 1302.

2. Adams, "Apprenticeship of Faulkner," pp. 153-55.

3. Conder, *Naturalism in American Fiction*, p. 161.

4. Joseph Blotner, ed., *William Faulkner's Library: A Catalogue* (Charlottesville: Univ. Press of Virginia, 1964).

5. Personal letter to the author, 28 April, 1980.

6. Cleanth Brooks, *William Faulkner: Toward Yoknapatawpha and Beyond* (New Haven: Yale Univ. Press, 1978), p. 255. Brooks's view is supported by Michel Gresset, who points out that the comment on Bergson came too late to prove any real influence. See *A Faulkner Chronology* (Univ. Press of Mississippi, 1985), p. 87.

7. The fact that Faulkner studied Eliot's work has been documented on many occasions. A fairly complete listing of some parallels between Faulkner's and Eliot's works is offered in Ida Fasel's "A 'Conversation' Between Faulkner and Eliot," *Mississippi Quarterly* 20 (Fall 1967): 195-206.

8. Ida Fasel develops the link between "endure" and *durée* in her "Spatial Form and Spatial Time," *Western Humanities Review* 16 (Summer 1962): 223-34.

9. Robert A. Jelliffe, ed., *Faulkner at Nagano* (Tokyo: Kenkyusha, 1956), p. 34.

10. Conrad Aiken, "The Novel as Form," *William Faulkner: Four Decades of Criticism*, ed. Linda Welshimer Wagner (Michigan State Univ. Press, 1973), pp. 136-7.

11. Clifton Fadiman, *Party of One: Selected Writings* (Cleveland: World Pub-

lishing Co., 1955), p. 113; and see Aiken, "Novel as Form," p. 136: "each sentence . . . a microcosm."

12. *Faulkner at Nagano*, p. 37.

13. Perrin Lowrey, "Concepts of Time in *The Sound and the Fury*," repr. in condensed form in *Twentieth-Century Interpretations of The Sound and the Fury*, ed. Michael H. Cowan, (Englewood Cliffs, N.J.: Prentice-Hall, 1968), pp. 61-62.

14. Peter Swiggart, "Time in Faulkner's Novels," *Modern Fiction Studies* 1 (May 1955): 25-29.

15. Zink, "Flux and Frozen Moments," pp. 298-30.

16. Darrel Abel, "Frozen Movement in *Light in August*," *Boston Univ. Studies in English* 3 (Spring 1957): 32-44.

17. Estella Schoenberg, *Old Tales and Talking: Quentin Compson in William Faulkner's Absalom, Absalom! and Related Works* (Jackson: Univ. Press of Mississippi, 1977), p. 124.

18. *Faulkner at Nagano*, pp. 38-39.

19. Walter Jacob Slatoff, *Quest for Failure: A Study of William Faulkner* (Ithaca: Cornell Univ. Press, 1960), pp. 244, 248, 97-101.

20. Ibid., pp. 97-101.

21. Shirley Parker Callen, "Bergsonian Dynamism in the Writings of William Faulkner," Ph.D. diss., Tulane University, 1962, pp. 126-27.

22. Agnes Pollock, "The Current of Time in the Novels of William Faulkner," Ph.D. diss., UCLA, 1965.

23. Margaret Church, *Time and Reality: Studies in Contemporary Fiction* (Univ. of North Carolina Press, 1963), pp. 240-45, 205.

24. Robert L. Nadeau, "Morality and Act: A Study of Faulkner's *As I Lay Dying*," *Mosaic* 6 (Spring 1966): 23-35.

25. Jesse C. Gatlin, "Of Time and Character in *The Sound and the Fury*," *Humanities Association Bulletin* (Canada) 17 (Autumn 1966): 27-35.

26. Eric Larson, "The Barrier of Language: The Irony of Language in Faulkner," *Modern Fiction Studies* 13 (Spring 1967): 30-31.

27. Richard P. Adams, *Faulkner: Myth and Motion* (Princeton: Princeton Univ. Press, 1968), pp. 59ff.

28. Ibid., pp. 10-11.

29. Ibid., pp. 7, 110-11, 5, 123.

30. Susan Dale Resneck Parr, "'And by Bergson, obviously': Faulkner's *The Sound and the Fury*, *As I Lay Dying*, and *Absalom, Absalom!* from a Bergsonian Perspective," Ph.D. diss., University of Wisconsin, 1972, pp. 122-23, 126.

31. Ibid., pp. 217, 221-22, 210-17.

32. James Joyce, *A Portrait of the Artist as a Young Man* (New York: Viking, 1972), p. 188.

33. Parr, "And by Bergson," p. 176; and see pp. 8-12.

34. Donald M. Kartiganer, *The Fragile Thread: The Meaning of Form in Faulkner's Novels* (Amherst: Univ. of Massachusetts Press, 1979), pp. xvii, 164, 195.

35. André Bleikasten, *The Most Splendid Failure: Faulkner's The Sound and the Fury* (Bloomington: Indiana Univ. Press, 1976), pp. 127-37.

36. Kartiganer, *Fragile Thread*, p. 167.

37. Bleikasten, *Splendid Failure*, p. 127.

38. Panthea Reid Broughton, *William Faulkner: The Abstract and the Actual* (Baton Rouge: Louisiana State Univ. Press, 1974), pp. 157, 177; my italics.

39. Ibid., pp. 41, 55, 199.

40. Ibid., pp. 34, 107; 199, 205; my italics.

41. Brooks, *Toward Yoknapatawpha and Beyond*, pp. 285-89, 265.

42. I except from the indictment Donald Kartiganer, who recognizes that Bergson knew "duration can be visible, even to intuition, only as materialization" (p. 165). Yet notice that Kartiganer still falls into the trap of thinking that materiality can mean only delineated *visible* form.

43. Brooks, *Toward Yoknapatawpha and Beyond*, p. 257.

44. Joseph Blotner and Frederick L. Gwynn, "Faulkner on *Light in August*," in *Light in August and the Critical Spectrum*, ed. Joseph Blotner and Olga W. Vickery (Belmont, Cal.: Wadsworth, 1971), p. 1.

45. Joseph Reed, *Faulkner's Narrative* (New Haven: Yale Univ. Press, 1973).

46. Charles Robert Anderson, "Faulkner's Moral Center," *Études Anglaises* 7 (1954): 48-49.

47. Henry Kucera and W. Nelson Francis, *Computational Analysis of Present-Day American English* (Providence: Brown Univ. Press, 1967).

48. William Faulkner, *Soldier's Pay* (New York: Boni and Liveright, 1926), p. 250.

49. William Faulkner, *The Unvanquished* (New York: Random House, 1938), p. 143.

50. *New Republic* 67 (May 20, 1931): 21.

51. William Faulkner, *Mosquitoes* (New York: Liveright, 1955), p. 210.

52. Kartiganer, *Fragile Thread*, p. 164.

53. See Francis Leaver, "Faulkner: The Word as Principle and Power," in *William Faulkner: Three Decades of Criticism*, ed. Frederick Hoffman and Olga W. Vickery (New York: Harcourt Brace Jovanovich, 1960), pp. 199-209.

54. William Faulkner, *Pylon* (New York: Random House, 1935), p. 56.

55. Hugh Kenner, "Faulkner and the Avant-Garde," in *Faulkner, Modernism, and Film: Faulkner and Yoknapatawpha, 1978*, ed. Evans Harrington and Ann J. Abadie (Jackson: Univ. Press of Mississippi, 1979), p. 188.

56. Bergson, *Genius of Lucretius*, p. 80.

57. See *The Faulkner-Cowley File: Letters and Memories, 1944-1962* (New York: Viking, 1966), p. 90.

58. *Notes Toward a Supreme Fiction*, "It Must Give Pleasure," VI.

Chapter Seven. Faulkner and the Bergsonian Self

1. The most helpful texts to consult on this topic, about which nearly everyone has something to say, have been cited in the discussions in chapter six. See especially Conder's and Broughton's books, but also Olga W. Vickery, *The Novels of William Faulkner: A Critical Interpretation* (Baton Rouge: Louisiana State Univ. Press, 1959).

2. Alfred North Whitehead, *Process and Reality* (New York: Macmillan, 1929), p. 184.

3. Maxwell Geismar, *Writers in Crisis: The American Novel, 1925-1940* (Boston: Houghton Mifflin, 1942), p. 168; and Richard Chase, *The American Novel and Its Tradition* (Garden City, N.Y.: Doubleday, 1957), p. 212.

4. Irving Malin, *William Faulkner: An Interpretation* (Stanford: Stanford Univ. Press, 1957), pp. 43, 46.

5. William Faulkner, *The Town* (New York: Random House, 1957), p. 193.

6. William Faulkner, *These Thirteen* (New York: Jonathan Cape and Harrison Smith, 1931), p. 355.

7. Faulkner, *The Town*, pp. 330-31.

8. Ibid., pp. 71-72.

9. William Faulkner, *The Mansion* (New York: Random House, 1955), pp. 187, 203.

10. See Edward Wasiolek, "*As I Lay Dying*: Distortion in the Slow Eddy of Current Opinion," *Critique* 3 (Spring 1959): 15-23.

11. John T. Irwin, *Doubling and Incest / Repetition and Revenge: A Speculative Reading of Faulkner* (Baltimore: Johns Hopkins Univ. Press, 1975). See esp. pp. 53-55.

12. Regina K. Fadiman, *Faulkner's Light in August: A Description and Interpretation of the Revisions* (Charlottesville: Univ. of Virginia Press, 1975), p. 206.

13. Jean-Paul Sartre, "Time in Faulkner: *The Sound and the Fury*," in *William Faulkner: Three Decades of Criticism*, p. 230.

14. Brooks, *Toward Yoknapatawpha and Beyond*, p. 257.

15. Quoted in Frederick L. Gwynn and Joseph P. Blotner, "Faulkner on *Light in August*," in *Light in August and the Critical Spectrum*, ed. John B. Vickery and Olga W. Vickery (Belmont, Calif.: Wadsworth, 1971), p. 1.

16. See Olga W. Vickery, "Faulkner and the Contours of Time," *Georgia Review* 12 (Summer 1958). Vickery points out that Hightower's realization stems from his "accepting responsibility" (p. 201).

Chapter Eight. Bergson and American Modernism

1. William Carlos Williams, *In the American Grain* (New York: New Directions, 1956), pp. 175, 177, 179. Further references to this edition will appear in the text with the abbreviation *Grain*.

2. Thomas Wolfe, *Look Homeward, Angel: A Story of the Buried Life* (New York: Charles Scribner's Sons, 1957), p. 159; orig. pub. 1929.

3. J.B. Priestley, *Literature and Western Man* (New York: Harper, 1960), p. 438.

4. Maurice Natanson, "The Privileged Moment: A Study in the Rhetoric of Thomas Wolfe," *Quarterly Journal of Speech* 43:144, 149.

5. Allegra Stewart, *Gertrude Stein and the Present* (Harvard Univ. Press, 1967), pp. 5, 6, 25.

6. Ibid., p. 16.

7. Sears, "James, Bergson, and Poetics of Frost," p. 342.

8. Dorothy Judd Hall, "The Height of Feeling Free: Frost and Bergson," *Texas Quarterly* 19, no. 1: 129.

9. Ibid., p. 141.

10. Letter to Lawrence Durrell, Big Sur, March 14, 1949, in *Lawrence Durrell and Henry Miller: A Private Correspondence*, ed. George Wickes (New York: E.P. Dutton, 1963), p. 261.

11. Henry Miller, *Tropic of Capricorn* (New York: Grove Press, 1961), pp. 346-47; orig. pub. Paris, 1939. Further references to this edition will appear in the text with the abbreviation *"Capricorn."*

12. Gertrude Stein, *Writings and Lectures, 1909-1945*, ed. Patricia Meyerowitz (Baltimore: Penguin, 1971), p. 84.

13. F. Scott Fitzgerald, *The Great Gatsby* (New York: Charles Scribner's Sons, 1925, 1953), p. 159.

14. Bergson, *Genius of Lucretius*, p. 82.

SELECTED BIBLIOGRAPHY

Works of Henri Bergson

Essai sur les données immédiates de la conscience. Paris: Felix Alcan, 1889. Translated as *Time and Free Will: An Essay on the Immediate Data of Consciousness,* by F.L. Pogson. New York: Macmillan, 1910.

Quid Aristoteles de Loco Senserit. Paris: Felix Alcan, 1889. Translated into French as *L'Idée de lieu chez Aristote,* by Robert Mosse-Bastide. In *Les Études Bergsoniennes,* 2 (1949).

Matière et mémoire: Essai sur la relation du corps a l'esprit. Paris: Felix Alcan, 1896. Translated as *Matter and Memory,* by Nancy Margaret Paul and W. Scott Palmer. New York: Macmillan, 1911.

Le Rire: Essai sur la signification du comique. Originally appeared in serial form in the *Revue Francaise,* 1900. Translated as *Laughter: An Essay on the Meaning of the Comic,* by C. Brereton and F. Rothwell. New York: Macmillan, 1911.

Introduction à la metaphysique. Originally appeared in the *Revue de Metaphysique et de Morale* in 1903. Translated as *Introduction to Metaphysics,* by T.E. Hulme. London: Macmillan, 1912.

L'Évolution créatrice. Paris: Felix Alcan, 1907. Translated as *Creative Evolution,* by A. Mitchell. New York: Henry Holt, 1911.

L'Énergie spirituelle: Essais et conférences. Paris: Felix Alcan, 1919. Translated as *Mind-Energy: Lectures and Essays,* by H.W. Carr. New York: Henry Holt, 1920.

Durée et simultanéité: À propos de la théorie d'Einstein. Paris: Felix Alcan, 1922.

Les Deux sources de la morale et de la religion. Paris: Felix Alcan, 1932. Translated as *The Two Sources of Morality and Religion*, by R.A. Audra and C. Brereton. New York: Henry Holt, 1935.

La Pensée et le mouvant: Essais et conférences. Paris: Felix Alcan, 1934. Translated as *The Creative Mind*, by M.L. Andison. New York: Philosophical Library, 1946.

Écrits et paroles. Textes rassembles par Rose-Marie Mossé- Bastide. 3 vols. Paris: Presses Universitaires de France, 1957-1959. (This is a collection of Bergson's writings—including letters—composed between 1877 and 1939.)

Oeuvres. Paris: Presses Universitaires de France, 1970, pp. xxx + 1682.

Selected Works of T.S. Eliot

For Lancelot Andrewes: Essays on Style and Order. Garden City, N.Y.: Doubleday, 1929.

The Use of Poetry and the Use of Criticism: Studies in the Relation of Criticism to Poetry in England. London: Faber and Faber, 1933.

After Strange Gods: A Primer of Modern Heresy. New York: Harcourt Brace, 1934.

Essays Ancient and Modern. London: Faber and Faber, 1936. *Selected Essays.* New ed. New York: Harcourt Brace, 1950.

On Poetry and Poets. New York: Farrar, Straus, and Cudahy, 1957.

Knowledge and Experience in the Philosophy of F.H. Bradley. London: Faber and Faber, 1964.

To Criticize the Critic and Other Writings. New York: Farrar, Straus, and Giroux, 1965.

Poems Written in Early Youth. New York: Farrar, Straus, and Giroux, 1967.

The Complete Poems and Plays: 1909-1950. New York: Harcourt Brace and World, 1971.

The Waste Land: A Facsimile and Transcript of the Original Drafts, including the Annotations of Ezra Pound. Edited by Valerie Eliot. New York: Harcourt Brace, 1971.

Selected Works of William Faulkner

Soldier's Pay. New York: Boni and Liveright, 1926.

The Sound and the Fury. New York: Random House, 1929.

As I Lay Dying. New York: Random House, 1930.

Sanctuary. New York: Random House, 1931.

These Thirteen. New York: Jonathan Cape and Harrison Smith, 1931.

Light in August. New York: Random House, 1932.

Pylon. New York: Random House, 1935.

Absalom, Absalom! New York: Random House, 1936.

Intruder in the Dust. New York: Random House, 1948.

The Mansion. New York: Random House, 1955.

Mosquitoes. New York: Liveright, 1955.

The Town. New York: Random House, 1957.

Faulkner in the University. Edited by Joseph Blotner and F.L. Gwynn. Charlottesville: Univ. of Virginia Press, 1959.

Early Prose and Poetry. Edited by Carvel Collins. Boston: Little, Brown, 1962.

Essays, Speeches, and Public Letters. Edited by James B. Meriwether. New York: Random House, 1965.

Lion in the Garden: Interviews with William Faulkner, 1926-1962. Edited by James B. Meriwether and Michael Millgate. New York: Random House, 1968.

Sanctuary: The Original Text. Edited by Noel Polk. New York: Random House, 1981.

Selected Criticism, Commentary, and Aesthetics

Abel, Darrel. "Frozen Movement in *Light in August.*" *Boston Univ. Studies in English* 3 (Spring 1957): 32-44.

Adams, Hazard. *Philosophy of the Literary Symbolic.* Gainesville: Univ. Presses of Florida, 1983.

Adams, Richard P. "The Apprenticeship of William Faulkner." *Tulane Studies in English* 12 (1962): 113-56.

—————. *Faulkner: Myth and Motion.* Princeton Univ. Press, 1968.

Aiken, Conrad. "William Faulkner: The Novel as Form." In *William Faulkner: Four Decades of Criticism,* edited by Linda Welshimer Wagner. East Lansing: Michigan State Univ. Press, 1973.

Alexander, I.W. *Bergson: Philosopher of Reflection.* London: Bowes and Bowes, 1957.

Bergsten, Staffan. *Time and Eternity: A Study in the Structure and Symbolism of T.S. Eliot's Four Quartets.* London: William Heinemann, 1960.

Bleikasten, André. *The Most Splendid Failure: Faulkner's The Sound and the Fury.* Bloomington: Indiana Univ. Press, 1976.

Blotner, Joseph L. *Faulkner: A Biography.* 2 vols. New York: Random House, 1974.

Bornstein, George. *Transformations of Romanticism in Yeats, Eliot, and Stevens.* Univ. of Chicago Press, 1976.

Bradley, F.H. *Appearance and Reality: A Metaphysical Essay.* 2nd ed., rev., with an appendix. New York: Macmillan, 1908.

Brooks, Cleanth. *William Faulkner: Toward Yoknapatawpha and Beyond.* Yale Univ. Press, 1978.

Broughton, Panthea Reid. *William Faulkner: The Abstract and the Actual.* Baton Rouge: Louisiana State Univ. Press, 1974.

Bush, Ronald. *T.S. Eliot: A Study in Character and Style.* Oxford Univ. Press, 1983.

Callen, Shirley Parker. "Bergsonian Dynamism in the Writings of William Faulkner." Ph.D. diss., Tulane University, 1962.

Campbell, SueEllen. "Equal Opposites: Wyndham Lewis, Henri Bergson, and Their Philosophies of Time." *Twentieth-Century Literature* 29 (Fall 1983): 351-69.

Čapek, Milič. *Bergson and Modern Physics: A Reinterpretation and Re-evaluation*. Dordrecht: D. Reidel, 1971.

Chiari, Joseph. *T.S. Eliot: A Memoir*. London: Enitharmon, 1982.

Church, Margaret. *Time and Reality: Studies in Contemporary Fiction*. Chapel Hill: Univ. of North Carolina Press, 1963.

Conder, John J. *Naturalism in American Fiction: The Classic Phase*. Lexington: Univ. Press of Kentucky, 1984.

Culler, Jonathan. *Structuralist Poetics*. Ithaca: Cornell Univ. Press, 1975.

De Man, Paul. *The Rhetoric of Romanticism*. New York: Columbia Univ. Press, 1984.

Elliott, Hugh Samuel R. *Modern Science and the Illusions of Professor Bergson*. London: Longmans, Green, 1912.

Farber, Marvin, ed. *Philosophic Thought in France and the United States: Essays Representing Major Trends in Contemporary French and American Philosophy*. Buffalo: Univ. of Buffalo Publications in Philosophy, 1950.

Fasel, Ida. "A 'Conversation' Between Faulkner and Eliot." *Mississippi Quarterly* 20 (Fall 1967): 195-206.

—————. "Spatial Form and Spatial Time." *Western Humanities Review* 16 (Summer 1962): 223-34.

Frank, Joseph, "Spatial Form in Modern Literature." In *The Widening Gyre: Crisis and Mastery in Modern Literature*. New Brunswick: Rutgers Univ. Press, 1963.

Freed, Lewis. *T.S. Eliot: The Critic as Philosopher*. Indiana: Purdue Univ. Press, 1979.

Friedman, Melvin. *Stream of Consciousness: A Study in Literary Method*. Yale Univ. Press, 1955.

Fulton, James Street. "Bergson's Religious Interpretation of Evolution," *Rice Institute Pamphlet* 43 (no. 3): 14-28.

Gardner, Dame Helen Louise. *The Art of T.S. Eliot*. London: Cresset, 1949.

—————. *The Composition of Four Quartets*. New York: Oxford Univ. Press, 1978.

Gish, Nancy K. *Time in the Poetry of T.S. Eliot: A Study in Structure and Theme*. Totowa, N.J.: Barnes and Noble, 1981.

Gouhier, Henri. *Bergson et le Christ des Évangiles*. Paris: Le Sign, Anthem Fayard, 1961.

Gordon, Lyndall. *Eliot's Early Years*. New York: Oxford Univ. Press, 1977.

Gray, Piers. *T.S. Eliot's Intellectual and Poetic Development, 1909-1922*. New Jersey: Humanities Press, 1982.

Greene, E.J.H. *T.S. Eliot et la France*. Paris: Boivin, 1951.

Gross, Harvey Seymour. *The Contrived Corridor: History and Fatality in Modern Literature*. Ann Arbor: Univ. of Michigan Press, 1971.

Gunter, P.A.Y. "Bergson and Jung." *Journal of the History of Ideas* 43 (Oct./Dec. 1982): 635-52.

—————. *Bergson and the Evolution of Physics*. Knoxville: Univ. of Tennessee Press, 1969.

Hagan, John. "*Déjà Vu* and the Effect of Timelessness in Faulkner's *Absalom, Absalom!*" *Bucknell Review* 11 (March, 1963: 31-52.

Hall, Dorothy Judd. "The Height of Feeling Free: Frost and Bergson." *Texas Quarterly* 19 (no. 1): 128-43.

Hanna, Thomas. *The Bergsonian Heritage*. New York: Columbia Univ. Press, 1962.

Hay, Eloise Knapp. *T.S. Eliot's Negative Way*. Cambridge: Harvard Univ. Press, 1982.

Herman, Daniel. *The Philosophy of Henri Bergson*. Washington, D.C.: Univ. Press of America, 1980.

Hulme, T.E. *Speculations: Essays in Humanism and the Philosophy of Art*. London: Kegan Paul, 1924.

Humphrey, Robert. *Stream of Consciousness in the Modern Novel*. Berkeley: Univ. of California Press, 1954.

Irwin, John T. *Doubling and Incest / Repetition and Revenge: A Speculative Reading of Faulkner*. Baltimore: Johns Hopkins Univ. Press, 1975.

Kartiganer, Donald M. *The Fragile Thread: The Meaning of Form in Faulkner's Novels*. Amherst: Univ. of Massachusetts Press, 1979.

Kawin, Bruce. *The Mind of the Novel: Reflexive Fiction and the Ineffable*. Princeton: Princeton Univ. Press, 1982.

Kenner, Hugh. *The Invisible Poet: T.S. Eliot*. New York: McDowell, Obolensky, 1959.

Kermode, Frank. *Romantic Image*. New York: Macmillan, 1958.

Kinney, Arthur F. *Faulkner's Narrative Poetics: Style as Vision*. Amherst: Univ. of Massachusetts Press, 1978.

Kirk, Russell. *Eliot and His Age: T.S. Eliot's Moral Imagination in the Twentieth Century*. New York: Random House, 1971.

Kolakowski, Leszek. *Bergson*. New York: Oxford Univ. Press, 1985.

Krieger, Murray. *Arts on the Level: The Fall of the Elite Object*. Knoxville: Univ. of Tennessee Press, 1981.

—————. *The New Apologists for Poetry*. Minneapolis: Univ. of Minnesota Press, 1956.

Kumar, Shiv K. *Bergson and the Stream of Consciousness Novel*. New York: New York Univ. Press, 1963.

—————. "Joyce's 'Epiphany' and Bergson's 'L'Intuition Philosophique.'" *Modern Language Quarterly* 20 (March 1959): 27-30.

Larson, Eric. "The Barrier of Language: The Irony of Language in Faulkner." *Modern Fiction Studies* 13 (Spring 1967): 19-31.

Le Brun, Philip. "T.S. Eliot and Henri Bergson." *Review of English Studies*, n.s., 18 (May 1967): 149-61; (August 1967): 274-86.

Lowrey, Perrin. "Concepts of Time in *The Sound and the Fury*." Reprinted in condensed form in *Twentieth-Century Interpretations of The Sound and the Fury*. Edited by Michael H. Cowan. Englewood Cliffs, N.J.: Prentice-Hall, 1968, pp. 53-62.

Lucy, Sean. *T.S. Eliot and the Idea of Tradition*. New York: Barnes and Noble, 1960.

Malin, Irving. *William Faulkner: An Interpretation*. Stanford: Stanford Univ. Press, 1957.

Margolis, John D. *T.S. Eliot's Intellectual Development, 1922-1939*. Univ. of Chicago Press, 1972.

Maritain, Jacques. *Bergsonian Philosophy and Thomism*. Translated by Mabelle L. Andison. 2d ed. New York: Pantheon, 1955.

Matthiessen, F.O. *The Achievement of T.S. Eliot: An Essay on the Nature of Poetry*. 3d ed. New York: Oxford Univ. Press, 1958.

Mendilow, Adam A. *Time and the Novel*. New York: Humanities Press, 1965.

Meyerhoff, Hans. *Time in Literature*. Los Angeles: Univ. of California Press, 1955.

Miller, J. Hillis. *Poets of Reality: Six Twentieth Century Writers*. Harvard Univ. Press, 1965.

Minter, David. *William Faulkner: His Life and Work*. Baltimore: Johns Hopkins Univ. Press, 1980.

Montgomery, Marion. *Eliot's Reflective Journey to the Garden*. Troy, N.Y.: Whitston, 1979.

Moody, A.D. *Thomas Stearns Eliot, Poet*. New York: Cambridge Univ. Press, 1979.

Mosse-Bastide, Rose Marie. *Bergson éducateur*. Paris: Presses Universitaires de France, 1955.

Mumford, Lewis. *The Myth of the Machine: The Pentagon of Power*. New York: Harcourt Brace Jovanovich, 1970.

Nadeau, Robert L. "Morality and Act: A Study of Faulkner's *As I Lay Dying*." *Mosaic* 6:23-35.

Nuttall, Anthony David. *A Common Sky: Philosophy and the Literary Imagination*. Los Angeles: Univ. of California Press, 1974.

Parr, Susan Dale Resneck. "'And by Bergson, Obviously': Faulkner's *The Sound and the Fury, As I Lay Dying*, and *Absalom, Absalom!* from a Bergsonian Perspective." Ph.D. diss., University of Wisconsin, 1972.

Pilkington, Anthony. *Bergson and His Influence: A Reassessment*. New York: Cambridge Univ. Press, 1976.

Pollock, Agnes. "The Current of Time in the Novels of William Faulkner." Ph.D. diss., University of California, Los Angeles, 1965.

Pondrom, Cyrena N. *The Road from Paris: French Influence on English Poetry 1900-1920*. Cambridge: Cambridge Univ. Press, 1974.

Poulet, Georges. *Studies in Human Time*. Baltimore: Johns Hopkins Univ. Press, 1956.

Pound, Ezra. *The Spirit of Romance*. 1912 Reprint. Norfolk, Conn.: New Directions, 1953.

Ransom, John Crowe, ed. *The Kenyon Critics: Studies in Modern Literature from the Kenyon Review*. New York: World Publishing Co., 1951.

—————. *The New Criticism*. Norfolk, Conn.: New Directions, 1941.

—————. *The World's Body*. New York: Charles Scribner's Sons, 1938.

Robinson, Daniel S. "The Bergson-Flewelling Correspondence, 1910-1940." *Coranto: Journal of the Friends of the Libraries—Univ. of Southern California* 10 (no. 2): 21-37.

Rosenthal, M.L., and Sally M. Gall. *The Modern Poetic Sequence: The Genius of Modern Poetry*. Oxford Univ. Press, 1983.

Russell, Bertrand. "The Philosophy of Bergson." *The Monist* 22:321-47.

Santayana, George. *The Winds of Doctrine: Studies in Contemporary Opinion.* New York: Charles Scribner's Sons, 1926. First pub. 1912.

Schneider, Elizabeth Wintersteen. *T.S. Eliot: The Pattern in the Carpet.* Los Angeles: Univ. of California Press, 1975.

Sears, John F. "William James, Henri Bergson, and the Poetics of Robert Frost." *New England Quarterly* 48 (Sept. 1975): 341- 61.

Schuchard, Ronald. "Eliot and Hulme in 1916: Toward a Revaluation of Eliot's Critical and Spiritual Development." *PMLA* 88 (Oct. 1973): 1083-94.

——————. "T.S. Eliot as an Extension Lecturer." *Review of English Studies* 25 (1974): 163-73, 292-304.

Schwartz, Sanford. *The Matrix of Modernism: Pound, Eliot, and Early Twentieth-Century Thought.* Princeton: Princeton Univ. Press, 1985.

Slatoff, Walter Jacob. *Quest for Failure: A Study of William Faulkner.* Ithaca: Cornell Univ. Press, 1960.

Spears, Monroe Kirklyndorf. *Dionysus and the City: Modernism in Twentieth Century Poetry.* New York: Oxford Univ. Press, 1970.

Stewart, John L. *The Burden of Time: The Fugitives and the Agrarians.* Princeton: Princeton Univ. Press, 1965.

Stonum, Gary Lee. *Faulkner's Career: An Internal Literary History.* Ithaca: Cornell Univ. Press, 1979.

Swiggart, Peter. "Time in Faulkner's Novels." *Modern Fiction Studies* 1 (May 1955): 25-29.

Szathmary, Arthur. *The Aesthetic Theory of Bergson.* Cambridge: Harvard Univ. Press, 1937.

Tate, Allen. *Reactionary Essays on Poetry and Ideas.* New York: Charles Scribner's Sons, 1936.

Thibaudet, Albert. *Le Bergsonisme.* Paris: Gallimard, 1923.

Thompson, Eric. *T.S. Eliot: The Metaphysical Perspective.* Carbondale: Southern Illinois Univ. Press, 1963.

Traversi, Derek Antona. *T.S. Eliot: The Longer Poems.* New York: Harcourt Brace Jovanovich, 1976.

Trethowan, Dom Illtyd. "Bergson and the Zeitgeist." *Downside Review,* 85 (1967): 138-47, 262-73.

Vickery, Olga W. "Faulkner and the Contours of Time." *Georgia Review* 12 (Summer 1958): 192-201.

——————. *The Novels of William Faulkner: A Critical Interpretation.* Baton Rouge: Louisiana State Univ. Press, 1959.

Underhill, Evelyn. "Bergson and the Mystics." *Littel's Living Age* 272:668-75.

——————. *Mysticism: A Study in the Nature and Development of Man's Spiritual Consciousness.* 12th rev. ed. New York: World, 1967).

——————. *Practical Mysticism: A Little Book for Normal People.* New York: E.P. Dutton, 1915.

Watkins, Floyd C. *The Flesh and the Word: Eliot, Hemingway, Faulkner.* Nashville: Vanderbilt Univ. Press, 1971.

Wittenberg, Judith Bryant. *Faulkner: The Transfiguration of Biography.* Lincoln: Univ. of Nebraska Press, 1979.

Zink, Karl E. "Flux and Frozen Moments." *PMLA* 71 (June 1956): 285-301.

INDEX

Abel, Darrel, 122, 123
Absolute, the, 24, 51-53, 60-63, 72, 83, 91, 94, 97, 104, 169
Adams, Hazard, 30-31, 116
Adams, Richard, 119, 125, 139
Addison, Joseph, 80
aesthetics, 23, 27-48 *passim*, 53, 64, 67, 73-74, 107-8, 110-17, 166-67, 173-77
Agrarians, the, 108-9, 114
Aiken, Conrad, 121-22
Alexander, I.W., 25
Anderson, Charles, 129
Anderson, Sherwood, 168, 170
Andrewes, Lancelot, 50
Aristotle, 8, 36
Augustine, St., 25, 28-29, 31, 57, 96, 176

Benda, Julien, 14-15, 55
Bergson, Henri
—and the Absolute, 24, 60-63
—and Action Française, 15
—and aesthetic theory, 23, 43, 45, 47-8, 64, 110, 113-14, 116-17, 118, 173-77. *See also* Bergson: and the artist's role; and flux vs. form; and *intuition philosophique*

—and the artist's role, 32-35, 43-44, 57, 64; compared to God, 35-37, 45-46
—on automatism, 19, 158. *See also* Bergson: and *dédoublement*
—and Becoming, 2, 7-8, 19, 37, 43, 103, 104
—and "Bergsonism," 3, 11, 13, 55-56, 58
—and Bradley, F.H., 50-56, 61-62
—his career, 7-26 *passim*
—and change, 7-8, 20, 22, 35, 37, 45-47, 57, 61, 63, 64-66, 71, 79, 120, 141, 142, 145, 146, 148
—and creative evolution, 17-18, 20, 22-23, 28, 55, 61-62, 64-65, 69-72, 82, 91, 112, 114, 128, 165
—and creativity, 10, 22, 24, 30-31, 33, 35-37, 39, 41, 79, 122, 140-41, 142, 166, 170, 177
—and "cuttings" of reality, 7-8, 19-20, 111, 122, 169. *See also* Bergson: and intellect, falsifications of
—and *dédoublement* (splitting of the self), 2, 19-20, 30, 75, 81-82, 95, 102, 140, 152-53, 166
—and determinism, 16, 18, 71, 79
—and dialectic process, 23-24
—his dualism, vs. monism, 18, 25, 27,